Risk, Return, Resilience

The Three pillars of Sustainable Green Finance

Dr. Priyanka Verma

P&P academy

PEN AND PAPER PUBLICATION

An academic imprint of the Pen and Paper Academy Group

www.pnpacademy.in

TITLE

Risk, Return, Resilience: The Three Pillars of Sustainable Green Finance

AUTHOR

Dr. Priyanka Verma

PUBLISHER ADDRESS

Pen and Paper Publication, A-71/7, Govindpuram,
Ghaziabad – 201013, India

Published: 11 December 2025

Printed by: Thomson Press India Ltd, New Delhi

ISBN: 978-81-996257-2-3

Dedication

This book is dedicated, with love and gratitude, to the memory of my beloved Daddy, **Mr. Shiv Kumar Verma** - Chief Manager, Canara Bank, and Founder and CEO of PS Global (Forensic and Public Safety Company).

My journey began with him.

I still remember the early days when he would take me for my primary school inspections, holding my hand with quiet pride and hope. Later, when he admitted me to St. Paul Academy, he said, *"One day, you will write something meaningful for the world."* Those words stayed with me, growing silently over the years.

Today, as I write this book, I feel that I am walking along the path he showed me.

Every morning, he took me to school. Every evening, he brought me back home, regardless of how full his day was. Those short walks became lifelong lessons. Through them, he taught me discipline, courage, and the importance of choosing what is right, always.

One memory lives especially close to my heart. The day he came to the airport with a large bouquet of flowers, his face glowing with pride. That moment remains with me as a blessing, reminding me that his presence continues to guide my professional journey.

When I completed my PhD, his happiness surpassed my own. That joy still gives me strength and clarity.

His influence lives on in my thinking, my values, and my work. From him, I inherited the foundation of my understanding of Green Finance - shaped by his sharp banking mind and his deep respect for compliance, transparency, and responsibility. His work at PS Global instilled in me a lasting appreciation for ethics and good governance.

He taught me what truly matters:

- To value people, the planet, and honest work
- To respect rules and institutions with integrity and discipline
- To see finance as a tool for fairness, responsibility, and sustainability

These teachings became the roots of my interest in Green Finance and continue to guide every decision I make.

As his only favourite child, I know that no book can fully honour the magnitude of his life. Still, with all his blessings and memories, I offer this work as a heartfelt tribute to the values he lived by.

May this book carry his legacy forward.

May every page reflect his principles.

May his light continue to inspire a more sustainable and meaningful world.

Daddy, this book is for you.

Everything I do carries your blessings.

Yours, Neelu

About The Author

Dr. Priyanka Verma, Assistant Professor, College of Business Administration, Fujairah University, UAE, is a sustainability-focused finance expert whose work bridges green finance, responsible investing, emerging technologies, and ethical leadership. For more than a decade, she has remained committed to a single purpose: enabling finance to serve People, Planet, and Profit (PPP), the true triple bottom line of sustainable development.

An engaged educator and sustainability research practitioner, Dr. Verma has taught students across India and the UAE, contributing to the growth of a new generation of values-driven finance professionals.

She is actively associated with the UAE's authorized training ecosystem, where she has trained professionals across sectors and contributed to development programs linked with the Central Bank of the UAE. Her work is recognised for its clarity, practicality, and strong alignment with ethical and sustainability-centred thinking.

As a SCOPUS indexed researcher, Dr. Verma has developed sustainability assessment models, ESG frameworks, and decision-support tools that connect theory with application. Her innovative work has received international recognition, including registered industrial design contributions in the United Kingdom and Germany.

Dr. Verma also works as an emerging-technology enabler, integrating advanced tools into sustainability practice. Her work spans artificial intelligence for sustainable finance, FinTech and GreenTech applications, ESG analytics, climate-risk modelling, data-driven sustainability assessments, and structured approaches to greenwashing detection.

She brings strong expertise in statistics, data analysis, and visualisation platforms such as Power BI, using these tools to help students and professionals interpret data with confidence and apply insights effectively in decision-making.

Her distinctive strength lies in blending academic depth with real-world engagement. She actively participates in community development, industry collaboration, and sustainability initiatives within her university ecosystem, supporting institutions and organisations as they move toward greener policies and more responsible financial decisions.

Dr. Verma's expertise also extends to Public–Private Partnership (PPP) applications, where she explores how collaborative financial models can advance green infrastructure, renewable energy, and community-centred development.

She is widely respected for her ability to simplify complex concepts and make sustainability meaningful and accessible to students, professionals, policymakers, and business leaders.

Her areas of expertise include:

- Green Finance and Sustainable Banking
- ESG, Corporate Responsibility, and Ethical Investing
- Triple Bottom Line (People–Planet–Profit) Strategy
- AI, FinTech, and GreenTech for Sustainability
- Greenwashing Risk Identification and Prevention
- Climate Risk, Carbon Accounting, and Impact Measurement
- PPP Applications for Sustainable Business Models

- Community Engagement and Industry Collaboration
- Policy Support for Green Development Initiatives

Guided by empathy, curiosity, and purpose, Dr. Verma writes to encourage deeper thinking, thoughtful questioning, and responsible action. Her work invites the finance community to look beyond short-term outcomes and contribute to a cleaner, fairer, and more resilient economic future.

Her belief is clear and steady:

Green finance is no longer a distant idea. It is one of the strongest forces shaping today's global economy. Sustainability, therefore, stands as a shared responsibility.

Dr. Priyanka Verma writes with a clear mission: to empower the next generation of finance leaders to build a greener, smarter, and more equitable economic future, one decision at a time.

Acknowledgements

This book carries the quiet presence of guidance, care, and support that shaped my journey over the years.

I begin with my mentor, whose wisdom, patience, and thoughtful direction played a defining role in my academic and professional growth. The guidance I received helped me sharpen my thinking, deepen my values, and approach finance with responsibility and clarity. This book reflects that influence in every chapter.

I express my heartfelt gratitude to my mother, whose strength, belief, and constant encouragement formed the emotional foundation of my work. Her faith in my purpose gave me confidence, resilience, and balance throughout this journey. Her presence remains a steady source of inspiration behind every step I take.

I am deeply thankful to my family, whose love, understanding, and quiet support made this work possible. Their trust, patience, and shared belief in my vision allowed me the space to think, write, and grow. This book stands as much on their support as on my effort.

With gratitude, I acknowledge each of them for being an integral part of this journey.

Who This Book Is For

This book introduces Green Finance as a practical field that links money with the conditions in which people live and work. It is written for readers who wish to understand how financial decisions shape projects, policies and everyday infrastructure, especially in emerging markets.

The book speaks to several groups at the same time:

- students of finance, management and economics who want a clear and applied entry into green finance
- students of engineering, planning, architecture, environmental science, health and social sciences who wish to see how finance interacts with technical and social choices
- young professionals in banks, funds, companies, consultancies and public institutions who already work with projects that have environmental and social dimensions
- teachers and trainers who are designing courses on sustainability and development and need a structured, classroom friendly text

What makes this book different?

The chapters are written as a cross discipline guide for emerging markets. Ideas are explained in straightforward language and then placed in settings that feel familiar to readers who deal with projects, policies or financial products in their daily work. The focus stays on how actual decisions are taken inside banks, companies, cities and ministries, and how those decisions influence power systems, buildings, transport, industry, agriculture and social infrastructure over time.

The lens of the book is global, and the centre of gravity lies in regions where development needs are high and green finance is growing quickly. Examples draw from India, the UAE, the wider Gulf region, South Asia and other parts of Asia, Africa and Latin America, so that a reader in Mumbai, Dubai or any other emerging city can recognise their own context while still gaining a wider view of the subject.

The material grows from years of teaching and research in green finance, shaped by regular dialogue with practitioners across banks, companies, development agencies and public institutions. Each chapter is designed to move from context to concept and then to practice through short illustrations and sector applications. A glossary at the end of the book supports readers who come from non-finance backgrounds.

In simple terms, this book serves readers who wish to move from general awareness of environmental issues to a working comfort with the language and logic of green finance. It invites people from different disciplines to share one table and think together about how emerging economies can grow in ways that respect both people and the planet.

NOTE: Some images in this book have been generated using artificial intelligence tools for illustrative purposes. These images are original creations and do not depict real persons, institutions, or proprietary designs

Finance that Counts the Planet In

Every financial decision quietly answers a deeper question: what kind of world are we willing to finance. Capital does more than move between accounts. It shapes skylines, landscapes, jobs, and the quality of air and water that future generation will inherit. Green finance begins at this meeting point of numbers and responsibility.

For a long time, conversations about climate and capital ran on parallel tracks. One belonged to scientists, activists, and policy makers, who spoke of rising temperatures, vulnerable communities, and planetary limits. The other belonged to bankers, investors, and corporate leaders, who spoke of risk, return, and growth. Today, these tracks are converging. Climate risk has become financial risk. Environmental performance influences credit quality, asset values, and long-term stability.

The idea for this book grew from observing how different disciplines were beginning to meet at a common point. In academic settings and professional workshops, scholars of finance and sustainability wanted to understand how environmental considerations shape real valuation models and portfolio construction. Engineers and urban planners questioned why technically sound solar parks, green buildings, or low-carbon transport systems still faced delays in securing capital, even with strong feasibility assessments.

Across companies, young professionals tasked with ESG reporting looked for a clearer map of instruments, metrics, and global standards that guide these disclosures. Policy researchers could explain international climate agreements, yet felt disconnected from the daily mechanics through which capital actually moves, absorbs risk, and supports sustainable transitions.

The interest was genuine. The concerns were serious. Yet the language was scattered and the dialogue fragmented.

At the same time, the field of green finance has been evolving with unusual speed. Markets have seen the growth of green bonds, sustainability linked loans, blended finance structures, and transition instruments. Central banks have begun to include climate in stress tests and supervision. Countries are building taxonomies that define what qualifies as green. Multilateral institutions are redesigning portfolios.

Behind these changes lies a simple recognition: the stability of financial systems now depends on how well they account for environmental realities. This book speaks to readers who are ready to stand inside that transition.

If you study finance or management, these chapters will show how core ideas of risk, return, and price discovery adapt when environmental and social outcomes become explicit and measurable. If you come from engineering, architecture, planning, or infrastructure, you will see how design choices affect cash flows, risk profiles, and access to specialized instruments. If your work touches IT, healthcare, agriculture, textiles, logistics, tourism, or public policy, you will find examples that connect your sector with the language of green finance in a concrete way.

The structure of the book follows the natural journey of the subject. It begins with the foundations: what green finance means, how it emerged, and why it moved from a niche concern to a central part of financial discussion. It then examines the main building blocks, including instruments, risk perspectives, disclosure regimes, and regulatory trends. From there, the focus widens to sectors where capital decisions are already reshaping real projects, such as energy, buildings, transport, industry, agriculture, cities, and digital infrastructure.

Throughout this journey, the aim is to keep three elements in view at the same time: financial performance, environmental impact, and social consequence. Concepts are introduced in clear language, then anchored in practice through scenarios and case style illustrations drawn from different regions.

The book rests on two pillars:

- The first is ongoing research on green finance and sustainability, which provides structure, evidence, and conceptual depth.
- The second is continuous interaction with scholars, researchers, and professionals across multiple disciplines, which keeps the narrative grounded in practical questions, institutional realities, and the complexities observed in real projects.

This is an invitation to think more carefully about the link between capital and the conditions of life that capital creates.

If you see your future in designing, advising, regulating, or funding projects that must align economic goals with environmental responsibility, this book is written with you in mind. By the end of this journey, you will be able to read, design, and evaluate green finance decisions with greater clarity, and to recognize that each decision is part of a larger ethical commitment to the world we leave for others.

Table of Contents

1

Why Green Finance, Why Now

Green Finance has reached a pivotal moment in global conversations, and this moment carries a quiet but powerful urgency. Environmental concerns and financial decisions once moved in separate worlds, one guided by scientific observations and ecological warnings while the other worked through balance sheets, credit flows and investment expectations.

Over the years they grew side by side without touching each other deeply. Today, however, the world stands in a place where these two streams merge with clarity.

This chapter opens with an invitation to understand why this convergence matters and how this alignment has reshaped the way every country, company, institution and citizen thinks about the future.

Global climate finance crossed USD 1.3 trillion in 2022, according to Climate Policy Initiative (CPI) [1].

---

[1] *Climate Policy Initiative (CPI), Global Landscape of Climate Finance 2024, Climate Policy Initiative, 2024,*

The shift did not appear suddenly. It evolved through decades of climate observations, technological progress, financial crises, policy reforms and changing societal expectations.

In this journey, professionals from finance realised that climate patterns influence economic structures, and environmental researchers recognised that financial systems shape real-world outcomes. A shared agenda emerged, rooted in the understanding that economic resilience and planetary health rise together. This chapter begins by exploring why this moment is the right time to embrace green finance as a central pillar of global progress.

Objectives of the Chapter

This chapter helps the reader:

1. Understand how environmental and financial discussions gradually aligned into a unified global conversation.

2. Recognise the direct link between climate patterns and financial decisions.

3. Trace the journey of green finance from a niche idea to an essential topic in investment and policy.

4. Understand how risk, return and impact now form the core lens for financial analysis.

5. See why green finance thrives through a blend of disciplines ranging from engineering and economics to data science and public policy.

---

https://www.climatepolicyinitiative.org/wp-content/uploads/2024/10/Global-Landscape-of-Climate-Finance-2024.pdf, accessed 4 December 2025.

The Connecting Threads of Two Worlds

For many decades, environmental studies spoke a language shaped by ecosystems, emissions, biodiversity and the planet's limits. Finance used a vocabulary built around interest rates, asset prices, investment horizons and credit flows. These two worlds rarely crossed paths in meaningful ways. The environment was often viewed as an external backdrop to economic activity, and financial decisions were guided by short-term gains rather than long-term societal stability.

As research deepened, a clearer picture emerged. Climate events were affecting agricultural cycles, infrastructure durability, health outcomes and national budgets.

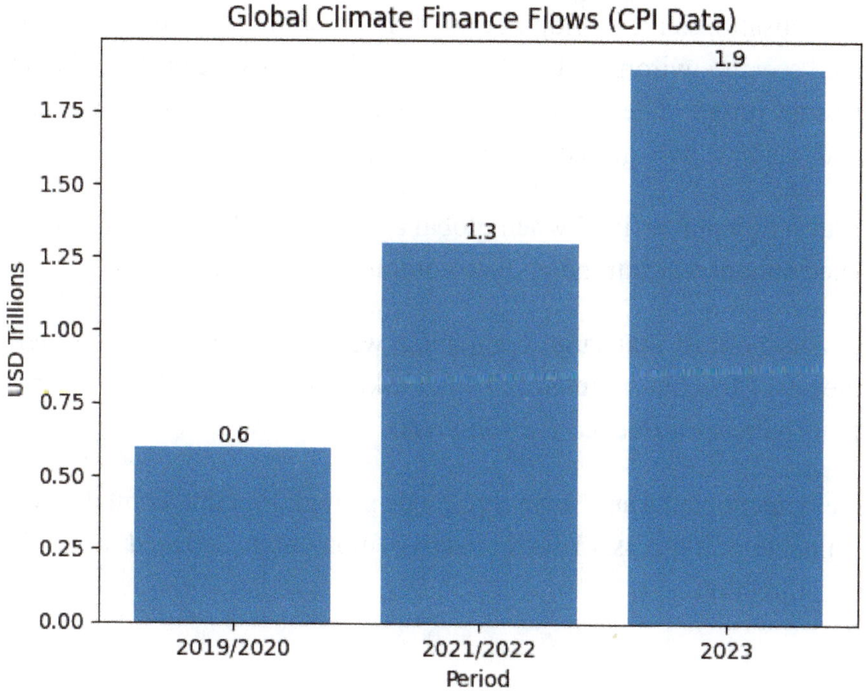

Source: Climate Policy Initiative, Global Landscape of Climate Finance 2023

At the same time, new policies, global agreements and technological advances began to reshape market behaviour. Gradually, the distance between these two worlds narrowed. Conversations started shifting from environmental responsibility to shared economic resilience.

The financial sector realised that every drought, flood, heatwave or storm influences business viability, and environmental experts observed that finance plays a vital role in creating cleaner technologies and sustainable systems.

Extreme weather displaced more than 20 million people annually in the last decade, influencing housing, infrastructure and insurance systems[2].

This realisation built a bridge between two parallel streams. The world started seeing environment and finance as interwoven elements shaping the same future. The journey from parallel conversations to a shared agenda reflects how global priorities matured.

The turning point arrived when global agreements like the Paris Accord pushed nations to examine climate commitments closely.

Investors noticed that large companies were revisiting their long-term strategies. Financial regulators began asking institutions to assess how climate patterns influence portfolio risks.

Development banks and sovereign funds started directing capital toward sustainable initiatives. This collective momentum created a unified global direction.

---

[2] *United Nations High Commissioner for Refugees (UNHCR), Climate Change and Disaster Displacement,* *https://www.unhcr.org/in/what-we-do/how-we-work/climate-change-and-disaster-displacement, accessed 4 December 2025.*

Climate Patterns and Financial Choices

Every climate event leaves an imprint on markets. Heavy rains influence crop yields, which shape food prices and affect household budgets. A heatwave stresses power systems, influencing energy prices and industrial production.

A cyclone damages infrastructure, influencing insurance payouts and government budgets. These examples reveal how weather-related shifts become financial realities.

Over time, such events accumulated enough data to show clear and measurable financial exposure. Banks observed that certain regions faced recurring climate-related credit challenges. Insurers reassessed how they calculated premiums. Companies recalculated long-term operating costs as temperatures, rainfall patterns and resource availability shifted.

For instance, several coastal regions around the world witnessed rising flood-related losses. This influenced real estate decisions, infrastructure planning and the cost of capital for long-term projects. Investment funds studying global markets found that companies with better climate resilience performed more steadily than those with weaker strategies. These observations created a deeper understanding within financial circles.

Climate risk became visible as financial risk through two primary pathways: physical risk and transition risk. To understand this link more clearly, two observations often guide professionals:

- Climate patterns influence operational continuity, supply stability and long-term asset strength.
- Policy shifts, technological changes and investor expectations influence how companies position themselves for the future.

Physical risk arises from climate events affecting assets directly. A drought reduces availability of water for agriculture and industry. A storm damages structures. Rising temperatures influence productivity and public health. Companies with strong climate adaptation strategies show **lower volatility and more stable long-term performance**.

These impacts influence cash flows and valuations. Transition risk appears when economies shift toward cleaner systems. New regulations, new technologies and new expectations influence how companies operate. Industries with heavy emissions face new pressures, while sectors aligned with sustainable innovation experience fresh opportunities.

A strong example of this alignment came when major global insurers recalculated their exposure to climate-related losses and shifted their underwriting models. Their approach influenced investments across multiple sectors and encouraged companies to improve climate resilience. The financial system absorbed this shift as a necessary adaptation.

How Green Finance Reached the Centre Stage

Green finance began as a small stream supported by development banks, specialised funds and early policy frameworks. Its early activity focused on renewable energy, basic environmental projects and research grants. Over time, this stream broadened into a larger, more dynamic ecosystem. Institutional investors began recognising long-term opportunities in energy transition, nature-based solutions, sustainable agriculture and resilient infrastructure. Pension funds and sovereign wealth funds reviewed their long-term portfolios and aligned them with sustainability priorities. Banks introduced new lending practices that encouraged companies to pursue greener technologies. Meanwhile, global markets witnessed a steady rise in labelled bonds and sustainability-linked instruments.

The journey from niche to mainstream can be understood through a few significant shifts. Among researchers and practitioners, two drivers often receive attention due to their lasting influence:

- Steady technological progress that improved renewable energy economics.

- Policy commitments and financial reforms that directed global markets toward cleaner and more resilient systems.

First, governments introduced policy commitments that pushed economy-wide transitions. Second, technology reduced the cost of renewable energy and encouraged large-scale adoption. Third, global investors realised that sustainable assets carry long-term stability and lower risk in uncertain climates. Finally, public expectations evolved and encouraged companies to adopt more responsible strategies.

For example, several emerging markets witnessed a rise in green bonds that supported solar parks, water systems and clean transport. Financial centres in Europe and Asia created new platforms for sustainability-related investments. These developments helped shift green finance from specialised discussions to everyday business conversations.

A key moment arrived when companies across sectors included sustainability performance in their board-level priorities. This step ensured that climate resilience and sustainability strategies shaped corporate growth.

Solar energy costs dropped by **over 85% in a decade**, transforming renewable economics **(IRENA)** [3]**.**

Financial analysts responded by studying how environmental performance influences valuations, cost of capital and long-term market perception.

Understanding Risk, Return and Impact Together

Understanding risk, return and impact together means looking at every financial decision through a wider window where numbers, people and the planet stand side by side in the same frame, where traditional analysis still offers a useful map with two co-ordinates that describe how much uncertainty surrounds an investment and how much gain it is expected to bring, and green finance gently stretches that map further by asking what each decision does to air and water, to communities and ecosystems, and to the capacity of future generations to live well, so that value grows into something larger than cash flows alone and performance begins to reflect both resilience in markets and responsibility toward the world those

[3] *International Renewable Energy Agency (IRENA), Renewable Power Generation Costs in 2020, IRENA, 2021,* *https://www.irena.org/publications/2021/Jun/Renewable-Power-Costs-in-2020, accessed 4 December 2025.*

markets operate in. Companies with strong ESG performance enjoy **10-20% lower cost of capital**[4].

1. The Evolution of Financial Thinking

Traditional financial analysis focused on two elements: risk and return. Investors assessed how much uncertainty surrounded an investment and how much gain they expected in exchange.

This framework guided markets for decades and shaped how institutions examined every loan, bond or equity decision.

[4] *McKinsey & Company, Why ESG Is Here to Stay, McKinsey,* *https://www.mckinsey.com/capabilities/strategy-and-corporate-finance/our-insights/why-esg-is-here-to-stay, accessed 4 December 2025.*

As global priorities evolved, a richer understanding emerged. Green finance broadened this foundation by adding a third pillar: impact. Impact reflects how an investment shapes communities, ecosystems, resources and long-term societal wellbeing. It allows financial decisions to be studied through a lens that measures value beyond immediate monetary outcomes.

2. How Impact Shapes Real-World Value

This wider approach encourages decision-makers to study each initiative with deeper intention. A renewable energy facility contributes stable revenue along with low emissions, cleaner air and long-term energy independence. A sustainable agriculture programme strengthens soil health, protects livelihoods and supports national food security while generating economic value for farmers and supply-chain participants. Climate-resilient infrastructure protects lives, strengthens essential systems and reduces future financial strain. These layers reveal that investments carry outcomes far beyond profit and loss statements.

3. What Analysts Look for Today

Analysts increasingly study companies through this expanded lens. They examine how an organisation:

- Manages emissions and resource cycles
- Protects biodiversity and ecological stability
- Supports communities through inclusive practices
- Adapts to evolving climate patterns and regulatory expectations

These elements influence productivity, market perception and long-term resilience. Organisations that integrate these considerations into their strategies inspire confidence among investors who value stability, credibility and responsible growth.

4. Measuring Integrated Performance

Several financial institutions around the world created internal systems that measure environmental and social contributions alongside financial performance. These systems combine data science, sector expertise and long-term scenario planning. They help institutions identify projects that deliver lasting economic strength along with meaningful environmental and social benefits. This approach supports clearer decision-making, stronger accountability and better alignment between institutional goals and global priorities.

5. A Foundation That Encourages Collaboration

The risk-return-impact lens encourages innovation across the financial world. It inspires collaborations where engineers, economists, investors and policymakers work together to design solutions that serve both markets and society. It strengthens financial systems by aligning capital with long-term resilience, encourages businesses to adopt forward-looking strategies and creates a foundation where economic and environmental progress grow together.

Why Multiple Disciplines Shape Green Finance

Green finance stands strong because it draws wisdom from various fields. Engineering offers clarity on technology, energy systems and infrastructure resilience. Environmental science explains climate patterns, resource cycles and ecological limits. Economics studies incentives, market behaviour and policy.

Data science brings precision through advanced modelling and analysis. Public policy shapes regulatory expectations and long-term national directions. This interdisciplinary nature helps green finance deliver real impact. Consider a renewable energy project. Engineers design the system, economists study cost structures, finance professionals design investment models, policymakers define regulations, and data experts monitor performance.

Together they create a solution that is efficient, resilient and scalable. A powerful example is the global shift toward green hydrogen. This transition brings together electrochemistry, engineering, policy support, finance models, infrastructure planning and international cooperation. Such projects grow through collaboration rather than isolated efforts.

Green finance thrives when students, researchers, bankers, engineers, entrepreneurs, planners and community members contribute their strengths. This diversity builds stronger systems and encourages innovative solutions.

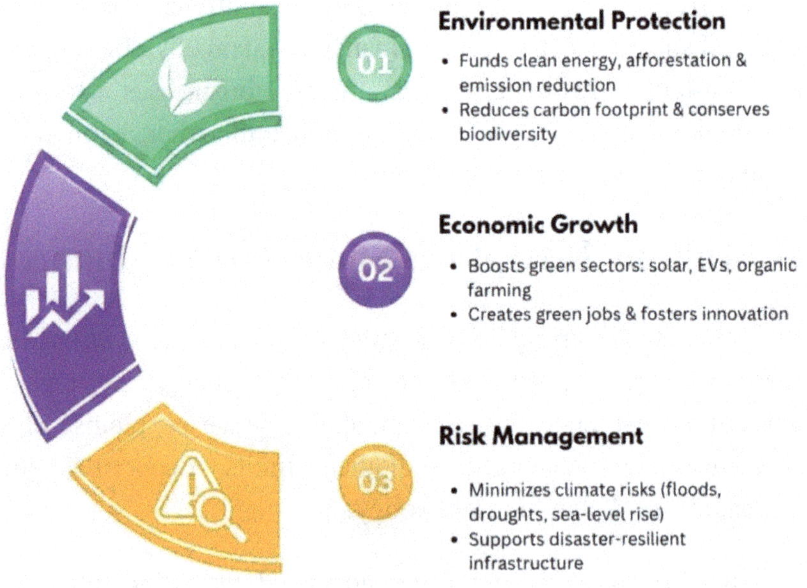

Key Takeaways

- Environmental and financial conversations gradually moved toward a unified global dialogue supported by scientific evidence, policy commitments and public expectations.
- Climate patterns began influencing business decisions, investment flows and national planning, bringing financial systems closer to environmental realities.
- Green finance grew from a small initiative into a central force shaping global markets and guiding long-term strategy across sectors.
- The lens of risk, return and impact strengthened professional decision-making and encouraged responsible, forward-looking financial approaches.
- Collaboration across disciplines created stronger, more resilient economic systems that support innovation, stability and long-term societal wellbeing.
- These ideas set the stage for deeper exploration in future chapters as the world continues to evolve and uncover new possibilities in sustainable finance.

2

Core Concepts of Green Finance

Green finance takes on real meaning when seen as more than a category of financial products. It reflects a shift in how capital understands responsibility, opportunity, and long-term resilience.

As markets evolve, the language around sustainability grows more precise, and clarity becomes essential.

Investors, institutions, and policymakers increasingly look for direction rooted in shared definitions and credible standards. Without this foundation, it becomes difficult to recognise what truly contributes to environmental progress and what merely appears to.

The global momentum around sustainable finance has created an ecosystem filled with new terms, instruments, and classifications. Green bonds, social loans, transition pathways, sustainability-linked structures - each carries its own purpose and logic.

More than **70 countries** introduced or drafted green taxonomies to guide credible classifications[5].

When the underlying principles are understood, these tools stop feeling like technical labels and start becoming clear signals of how capital shapes environmental outcomes. This understanding builds confidence and helps readers interpret how the financial world is adapting to climate priorities.

Green finance continues to expand through international taxonomies, emerging market practices, and rapid innovation in reporting systems. For example, the early success of green bonds in Europe set the stage for Asia's rise in transition financing, where hard-to-abate sectors began designing structured pathways for emission reduction.

These developments show how ideas turn into frameworks, and how frameworks evolve into global standards.

With an organised view of these building blocks, the entire field becomes easier to navigate.

A strong understanding of sustainable finance begins with clarity around its core classifications. These classifications guide global capital flows and shape how financial systems respond to environmental and social priorities.

Over the years, international cooperation, market evolution, and continuous refinement of standards have given each category a distinct identity. When these foundations are clear, the entire ecosystem becomes

---

[5] *World Bank Group, International Developments in Sustainable Finance Taxonomies, World Bank Group, 2023, available via World Bank Documents & Reports,* https://documents.worldbank.org/en/publication/documents-reports, *accessed 4 December 2025.*

easier to navigate, and investors gain a sharper appreciation of how capital advances meaningful outcomes.

Objectives

- Provide a clear understanding of the main classifications within sustainable finance.
- Explain how different financing tools are structured and why these distinctions matter.
- Build familiarity with safeguards and verification practices that strengthen market credibility.
- Equip the reader to interpret green finance within the broader landscape of sustainable financial systems.
- Offer a structured conceptual base that supports deeper learning in upcoming sections.
- Strengthen the reader's confidence in identifying credible sustainability claims.
- Clarify the relationship between environmental goals and financial decision-making.
- Highlight how global frameworks influence market behaviour and industry standards.
- Prepare the reader to evaluate instruments, disclosures, and outcomes with balanced judgment.

The Core Classifications in Sustainable Finance

Green Finance

Green finance focuses on activities that uplift environmental wellbeing. It channels capital into renewable energy, efficient mobility, sustainable land management, clean buildings, water stewardship, and climate-resilient development. The intention is always aligned with ecological improvement and resource harmony.

A pivotal moment in the rise of green finance came through the global discussions surrounding the EU Green Bond Standard. These discussions encouraged countries and issuers to refine definitions, align with transparent taxonomies, and strengthen the quality of disclosures. As these frameworks gained recognition, green finance expanded with confidence.

Multilateral development banks played a major role as well. Their early issuances of labelled green bonds introduced structured reporting and clear project categorisation. This helped create market discipline, encouraged reliable communication, and set expectations for future issuers. Investments in renewable energy reached nearly **USD 495 billion in 2022**, marking one of the strongest years of clean energy financing[6].

With these foundations, green finance grew steadily across continents, gaining respect from policymakers, investors, and corporates alike.

Social Finance

Social finance strengthens communities and human development. It directs capital toward healthcare infrastructure, inclusive education, skill development, affordable housing, social protection systems, and essential public services. Every element supports stability, dignity, and progress. Affordable housing finance has grown to a **USD 1 trillion global market opportunity**, especially in emerging economies[7].

---

[6] *REN21, Renewables 2023 Global Status Report: Investment, REN21 Secretariat, 2023,* https://www.ren21.net/gsr-2023/modules/energy_supply/01_energy_supply/03_investment/, *accessed 4 December 2025.*

[7] *World Bank Group, Housing Finance: A New Way Forward, World Bank Group, available via World Bank Documents & Reports,* https://documents.worldbank.org/en/publication/documents-reports, *accessed 4 December 2025.*

The expansion of social finance became especially visible when institutions worldwide recognised the importance of resilient community frameworks.

Social bonds emerged as a vehicle for uplifting essential services and expanding access to opportunities. These instruments highlighted how finance can nurture human wellbeing at scale.

Eventually, global organisations introduced guidelines that brought coherence to social impact measurement. These guidelines allowed issuers to structure their approaches with clarity and helped investors appreciate how their capital contributed to meaningful improvements in people's lives. This growth transformed social finance into a respected pillar of sustainable investing.

Sustainability Finance

Sustainability finance brings environmental and social priorities together within a unified framework. It recognises that ecosystems and communities flourish together, and sustainable outcomes arise when both are strengthened simultaneously.

A key point in its evolution came when major financial institutions introduced sustainability bonds that blended green and social project categories. Corporates issuing sustainability bonds report **higher multi-sector impact diversification**, with nearly **60%** allocating to mixed green and social outcomes[8].

---

[8] ***World Bank****, Title of Report, World Bank Group, Year, available via World Bank Documents & Reports,* [*https://documents.worldbank.org/en/publication/documents-reports*](https://documents.worldbank.org/en/publication/documents-reports)*, accessed 4 December 2025.*

This approach provided issuers with flexibility and encouraged integrated planning. Investors gained access to instruments that supported comprehensive development goals, spanning both ecological and social progress. Over time, sustainability finance has become a bridge connecting environmental stewardship with community wellbeing.

Transition Finance

Transition finance accelerates the journey of industries that play a vital role in the global economy yet require structured pathways toward lower emissions. These sectors include steel, cement, heavy mobility, aviation, and maritime operations.

Transition finance guides them through long-term improvement by supporting technological upgrades, energy efficiency, cleaner processes, and transparent progress tracking. Hard-to-abate sectors (steel, cement, heavy transport) account for nearly **30% of global CO_2 emissions**, making transition finance critical [9].

Japan played a pioneering role in developing this area. Through clear transition pathways and sector-specific guidance, Japan encouraged organisations to publish credible strategies and work steadily toward lower-emission operations. These steps gave transition finance its early shape and inspired similar efforts across other regions.

Transition finance occupies a unique space. It supports ambition and practicality together, recognising that meaningful progress arises from gradual, well-planned advancement. By offering structured direction,

---

[9] *World Economic Forum, Net-Zero Industry Tracker 2024: Cross-Sector Findings, World Economic Forum, 2024, https://www.weforum.org/publications/net-zero-industry-tracker-2024/cross-sector-findings-net-zero-tracker-2024/, accessed 4 December 2025.*

this category ensures that essential industries move toward greener futures with confidence.

Understanding Instrument Structures

Sustainable finance instruments follow two core architectures. Each serves a distinct purpose and helps investors interpret how issuers plan their sustainability actions.

Use of Proceeds Instruments

Use of proceeds instruments focus on the destination of the funds. Issuers outline eligible project categories and dedicate the capital entirely to those activities. Green bonds are the most established examples in this category. They come with documented frameworks, allocation plans, and impact reporting commitments.

Green, social, and sustainability bonds (use of proceeds instruments) represent more than **60% of all sustainable debt issued globally**[10].

These instruments gained prominence when international principles provided clear criteria for project evaluation, management of proceeds, and transparency. As these principles spread across regions, use of proceeds instruments gained strong credibility. They support project-level clarity and give investors a direct understanding of the environmental or social outcomes financed through their capital.

Growing taxonomies added further confidence to this model. When issuers align projects with recognised classification systems, investors receive a structured and comparable view of sustainability efforts. Over

---

[10] *Climate Bonds Initiative (CBI), Global State of the Market Report 2023, Climate Bonds Initiative, 2023,* *https://www.climatebonds.net/files/documents/publications/Global-State-of-the-Market-Report-2023.pdf, accessed 4 December 2025.*

time, this encouraged more organisations to prepare eligible pipelines and explore labelled issuances.

Performance-based Instruments

Performance-based instruments build around the idea of organisational improvement. Instead of limiting funds to specific projects, they link financial terms to measurable sustainability outcomes. Organisations commit to key performance indicators-such as emission reduction, energy efficiency improvement, water stewardship progress, or diversity enhancement-and track their advancement openly.

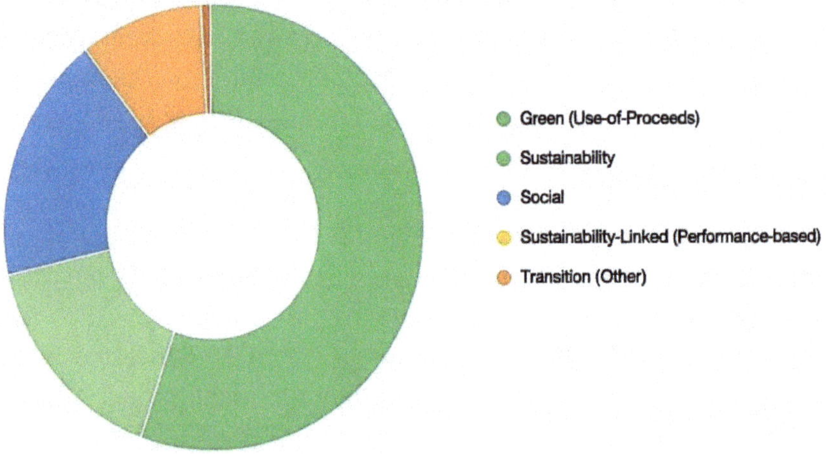

Source: Climate Bonds Initiative (2025). Sustainable Debt Global State of the Market 2024. London: Climate Bonds Initiative

Sustainability-linked bonds and loans are the clearest examples of this approach. They offer flexibility in fund utilisation while encouraging ambitious, measurable results. More than **80% of performance-based instruments** link financial terms to emission reduction KPIs[11].

[11] *International Capital Market Association (ICMA), Sustainability-Linked Bond Principles – Market Practice and KPI Characteristics, ICMA,* https://www.icmagroup.org/sustainable-finance/the-principles-guidelines-and-handbooks/sustainability-linked-bond-principles-slbp/, *accessed 4 December 2025.*

Performance-based instruments gained widespread attention when an Asian borrower introduced a sustainability-linked loan with interest adjustments directly tied to its ESG scoring. This innovation demonstrated how financial incentives can strengthen corporate sustainability commitments.

These instruments encourage disciplined planning. Issuers define baselines, set realistic improvement pathways, and disclose progress consistently. Investors gain assurance through verified metrics and transparent milestones. As a result, performance-based financing has become a powerful tool for organisations aiming to transform their entire operations.

How These Approaches Shape Market Behaviour

Instrument	Focus	Structure	Typical KPIs / Categories	Issuance (USD tn)	Market Share
Green	Environmental only	Use-of-Proceeds	Renewables, green buildings, clean transport, pollution prevention	3.40	56 %
Sustainability	Environmental + Social	Use-of-Proceeds	Mixed green & social projects	1.02	17 %

Social	Social only	Use-of-Proceeds	Healthcare, education, affordable housing	0.48	8 %
Sustainability-Linked (SLB)	Corporate-wide ESG improvement	Performance-based	GHG reduction, diversity, water use, science-based targets	0.71	12 %
Transition	High-emitting sector decarbonisation	Mostly Use-of-Proceeds	Low carbon steel, SAF, cement CCS, green shipping	0.04	<1 %

The distinction between use of proceeds and performance-based instruments plays a central role in shaping sustainable finance. Use of proceeds structures highlight project-level clarity. Performance-based structures emphasise organisational evolution. Both encourage transparency, encourage thoughtful planning, and strengthen accountability.

Issuers with a pipeline of well-designed green or social projects may find use of proceeds instruments ideal for targeted outcomes. Organisations seeking a broader operational shift may consider performance-based tools, which allow them to pursue multi-dimensional improvements.

Together, these two models expand opportunities for sustainability-oriented investment. They encourage both precise action and long-term transformation, giving markets the flexibility required to advance environmental and social progress at scale.

Why These Classifications and Structures Matter

Clear classification empowers investors, issuers, and policymakers to communicate effectively. Each category offers a lens through which stakeholders understand environmental and social ambition. These foundations support stronger reporting, clearer expectations, and a shared vocabulary that enhances global cooperation.

Instrument structures influence behaviour across industries. Project-aligned frameworks encourage tangible, on-ground action, while performance-linked frameworks inspire organisational maturity. Both uplift accountability and reflect the growing alignment between capital markets and sustainability goals.

By understanding these foundational elements, readers gain the ability to interpret market signals with ease, recognise credible sustainability commitments, and appreciate the thoughtful evolution of global sustainable finance. These concepts form the base upon which advanced discussions around verification, metrics, safeguards, and systems-level frameworks will naturally build.

Seeing Real Change - Impact, Additionality and Materiality

Green finance gains its real strength when the underlying principles guiding capital decisions become clear. The field relies on concepts that shape how outcomes are measured, how progress is recognised, and how market behaviour aligns with environmental aspirations. These ideas form the deeper layer of sustainable finance, the layer that ensures every action carries substance and intention. When understood well, they give investors the confidence to interpret sustainability commitments with clarity and help issuers design more meaningful frameworks.

Impact

Impact represents the measurable change created through the flow of capital. It reflects the direct influence of financing on environmental or social progress. This can include reduced emissions, restored habitats, improved resource efficiency, or enhanced community wellbeing. The essence of impact lies in visibility and measurement; progress becomes clear when outcomes can be observed and documented.

An influential example comes from the early work of the International Finance Corporation. When the IFC introduced structured impact reporting templates, the practice provided a practical foundation for consistent measurement. This encouraged financial institutions across regions to adopt similar templates, eventually shaping how global markets evaluate sustainability results. The IFC's contribution became a reference point that guided the industry toward greater clarity.

A simple analogy helps: impact is like the growth of a plant after receiving water. The watering represents capital; the visible growth represents the outcome. When the growth is measured, the effect becomes clear.

Additionality

Additionality refers to the value created through financing that would not have emerged otherwise. It reflects the idea that capital has unlocked opportunities, improvements, or progress that remained untapped earlier. Additionality is especially important for projects that require support to become viable, such as early-stage clean technologies or community-focused initiatives.

Consider the structure of blended finance used by development banks. These institutions often provide foundational capital, creating a supportive environment that attracts private investors. This combination allows projects to move forward even when market conditions are evolving. The additional capital acts like a supportive boost, enhancing the overall outcome.

A simple analogy explains it well: additionality is similar to tutoring given to a student who already works hard. The student progresses faster because of the extra guidance. The improvement created by that extra support reflects additionality.

Materiality

Materiality focuses on how sustainability factors influence financial decision-making. It highlights the aspects of environmental and social performance that hold genuine relevance for the long-term stability of a company or project. Materiality encourages organisations to focus on the areas where their decisions create the greatest impact.

A significant shift occurred when global reporting frameworks placed materiality at the center of their guidelines. This encouraged companies across industries to identify their most influential sustainability factors and integrate them into strategy. As a result, sustainability reporting became more purposeful and aligned with business realities.

A simple analogy clarifies the idea: materiality is like selecting the key ingredients in a recipe. Many items can be added, yet only a few decide the flavour. Those few represent the material factors that shape the final outcome.

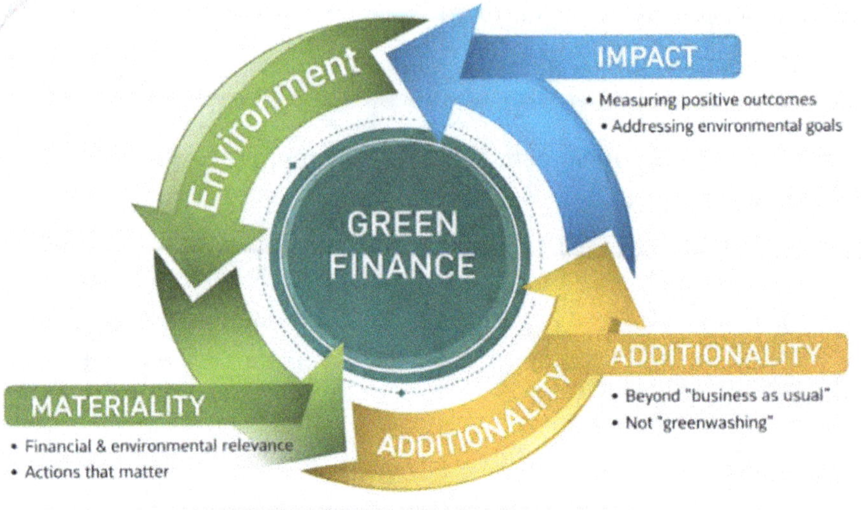

The core principles that build trust in sustainable finance

Together, these three concepts - impact, additionality, and materiality - provide the intellectual foundation of modern sustainable finance. They help investors interpret sustainability commitments with clarity and support issuers in structuring actions that create meaningful progress.

Moving Toward Clarity: Addressing Greenwashing Through Strengthened Safeguards

Greenwashing arises when sustainability claims do not align with actual outcomes. This usually takes place when definitions remain broad, reporting stays general, or communication focuses more on branding than measurable progress. As sustainable finance gained momentum, the need for stronger guardrails became clear. Markets responded by building safeguards that guide issuers toward clarity and investors toward confidence.

One well-known event in the evolution of safeguards occurred when a large global fund revisited its classification of labelled products. Through a detailed review, the fund refined its frameworks, realigned its instruments with established standards, and strengthened the quality of disclosures. This step encouraged many other institutions to elevate their own approach to classification and verification. The ripple effect allowed sustainable finance to move forward with stronger foundations.

Key Safeguards Strengthening Market Integrity

Taxonomies

Taxonomies provide structured definitions for sustainability activities. They outline which projects qualify as green or socially beneficial, helping both issuers and investors follow clear guidelines. As taxonomies evolved across regions, transparency increased and interpretive uncertainty reduced.

Independent Verification: External reviewers play a central role in strengthening credibility. Their assessments ensure that issuers align with recognised frameworks and maintain quality in reporting. Independent verification enhances trust across markets and provides investors with added assurance.

Standardised Impact Reporting: Reporting templates encourage issuers to share results consistently. Standardised impact reports allow investors to evaluate outcomes across markets and sectors. This consistency supports comparability and strengthens the long-term credibility of sustainable finance.

Science-Based Targets: Targets grounded in scientific pathways guide organisations toward emission-aligned strategies. They help companies plan transitions that reflect global climate ambitions. Science-based targets create a clear roadmap and encourage disciplined progress.

These safeguards nurture a culture of transparency, clarity, and accountability. They bring structure to ambition and allow sustainable finance to grow with integrity.

Measuring What Matters: Metrics, Verification and the Position of Green Finance in the Wider Framework

Measurement sits at the heart of sustainable finance because it transforms intention into observable progress. Metrics give form to goals, help issuers track improvements, and support investors in evaluating performance. Verification strengthens this system by ensuring that information remains aligned with recognised frameworks.

The Role of Metrics and Verification

Global verification practices have evolved steadily. The ICMA principles guide issuers through clear processes for project evaluation, management of proceeds, and reporting. External reviewers verify alignment with these principles. Key performance indicators provide measurable targets, while baseline-setting establishes a reference point for progress.

An important moment in verification history came when early green bonds introduced third-party review models between 2014 and 2015. These reviews were adopted by several large issuers and helped shape the practice of external assessment. The approach demonstrated how independent evaluation could elevate trust and encourage disciplined reporting. These early frameworks became a foundation for the verification structures used today.

Metrics and verification together promote clarity. They encourage precise communication, support alignment with global sustainability pathways, and create a common language that strengthens market confidence.

Where Green Finance Fits Within Sustainable Finance

Green finance belongs to a broader ecosystem that includes ESG investing, thematic financing, and sector-specific sustainability instruments. Understanding its position helps readers appreciate how different components of sustainable finance work together.

Sustainable finance represents the full spectrum of environmental, social, and governance considerations. ESG focuses on strategic decision-making and long-term resilience. Thematic financing brings specific goals into focus, such as gender inclusion, climate adaptation, clean mobility, or digital access. Within this thematic universe, green, social, sustainability, and transition instruments offer structured ways for capital to support targeted outcomes. Third-party reviews (Second Party Opinions) accompany **over 90%** of labelled sustainable bonds[12].

Green finance holds a central position because environmental outcomes anchor climate goals. It serves as a catalyst for clean technologies, a driver of innovation, and a foundation for large-scale ecological restoration. It reinforces corporate sustainability strategies and aligns strongly with policy commitments from governments worldwide.

As markets progress, green finance continues to influence regulation, investor preferences, and long-term planning. Its principles inspire related fields such as blue finance, circular economy financing, and nature-based solutions. By understanding where green finance sits within the wider sustainability landscape, readers gain a complete view of how capital shapes the transition to a more balanced and resilient global economy.

---

[12] *Eco-Business, "Second party opinions: a greenwash safeguard or just for show?," Eco-Business, https://www.eco-business.com/news/second-party-opinions-a-greenwash-safeguard-or-just-for-show/, accessed 4 December 2025.*

Key Takeaways

- Green, social, sustainability, and transition finance form the foundational classifications that guide global capital toward environmental and social progress.
- Use of proceeds and performance-based instruments create the two main structures through which sustainable finance operates, shaping how issuers plan and how investors interpret outcomes.
- Impact, additionality, and materiality serve as the conceptual anchors of sustainability evaluation, helping markets identify meaningful results, accelerated progress, and factors that influence long-term value.
- Safeguards such as taxonomies, external reviews, science-aligned targets, and structured impact reporting strengthen clarity, enhance trust, and support responsible financial behaviour.
- Metrics and verification elevate the credibility of sustainable finance by turning goals into measurable progress and aligning issuers with globally recognised frameworks.
- Green finance occupies a central place within the broader sustainable finance landscape, driving innovation, supporting climate commitments, and helping markets transition toward more balanced and resilient systems.

3

The Global Landscape of Green Finance

The movement toward sustainability gains momentum each year as countries refine their priorities and financial systems reshape long-term development paths. Across global markets, innovative policies and collaborative frameworks continue to guide investment decisions that support environmental progress.

What once felt like a specialised segment of finance now stands as a central pillar of economic strategy, shaping how nations plan for growth and resilience.

Across continents, distinct pathways have emerged. Europe continues to lead with structured regulatory systems. North America blends innovation with market-driven approaches. India advances large-scale transition strategies. The GCC and the wider Middle East, especially the UAE, pursue rapid progress in clean energy and sustainable finance. East Asia scales green initiatives at remarkable speed, while Africa fosters solutions shaped by resilience and resource stewardship.

Latin America brings biodiversity and natural capital into financial architecture. These regional stories prepare readers for a deeper exploration of how global frameworks guide local transformation.

Objectives

- Explain the global context surrounding climate finance commitments.
- Introduce the role and influence of multilateral and development finance institutions.
- Present structured regional insights that highlight the evolution of green finance across continents.
- Highlight global precedents, influential agreements, and moments that shaped international climate finance.
- Build understanding of how regions differ in approach while moving toward shared environmental goals.
- Equip readers to interpret global sustainable finance trends with clarity and confidence.
- Strengthen awareness of how policy frameworks influence market behaviour.
- Offer perspective on how global collaboration accelerates sustainable development.

Agreements That Shape Global Momentum

Global green finance rests on a foundation shaped through decades of dialogue, evolving commitments, and the steady rise of institutions that brought structure to ambition.

When countries pledged to move toward climate-aligned growth, financial systems didn't simply adjust-they began redesigning the pathways through which capital meets environmental priorities. These shifts didn't happen suddenly; they unfolded through steady cooperation, shared scientific understanding, and a global sense of direction that continues to mature every year.

The world's major climate agreements play a central role in this story. They create a unified language through which nations, investors, and institutions understand both the urgency and the opportunity available in sustainable transformation.

Once these agreements were established, market innovation naturally followed, and financial commitments began aligning themselves with long-term climate goals.

Global Commitments That Guide Financial Ambition

The Paris Agreement stands as one of the most influential inflection points. It didn't merely outline temperature goals-it introduced a shared vision for a climate-resilient future. The clarity of its scientific thresholds encouraged governments to rethink policy strategy and financial institutions to create instruments that mirror those pathways.

Capital began flowing toward projects that align with long-term ecological balance, creating a new sense of direction for markets around the world.

Nationally Determined Contributions widened this momentum. By encouraging each country to articulate its own climate pathway, they brought structure to ambition.

Loss and damage from climate-related **events now exceed USD 300 billion per year in global economic impact, reflecting the growing financial consequences of extreme weather and climate risks**[13].

Once NDCs became part of national planning, investors gained a clearer view of long-term opportunities. Project pipelines expanded, regulations strengthened, and countries began designing financial systems capable of supporting transition-focused investments.

The introduction of long-term net-zero commitments brought another layer of depth. These commitments encouraged institutions to design instruments that stretch across decades-transition-focused bonds, technology-linked funds, and other long-horizon structures that match the scale of environmental transformation.

Climate finance transitions from reactive to proactive investment.

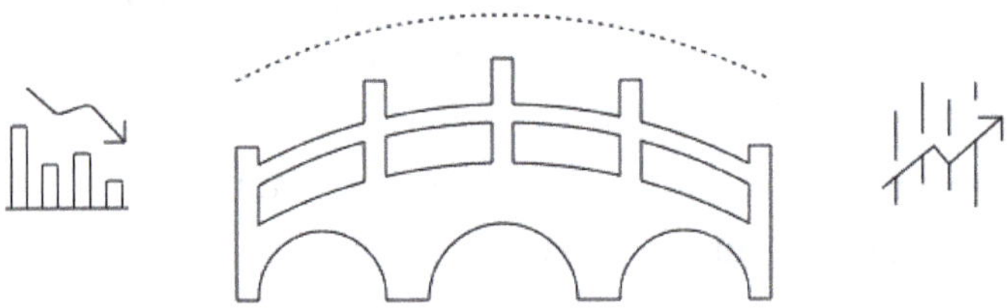

[13] *United Nations Office for Disaster Risk Reduction (UNDRR), Global Assessment Report on Disaster Risk Reduction 2022, United Nations,* https://www.undrr.org/publication/global-assessment-report-disaster-risk-reduction-2022, *accessed 4 December 2025.*

Certain global moments helped accelerate this transition. When climate finance tracking reports showed flows surpassing USD 600 billion, it marked a shift in global confidence.

And when international discussions began acknowledging the importance of loss-and-damage finance, it expanded the conversation to include resilience and community protection.

These developments show how agreements evolve into commitments, and commitments evolve into structured financial pathways.

How Agreements Influence Market Behaviour

These global frameworks do more than set direction; they shape expectations. Investors look for alignment with long-term climate plans. Companies design strategies that reflect future regulatory landscapes.

Governments build incentives that match international commitments. Through these layers, agreements guide the architecture of global finance, turning high-level ambitions into structured investment flows.

Institutions That Build the Architecture of Sustainable Finance

Climate agreements provide the direction, but institutions create the systems through which capital flows. They serve as architects-designing financial structures, validating methodologies, and demonstrating how ambitious goals can be translated into tangible outcomes.

Institutions Driving Global Sustainability Pathways

The World Bank Group has long supported environmental progress through green lending programs, blended finance solutions, and impact-focused advisory support. Its efforts help countries integrate sustainability into long-term development strategies, especially in infrastructure and energy transformation.

The Asian Development Bank has shaped Asia's sustainability landscape by supporting renewable energy expansion, urban green development, and region-wide cooperation. ADB's approach reflects the diverse economic realities of Asia while encouraging countries to adopt cleaner pathways at scale.

In Africa, the African Development Bank plays a pivotal role in building climate resilience. Its work on sustainable water systems, land restoration, clean energy access, and nature-focused financing lays the ground for long-term ecological stability. AfDB consistently blends innovation with community-centered development.

Latin America's progress has been strengthened through the Inter-American Development Bank. Through environmental lending, conservation financing, and support for nature-positive initiatives, IDB helps integrate climate action with economic advancement.

The Green Climate Fund and the Global Environment Facility expand global capacity through catalytic funding. They provide early-stage financing for climate solutions, support innovative technologies, and encourage national institutions to adopt structured climate investment frameworks.

A Turning Point in Impact Measurement

One of the most influential developments came from the International Finance Corporation. Its impact reporting templates offered clarity on how to measure environmental and social progress.

Countries representing over 90% of global GDP now have net-zero commitments (national or corporate[14]).

---

[14] ***Net Zero Tracker*** *(Oxford Net Zero, Energy & Climate Intelligence Unit, NewClimate Institute), Global Net-Zero Coverage,* *https://zerotracker.net, accessed 4 December 2025.*

This framework became an international reference, guiding issuers, investors, and regulators toward structured reporting practices. It helped introduce discipline into the way markets communicate sustainability results, influencing everything from green bonds to blended finance models.

What These Institutions Enable

By creating clear structures, these institutions help countries access global markets, adopt modern sustainability tools, and design long-term ecological strategies. Their work blends technical expertise, financial innovation, and global cooperation, allowing sustainable finance to grow with stability and direction.

How Global Institutions Influence Market Behaviour

Institutions do far more than finance projects; they strengthen the habits, expectations, and strategic choices that shape sustainability-oriented markets.

Setting Standards That Guide the Market

Guidelines and frameworks created by institutions offer reference points for project evaluation, reporting, and transparency. When issuers follow these structures, investors gain clarity. Over time, these guidelines help markets mature and adopt practices that reinforce accountability and purpose.

Supporting Policy and National Planning

Countries developing their climate strategies often rely on institutional expertise. Development banks provide insights on taxonomies, sustainable finance regulations, and policy design. These contributions help governments shape programs that attract investment and build long-term environmental resilience.

Strengthening Sustainable Project Pipelines

Sustainable development requires ready, well-designed projects. Institutions help countries identify opportunities, assess viability, and prepare projects for financing. This support encourages the development of renewable energy corridors, nature-restoration programs, and resilient infrastructure.

Creating Confidence for Private Capital

When institutions participate in early-stage or complex sustainability initiatives, they provide assurance. Their presence signals reliability, encourages knowledge transfer, and reduces uncertainty for private investors. This multiplier effect allows clean energy, adaptation, and transition-focused initiatives to expand rapidly.

Through global frameworks and institutional leadership, green finance gains structure, clarity, and shared purpose. The next perspective emerges when these foundations meet regional priorities-each region interpreting global direction through its own economic realities, innovation pathways, and sustainability ambitions.

Regional dynamics give green finance its character. While global agreements and institutions lay the foundation, the vitality of the movement becomes clearer when we see how different geographies shape their own pathways.

Each region reflects its history, regulatory strength, technological capacity, and environmental priorities. Together, they create a mosaic of progress that strengthens the global transition.

Europe's Structured Clarity and Influence

Europe continues to stand out for its ability to transform climate ambition into well-organised financial systems. The region approaches sustainability through frameworks that guide both public and private markets, creating a structured ecosystem many countries look to for direction.

EU Taxonomy: A Shared Vocabulary for Sustainability

The EU taxonomy gives issuers and investors a common understanding of what qualifies as environmentally aligned economic activity. Its technical criteria create consistency, allowing capital to flow into areas that clearly support long-term ecological progress. The taxonomy's influence extends far beyond Europe, inspiring several countries to develop similar classification frameworks.

Sustainable Finance Disclosure Regulation (SFDR)

SFDR brings clarity to how financial institutions communicate their sustainability practices. It guides disclosures on strategies, risk integration, and impact alignment. This transparency strengthens investor confidence and encourages organisations to refine their sustainability approach with more precision.

EU Green Bond Standard

The EU Green Bond Standard complements the taxonomy by outlining how green bonds should be structured and reported. Its alignment requirements and impact-related disclosures help create stronger trust in green-labelled instruments. Many issuers across the world draw inspiration from its design.

Green Bond Leadership Across Europe

France, Germany, and several Nordic countries have cultivated deep green bond markets. The Nordic region, in particular, gained early attention when it introduced some of the world's first sovereign green bonds. These issuances helped set expectations for credibility, reporting, and environmental alignment, motivating other regions to enhance their sustainable finance frameworks.

Europe's approach shows how regulations, disclosures, and active markets can work together to strengthen long-term environmental planning.

North America's Innovation-Driven Sustainability Momentum

North America's contribution to green finance emerges through innovation, strong investor participation, and technological ambition. While its approach differs from Europe's structured clarity, it carries its own strengths that have shaped global markets in meaningful ways.

A Growing Market for Sustainability-Linked Instruments

Across the United States and Canada, sustainability-linked bonds and loans have gained remarkable traction. These instruments allow issuers to follow broad financial strategies while moving toward measurable sustainability outcomes. One of the earliest sustainability-linked loans originated in this region, demonstrating how creative financing models can influence global trends.

Role of Asset Managers and Pension Funds

Large asset managers play an essential part in shaping North American financial behaviour. Their sustainability perspectives influence capital allocation, corporate engagement, and long-term strategy formation. Pension funds also contribute significantly by supporting clean energy, green infrastructure, and outcome-focused investment programs.

Federal and State-Level Climate Action

Climate ambition in North America emerges through multiple channels. Federal programs encourage clean technology, while several states follow their own high-impact climate strategies. This combination creates a diverse landscape where innovation, regulation, and community-level initiatives evolve together.

Investment in Green Technology

Technological advancement continues to be one of North America's defining strengths. Sizable investments in electric mobility, renewable energy storage, carbon utilisation, and advanced materials demonstrate how financial and technological progress reinforce each other. These developments shape global expectations around climate-aligned innovation.

India: A Transformative Transition Story

India's place in the global green finance landscape continues to grow, driven by large-scale renewable energy expansion and steady policy alignment.

Solar and wind capacity reached global recognition due to the country's ability to scale projects rapidly. This achievement became a reference point for emerging market transition frameworks.

India's sovereign green bonds represent a strong commitment to climate-aligned development. Corporates also participate actively, issuing a range of green and sustainability-themed instruments. As the market evolves, national hydrogen ambitions add another dimension, encouraging industries to explore cleaner production pathways.

South Asia: Regional Approaches Shaped by Development Priorities

Bangladesh has demonstrated notable leadership through its green refinancing programs, enabling local banks to support environmentally aligned projects. Bangladesh Bank stands out for being among the earliest central banks anywhere to introduce green lending guidelines, a milestone that influenced the region's approach to sustainability.

Sri Lanka and Nepal follow development models anchored in renewable expansion, climate adaptation, and nature-aligned investments. Regional banks increasingly incorporate sustainability frameworks, offering structured pathways for businesses to adopt environmentally responsible strategies.

India added over 70 GW of solar capacity in a decade, placing it among the top global renewable markets [15].

South Asia's progress reflects a balance-one that supports development priorities while strengthening environmental stewardship. The region's financial systems continue evolving as institutions refine frameworks, adapt global ideas, and design local solutions.

These regional perspectives reveal how green finance adapts to local realities while contributing to global momentum. Different markets approach sustainability with distinct tools-regulation, innovation, large-scale infrastructure plans, and development-focused strategies.

Together, they create a dynamic landscape shaped by transition planning, technological expansion, and region-specific financial design.

Global green finance continues to mature through the distinct contributions of several fast-evolving regions.

These regions bring different strengths-some excel in scale, others in speed, and some in the creativity of their environmental finance models.

---

[15] *Ministry of New and Renewable Energy (MNRE), Government of India, Solar Energy Overview,*
https://mnre.gov.in/en/solar-overview/, accessed 4 December 2025.

Their efforts reveal how sustainability ambitions adapt to local conditions yet still move in harmony with global goals. With each new policy, investment framework, or financial instrument, the global landscape becomes more diverse, resilient, and capable of addressing long-term ecological challenges.

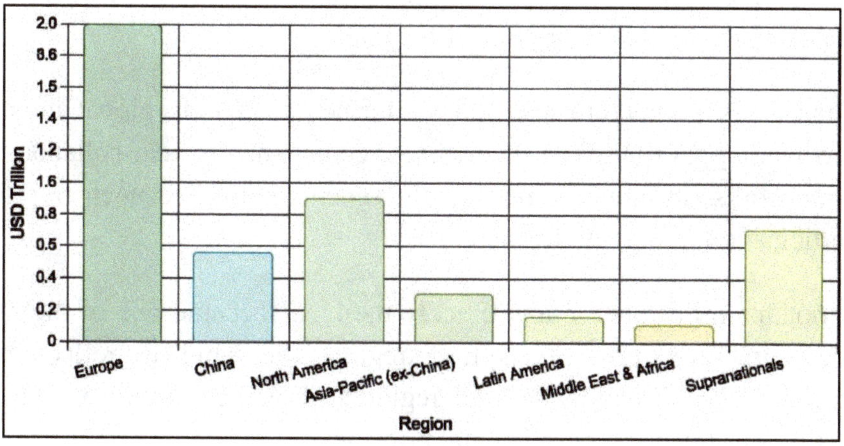

Source: Climate Bonds Initiative. (2025). Sustainable Debt Global State of the Market 2024. London: Climate Bonds Initiative.

GCC and the UAE - Momentum, Vision, and Strategic Clarity

The GCC region has emerged as a powerful participant in sustainable finance, combining long-term economic planning with forward-looking climate strategy. Within this region, the UAE stands out for shaping one of the most proactive sustainability pathways.

UAE's Expanding Sustainability Ambition

The UAE's net-zero vision encourages coordinated action across government agencies, financial institutions, and corporates. Its national strategies highlight renewable energy leadership, low-carbon infrastructure, and emerging green technology programs. These ambitions translate into active financial markets, where green bonds, sustainability-linked instruments, and thematic funds continue to gain traction. **The UAE's clean energy investments exceed USD 40 billion**, including solar mega-projects and hydrogen pilots. [16]

Issuers across sectors participate in this transition. Banks adopt sustainability-linked financing frameworks, real estate developers explore green-certified project financing, and infrastructure entities issue bonds aligned with energy transition goals.

The UAE's momentum strengthened further through the global attention surrounding COP28. The discussions, commitments, and collaborative frameworks introduced during the event helped deepen regional participation in climate finance.

A notable milestone is how quickly the UAE became one of the most active green finance markets in the region. This rapid rise reflects both strong policy direction and the region's ability to mobilise financial institutions toward environmental priorities.

Saudi Arabia's Transition Finance Vision

Saudi Arabia's sustainability journey emphasises large-scale transformation.

Its initiatives focus on green energy corridors, transition pathways for carbon-intensive sectors, and frameworks that encourage organisations to adopt clearer environmental strategies.

By integrating transition finance models into national plans, Saudi Arabia supports long-term diversification and creates opportunities for innovative financing tools.

---

[16] *World Economic Forum, Fostering Effective Energy Transition 2023: United Arab Emirates, World Economic Forum, 2023,* *https://www.weforum.org/publications/fostering-effective-energy-transition-2023/in-full/united-arab-emirates/, accessed 4 December 2025.*

Green Hydrogen Hubs Across the Region

The GCC's interest in green hydrogen has attracted global attention. Projects in the UAE, Saudi Arabia, and Oman highlight the region's potential to become a major producer of clean hydrogen. These hubs encourage collaboration between public and private actors and create demand for new financing structures that support technology deployment, renewable energy integration, and large-scale export infrastructure.

Together, GCC countries demonstrate how strong national visions, coordinated planning, and resource advantages can shape a sustainable financial ecosystem.

East Asia's Scale, Precision, and System-Level Approach

East Asia plays a central role in global green finance due to its scale, manufacturing strength, and coordinated policy design. The region's approach combines regulatory clarity with system-wide innovation, creating one of the most dynamic sustainability environments in the world.

China's Leadership in Green Finance

China established one of the world's earliest and most comprehensive green bond taxonomies. This classification system influences how issuers design projects and how investors interpret environmental alignment.

The taxonomy covers a wide range of activities, from renewable energy and clean transportation to pollution control and ecological restoration. **China holds the world's largest green loan portfolio, exceeding USD 3 trillion equivalent[17].**

---

[17] *Griffith Asia Institute, China's Green Finance: Status and Trends 2023–2024, Griffith University, 2024,*

China also built an extensive green loan portfolio-one of the largest globally. Banks integrate sustainability considerations into credit decisions, encouraging industries to adopt cleaner technologies. This scale makes China a major driver of global sustainable finance trends.

Japan's Transition Finance Guidelines

Japan's approach focuses on gradual, strategic transformation. Its transition finance guidelines help companies design pathways that reflect their industry realities while still aligning with long-term climate goals.

By supporting technology upgrades, energy efficiency, and innovation-led change, Japan provides a structured approach that suits sectors requiring staged transformation.

South Korea's Green Innovation Ecosystem

South Korea advances sustainability through its strength in technology-driven markets. Its national strategies emphasise green mobility, renewable energy expansion, smart cities, and low-carbon manufacturing. Korean institutions actively participate in green bond markets and support financing frameworks that accelerate innovation across industries.

East Asia's coordinated yet diverse approaches show how scale and systematic planning can reshape global financing patterns.

Africa: Integrating Resilience and Innovation

Africa's green finance landscape grows through strategies that balance environmental priorities with socio-economic development. Climate adaptation finance plays a central role. **Africa's climate financing needs**

---

https://blogs.griffith.edu.au/asiainsights/china-green-finance-status-and-trends-2023-2024/, accessed 4 December 2025.

are estimated at USD 250 billion annually between by 2020 and 2030, far above current flows[18].

Countries across the region invest in early-warning systems, drought resilience projects, water infrastructure, and agricultural transformation to support long-term stability.

Green mini-grids have become one of Africa's most influential contributions to global sustainability.

These systems provide clean energy solutions for rural and underserved communities, demonstrating how decentralised models can support both development and climate goals.

Several African nations, including Nigeria and Egypt, issued sovereign green bonds to finance renewable energy, transportation networks, and environmental restoration. These issuances helped strengthen credibility for sustainable finance across the region.

Africa also contributed significantly to nature-based finance. Land restoration programs, biodiversity conservation models, and community-centred financing frameworks gained global recognition.

These models show how ecological stewardship can support livelihoods while strengthening climate resilience.

---

[18] *Climate Policy Initiative (CPI), Climate Finance Innovation for Africa, CPI, 2023, https://www.climatepolicyinitiative.org/publication/climate-finance-innovation-for-africa/, accessed 4 December 2025.*

Region	Policy Maturity	First-of-its-Kind Milestone (Year)	Dominant Instrument 2024	2024 Issuance (USD bn)	Signature Strength
Europe	5/5	Sovereign green bond, Poland (2016)	Green Use-of-Proceeds	380	EU Taxonomy & SFDR, global benchmark
China	4/5	National green bond catalogue (2015)	Green Use-of-Proceeds + Loans	280	Scale & world's largest green loan stock
North America	4/5	First sustainability-linked loan (2017)	Sustainability-Linked (SLB)	180	Private-sector innovation & asset managers
Asia-Pacific (ex-China)	4/5	Japan Transition Finance Guidelines (2021)	Transition & Green	95	Transition finance leadership
Latin America	3/5	Chile SL sovereign bond (2022)	Sustainability-Linked Sovereign	38	Biodiversity & natural-capital finance
Middle East & GCC	3/5	UAE sovereign green bond (2022)	Green & Transition	42	Green hydrogen hubs & rapid growth

Africa	2/5	Egypt sovereign green bond (2020)	Sovereign Green	18	Adaptation & off-grid renewables

Latin America: Biodiversity and Natural Capital in Financial Design

Latin America integrates sustainability into economic planning through deep experience with natural ecosystems. Brazil's environmental finance initiatives include conservation-linked lending, regional sustainability funds, and programs that support forest protection. These initiatives highlight the region's ability to align financial structures with natural capital.

Chile made global headlines through its sustainability-linked sovereign bonds. These issuances tied national financing to measurable sustainability performance, signalling strong commitment to climate-aligned development.

Latin America contains over 40% of the world's biodiversity, making natural-capital finance one of its strongest market areas[19].

Across the region, financial models based on forests, water systems, and natural resources gained traction. These models encourage governments and private actors to view biodiversity as a long-term economic asset. Latin America's frameworks influenced international discussions on nature-positive finance, strengthening the link between ecological preservation and financial innovation.

[19] *Convention on Biological Diversity (CBD), Global Biodiversity Outlook 4: Regional Assessment for Latin America and the Caribbean (GRULAC), CBD, 2014,* https://www.cbd.int/gbo/gbo4/outlook-grulac-en.pdf, *accessed 4 December 2025.*

Key Takeaways

- Global climate agreements created direction for sustainable finance and shaped policy alignment across regions.
- Multilateral and development banks designed frameworks, instruments, and blended models that mobilised large-scale climate capital.
- Europe strengthened sustainable finance through structured regulation and transparent reporting standards.
- North America advanced market innovation and technology-driven sustainability pathways.
- India and South Asia broadened transition finance through renewable expansion and evolving market systems.
- The GCC and the UAE accelerated green finance momentum through ambitious national strategies, hydrogen hubs, and active bond markets.
- East Asia contributed scale, taxonomies, and transition frameworks that influenced global market behaviour.
- Africa and Latin America expanded nature-based and resilience-focused financial models that shaped global sustainability thinking.
- Together, these regions form an interconnected landscape where policy, innovation, and financial commitment guide the future of green finance.

4

Green Bonds and Sustainability-Linked Bonds

Green and sustainability-linked bonds have become two of the most influential instruments in modern climate finance. They began as specialised tools used mostly by development banks and a few pioneering governments.

Over the years, they matured into mainstream vehicles capable of shaping national transition strategies, influencing investor expectations, and guiding market behaviour. Their rise reflects a larger shift in how financial systems understand environmental responsibility-moving from fragmented initiatives to structured, transparent, and measurable commitments.

As the world increasingly plans its growth around climate resilience, these instruments now serve as anchors that connect ambition with long-term capital flows.

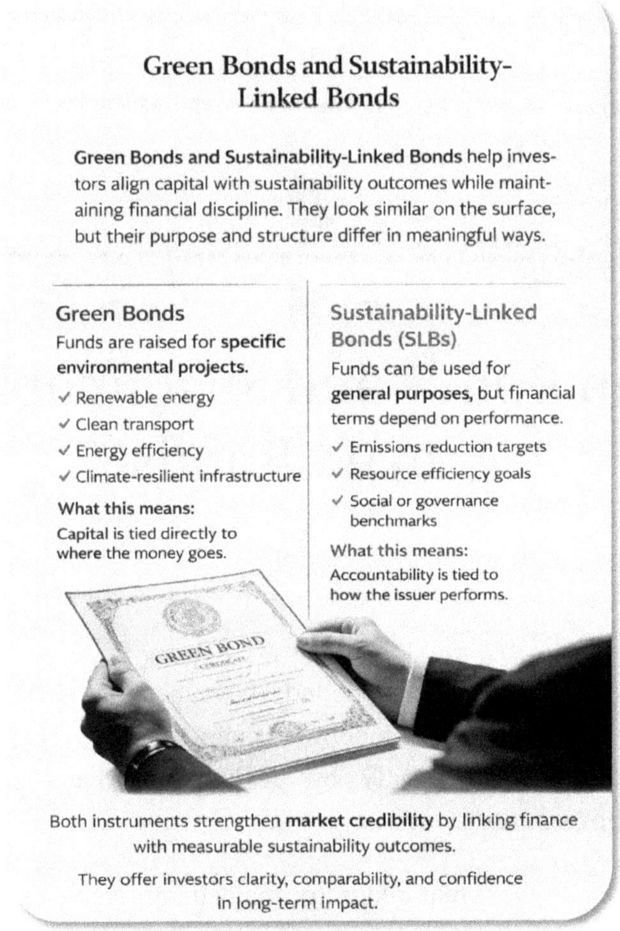

This evolution did not happen by chance.

Markets needed clarity as sustainability priorities grew more complex. Institutions around the world began seeking instruments that could articulate purpose clearly, demonstrate measurable progress, and offer investors a way to engage with transition pathways without uncertainty. Labelled bonds answered that need. They introduced well-defined categories, documented frameworks, and reporting practices that strengthened market confidence.

What began as a niche segment gained respect because it reduced ambiguity and encouraged disciplined financial behaviour.

A significant turning point came when cumulative issuance in the global labelled bond market - including green, social, sustainability, and sustainability-linked bond - crossed USD 2 trillion by 2023, according to the Climate Bonds Initiative. This milestone illustrated how rapidly investor appetite expanded and how central these instruments have become to sustainable finance[20].

That momentum continues to grow as institutions refine frameworks, introduce new structures, and explore innovations rooted in measurable performance.

The appeal of these instruments lies in their balance: they blend flexibility with discipline, ambition with verification, and long-term strategy with immediate transparency. They allow issuers to shape clear environmental or social outcomes while offering investors reliable insight into how funds are used and what progress is being achieved.

Bond frameworks, external reviews, market precedents, and evolving investor expectations now form a shared language that professionals across sectors rely on. This chapter opens the door to that landscape-its structures, its discipline, its practical nuances, and the opportunities it creates for both issuers and practitioners.

By understanding how these bonds work and what gives them credibility, readers gain the confidence to interpret market signals with clarity and depth.

---

[20] *Climate Bonds Initiative (CBI), Global State of the Market Report 2023, Climate Bonds Initiative, 2023,* *https://www.climatebonds.net/files/documents/publications/Global-State-of-the-Market-Report-2023.pdf, accessed 7 December 2025.*

OBJECTIVES OF THE CHAPTER

This chapter will help readers:

- Understand the purpose and design of labelled bonds within sustainable finance ecosystems.
- Differentiate with confidence between green, social, sustainability, and sustainability-linked bonds.
- Recognise why use-of-proceeds frameworks hold central importance in credible sustainable finance.
- Learn how sustainability-linked bonds anchor progress through KPIs, targets, and transparent tracking.
- Explore the forces behind global market growth, investor interest, and rising demand for credible instruments.
- See how external reviews and second-party opinions enhance trust and shape issuer behaviour.
- Discover meaningful global and emerging market examples that influenced the development of this field.
- Identify practical opportunities and challenges faced by issuers as they align with sustainability expectations.
- Develop a structured and analytical lens for evaluating any green or sustainability-linked bond framework.
- Build confidence in interpreting sustainable debt markets through well-designed instruments and disciplined reporting.

Understanding Labelled Bonds and Their Core Logic

Labelled bonds emerged as a natural response to the growing need for financial instruments that clearly stated their purpose. As sustainability ambitions expanded, investors wanted to know whether their capital supported environmental improvements, strengthened communities, or contributed to larger wellbeing goals.

Traditional bonds never revealed this level of intention. Green, social, and sustainability bonds filled that gap by introducing clarity, signalling alignment with broader development priorities, and strengthening the communication bridge between issuers and investors.

Green bonds channel capital into clearly defined environmental improvements like renewable energy, efficient buildings, clean mobility, and water systems.

- Social bonds focus on community outcomes such as healthcare, education, housing, and inclusive development.
- Sustainability bonds blend both aims, acknowledging that environmental and social progress reinforce each other.
- Each label signals an issuer's intentional shift toward integrating sustainability into core financial strategy.

Markets embraced these instruments because they created a shared vocabulary. When a bond is labelled, investors know precisely what kind of impact it aims to support and how the issuer intends to allocate funds. This clarity reduces ambiguity and encourages disciplined planning. It also allows institutions to design portfolios aligned with transition strategies, community support programmes, or integrated sustainability pathways.

The earliest phase of labelled bonds offers an important context. Development banks and supranational institutions introduced the first green bonds more than a decade ago, offering a template for the market to follow.

Their presence helped shape early expectations around reporting, project selection, and transparency.

A major inflection point arrived when governments began issuing sovereign green bonds, signaling that sustainability-aligned financing had become a core element of national development strategies rather than something confined to specialised institutions. This shift broadened participation and encouraged countries to examine how capital markets could support long-term ecological priorities.

The idea behind labelled bonds is simple but powerful: purpose-driven financing strengthens trust, encourages accountability, and shapes behaviour across markets. As sustainability became a central theme in economic planning, these instruments moved from experimentation to mainstream use, becoming one of the most recognised elements of modern sustainable finance.

Use of Proceeds, Frameworks, and Reporting Discipline

The credibility of labelled bonds rests on their structure. Investors need to know how funds will be used, how issuers define eligibility, how progress will be tracked, and how results will be communicated. This is where use-of-proceeds frameworks play a vital role. These frameworks outline the activities that qualify for financing, the internal processes used to evaluate projects, and the systems in place to manage and monitor allocations.

- Most labelled-bond frameworks follow ICMA principles for consistency and market credibility.
- The framework rests on four pillars:
    - how proceeds will be used
    - how projects are evaluated and selected
    - how proceeds are tracked
    - how reporting will be delivered
- Using these standards helps issuers communicate transparency and long-term intent.
- Investors gain a clearer view of ambition, direction, and reliability.

Eligible categories usually reflect national or sector priorities. A green bond may support solar parks, electric mobility infrastructure, sustainable agriculture, or circular economy initiatives.

A social bond may target affordable housing, inclusive financing for small entrepreneurs, or community health initiatives. What matters is that issuers describe these categories with precision, supported by robust internal processes that ensure funds reach their intended purpose.

Reporting forms the backbone of investor confidence. Allocation reporting shows where the money went, while impact reporting describes the outcomes achieved.

Strong reporting practices help investors understand both the scale and effectiveness of financed activities. When issuers present clear metrics, independent evaluations, and measurable progress, they enhance market credibility and strengthen long-term relationships with investors.

Transparency reduces uncertainty, and this is one reason labelled bonds continue to attract deep, long-term capital. When investors understand exactly how their capital contributes to environmental or social progress, they engage with greater confidence and remain aligned with issuers for future transactions.

A historical example highlights how this discipline shaped global expectations. The World Bank's early green bond issuances demonstrated how structured, transparent reporting frameworks could elevate credibility.

Their templates provided clarity on impact categories, monitoring systems, and project-level results, encouraging other institutions to adopt similar practices. This created a foundation for the broader adoption of use-of-proceeds frameworks across regions.

One milestone also illustrates the importance of structure: **ICMA's principles became the dominant global reference, influencing more than 90% of global labelled bond frameworks by the early 2020s (ICMA Market Survey).** This widespread adoption shows how aligned frameworks help markets grow with coherence and trust[21].

[21] *International Capital Market Association (ICMA), Green Bond Principles, ICMA, https://www.icmagroup.org/sustainable-finance/the-principles-guidelines-and-handbooks/green-bond-principles-gbp/, accessed 7 December 2025.*

Market Growth, Investor Appetite, and Evolving Demand

As sustainable finance matured, investor interest expanded rapidly. Long-term investors-pension funds, insurance companies, sovereign wealth funds-sought instruments that matched their horizon while also supporting climate and community resilience.

Labelled bonds offered that alignment, combining predictable cash flows with measurable impact. This created a natural synergy between long-term capital and long-term sustainability priorities.

Market growth has been steady and broad-based. Green bonds initiated the movement, but social and sustainability bonds soon followed, expanding the investor base and diversifying impact categories. What stands out is how investors evaluate these instruments. Beyond returns, they look at clarity of intention, strength of frameworks, and quality of reporting. Instruments backed by strong governance receive greater traction because investors place high value on transparent and credible commitments.

Demand strengthened across both developed and emerging markets. Europe continues to lead through regulatory support and structured taxonomies. North America shows strong interest driven by innovation and institutional preferences. Asia's role grows each year, supported by transition planning and large-scale infrastructure needs. Meanwhile, emerging markets attract investors who appreciate strong purpose-driven frameworks, especially when supported by development banks or national strategies.

Investor behaviour reveals a key insight: markets reward issuers who communicate clearly and report consistently. Strong frameworks attract repeat investors.

High-quality impact reporting encourages diversified participation. Instruments aligned with national climate or development strategies create confidence and strengthen long-term partnerships. This behaviour explains why labelled bonds continue expanding across sectors-from energy and transport to manufacturing, housing, and public services.

Interest also rises because labelled bonds help investors manage transition risk. By financing sustainable assets or encouraging organisations to adopt cleaner practices, these instruments help reduce long-term exposure to climate-related vulnerabilities. Investors increasingly incorporate sustainability considerations into mainstream financial analysis, viewing labelled bonds as integral to building resilient portfolios.

Regional dynamics enhance this story. Nordic issuers continue influencing best practices. Asian markets explore innovative structures. Latin American issuers design biodiversity-oriented financing models. African markets experiment with green mini-grid financing and adaptation-focused bonds. These developments illustrate how demand for labelled instruments adapts to local priorities while contributing to a global movement.

Overall, the rise of labelled bonds reflects a blend of clarity, transparency, and strategic alignment. Investors engage with them for financial stability and for the confidence that comes from measurable, purpose-driven outcomes. This balanced appeal ensures that labelled bonds remain central to global sustainable finance.

Sustainability-Linked Bonds: Performance Pathways and Organisational Signals

Sustainability-linked bonds introduced a different way of thinking about climate and social ambition. Instead of focusing on specific projects, these instruments encourage organisations to improve their overall performance through measurable commitments. Where use-of-proceeds bonds ask, "What will the funds support?" SLBs ask a deeper question: "How will the organisation evolve over time?" This shift elevates sustainability from an activity-level decision to a strategic priority integrated across the entire business.

Criteria	Green Bonds (Use-of-Proceeds)	Sustainability-Linked Bonds (Performance-Based)
Core Logic	Funds must be used for specific eligible green projects	Funds can be used for any purpose; performance is tied to sustainability KPIs
What Investors Evaluate	Project categories, eligibility rules, reporting quality	Strength of KPIs, ambition of targets, baseline clarity
Typical Use	Renewable energy, clean mobility, buildings, water systems	Emission reduction, energy efficiency, resource circularity
Framework Requirement	Mandatory clear use-of-proceeds framework aligned with ICMA	Mandatory KPI framework + SPT (sustainability performance targets)
Accountability Mechanism	Reporting on allocation and impact of financed projects	Coupon step-up if targets are missed; strong disclosure required
Ideal For	Issuers with clear green project pipelines	Issuers without project pipelines but with strong transition commitments
Investor Focus	Environmental contribution and project outcomes	Organisation-wide behavioural change and long-term pathway
Verification Style	Second-party opinion focuses on project categories & impact	SPO focuses on KPI relevance, ambition, baselines, methodologies

SLBs revolve around carefully chosen key performance indicators. These KPIs represent the areas where an organisation intends to demonstrate meaningful advancement-emission reduction, energy efficiency gains, water-use optimisation, or circularity improvements.

The targets connected to these KPIs must show ambition, credibility, and alignment with long-term transition planning. When done well, they serve as signals of an organisation's direction and maturity.

Designing KPIs requires thoughtful judgement. They must reflect areas material to the issuer's sector, measurable within defined timelines, and aligned with global sustainability pathways. Strong targets encourage better governance and operational discipline.

They also influence internal behaviour, because a missed target carries financial consequences through coupon step-ups. This dynamic creates a steady incentive for companies to integrate sustainability commitments into everyday decision-making.

SLBs created a clear pathway for sectors without ready green-bond project pipelines to actively show their transition commitment. Heavy industry, logistics, and manufacturing have used SLBs to show long-term improvement trajectories.

The structure gives them flexibility while maintaining accountability, which explains why SLBs have become one of the fastest-growing innovations in sustainable finance.

A moment often referenced when discussing SLB evolution comes from one early transaction in Asia that directly linked interest adjustments to ESG scoring improvements.

This deal showed how financial incentives could reinforce sustainability ambitions. The design was straightforward yet influential, inspiring other issuers to explore how organisational change could be tied to financing terms.

As markets mature, expectations around SLBs continue increasing. Investors study the strength of KPIs, the clarity of baselines, the transparency of methodologies, and the issuer's readiness to report frequently. Strong SLBs highlight a company's confidence in its long-term pathway.

Weak SLBs reveal hesitation. This difference influences investor behaviour and becomes an important part of market due diligence.

According to Climate Bonds Initiative, SLB issuance exceeded USD 90 billion globally by 2023, reflecting how quickly these instruments became central to transition-focused financing[22].

The appetite for SLBs indicates a broader trend-investors value commitments backed by measurable, time-bound action.

External Reviews, Independent Opinions, and Market Integrity

As labelled bonds expanded, so did the need for trust. Investors wanted assurance that the commitments presented by issuers were aligned with recognised standards and backed by credible methodologies. This is where external reviews and independent opinions gained importance.

They help verify alignment with established frameworks, strengthen communication, and elevate the overall integrity of sustainable finance markets.

---

[22] *Climate Bonds Initiative (CBI), Global State of the Market Report 2023, Climate Bonds Initiative, 2023,* *https://www.climatebonds.net/files/documents/publications/Global-State-of-the-Market-Report-2023.pdf, accessed 7 December 2025.*

Second-party opinions are one of the most familiar forms of external evaluation. Independent institutions study the issuer's framework, assess eligibility criteria, evaluate KPI selection, and confirm alignment with market principles. Their role is to offer analytical insight that investors can rely on. A well-prepared SPO gives depth to an issuer's strategy and helps stakeholders understand the thinking behind each element of the framework.

Verification also includes audits, impact assessments, and annual reporting reviews. These steps ensure that commitments translate into measurable outcomes. The independence of reviewers builds confidence, because it reduces interpretive uncertainty and encourages disciplined reporting from issuers. Investors appreciate this clarity; it allows them to compare instruments more effectively and understand the credibility of an issuer's commitments.

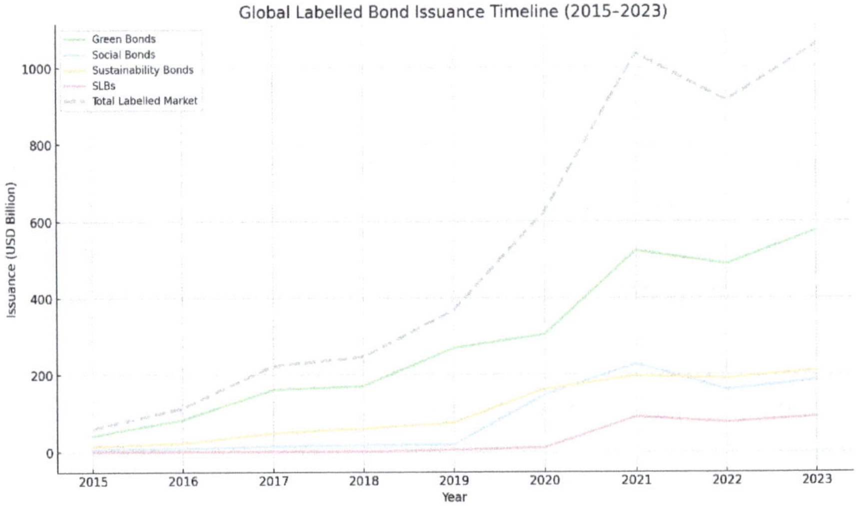

Source: Climate Bonds Initiative (Global State of the Market 2023; SLB Market Analysis 2023); ICMA Sustainable Bond Market Survey 2022.

Practitioners reading verification documents focus on several aspects. The strength of methodologies, the clarity of baselines, the ambition level of KPIs, and the transparency of data sources are among the primary areas of attention. A clear assessment helps investors evaluate whether an instrument aligns with global expectations and whether the issuer's approach reflects long-term resilience.

Different instruments require different review styles. Use-of-proceeds bonds often rely on project-level evaluation and impact alignment. SLBs need deeper organisational analysis because KPIs represent long-term commitments rather than isolated activities. Independent reviews help differentiate between promising structures and frameworks that require further refinement.

External reviews also influence issuer behaviour. They encourage organisations to strengthen internal data systems, improve governance, and prepare more robust measurement practices. Many issuers repeat their work with the same reviewer across multiple transactions because consistency helps build long-term credibility. These collaborative dynamic supports market maturity and enrich cross-industry knowledge sharing.

In practice, verification is part of building trust. Investors rely on independent insight, issuers use the process to refine their frameworks, and markets gain efficiency through aligned expectations. As sustainability commitments become more ambitious, the value of credible verification increases steadily.

Global Examples, Issuer Opportunities, Challenges & Practitioner Checklist

Across regions, issuers use labelled instruments to communicate direction, strengthen their sustainability agendas, and access broader pools of capital. These examples highlight how green and sustainability-linked bonds adapt to different priorities while reinforcing global trends.

European issuers continue demonstrating leadership by integrating taxonomies, detailed reporting systems, and strong KPI-based frameworks. North American issuers explore innovative structures tied to technology, clean mobility, and portfolio-level commitments.

Asian markets introduce transition-oriented KPIs, reflecting the diverse realities of energy systems and manufacturing sectors. Emerging markets increasingly participate by issuing sovereign and corporate green bonds that support renewable energy and infrastructure development.

These examples show how labelled bonds operate across economic models. In some regions, they highlight regulatory alignment. In others, they encourage innovation or strengthen access to international investors. Each issuance expands the knowledge base and broadens the understanding of how sustainable finance evolves globally.

Issuers benefit from several opportunities. Labelled bonds help strengthen market visibility, attract long-term capital, and communicate strategic priorities with clarity. They also support internal alignment because different teams-finance, sustainability, operations, and strategy-collaborate closely while preparing frameworks and reports.

Challenges also exist. Issuers need strong data systems, clearly defined KPIs, and the ability to report consistently. Preparing internal structures to track sustainability progress can take time. Investors expect high-quality disclosures, strong baseline logic, and transparency in methodologies. Meeting these expectations requires continuous refinement.

For students and practitioners evaluating a labelled bond framework, a simple checklist helps build confidence:

- Review the clarity of the issuer's sustainability strategy.
- Study the use-of-proceeds categories or KPIs for alignment with material issues.

- Examine baselines, timelines, and any underlying assumptions.
- Assess the transparency of reporting commitments.
- Check whether an external review provides clear and balanced analysis.
- Look for alignment with recognised principles and taxonomies.
- Consider whether the structure reflects ambition appropriate for the issuer's sector.
- Evaluate the issuer's capacity to measure, report, and verify outcomes.

This lens helps readers interpret labelled instruments thoughtfully and recognise the strengths and limitations of each structure. It also encourages practitioners to adopt balanced judgement rather than rely solely on labels or high-level claims.

Key Takeaways

- Labelled bonds create structured, transparent pathways for financing environmental and social priorities.
- Use-of-proceeds frameworks guide disciplined planning, allocation, and impact measurement.
- Sustainability-linked bonds encourage long-term organisational progress through measurable KPIs.
- External reviews support credibility, comparability, and clarity across markets.
- Global examples show how different regions use labelled instruments to advance transition goals.
- Issuers gain strategic advantage through improved visibility and access to deep investor pools.
- Strong frameworks depend on data quality, ambitious KPIs, and transparent reporting.
- Practitioners benefit by analysing frameworks through structure, ambition, and alignment with international standards.

5

Loans, Credit Lines and Project Finance with a Green Lens

Green loans and sustainability-linked loans have become essential instruments for climate-focused development. Their rise reflects a simple truth: lending decisions shape real outcomes on the ground.

Renewable energy projects, efficient manufacturing systems, resilient infrastructure networks, and cleaner mobility corridors all depend on access to structured, well-designed credit. Banks now operate as active partners in this transition.

Their policies guide which technologies gain scale, which organisations strengthen their sustainability pathways, and which sectors move toward more resilient models.

According to the Loan Market Association and the Climate Bonds Initiative, **cumulative global green loan issuance crossed USD 500**

billion by 2022[23], a milestone that shows how quickly lending aligned itself with long-term sustainability goals.

A quiet but important shift has taken place inside lending institutions. Credit assessments that once looked purely at financial ratios now incorporate environmental commitments, long-term operational resilience, and transition alignment.

[23] *International Energy Agency (IEA), World Energy Investment 2023: Overview and Key Findings, IEA, 2023,* https://www.iea.org/reports/world-energy-investment-2023/overview-and-key-findings, *accessed 7 December 2025.*

Lending teams study how a company manages emissions, handles resources, and prepares for new regulatory expectations. Internal due diligence touches areas that were never part of traditional credit conversations-baselines, sustainability targets, measurable outcomes, and governance strength.

Once these elements enter the credit process, they influence how covenants are structured, how performance triggers are designed, and how pricing reflects improvement pathways.

Alongside these internal changes, broader financing structures have also evolved. Project finance provides a stable backbone for capital-intensive green developments, from utility-scale solar parks to waste-to-energy facilities.

Structured credit lines-public, private, and blended-help institutions de-risk innovation, expand infrastructure, and open access for sectors that gain strength through concessional elements or multilateral participation. Performance-linked pricing adds another dimension by encouraging companies to move steadily toward sustainability commitments.

Risk-mitigation tools support these systems, ensuring that financial resilience grows in step with environmental ambition. All these elements work together, forming a comprehensive landscape where lending activity becomes a cornerstone of climate-aligned growth.

OBJECTIVES OF THE CHAPTER

This section supports a clear understanding of how green lending and project finance operate by offering guidance to:

- Understand green loans and sustainability-linked loans and how they differ from labelled bonds.
- Learn how banks integrate sustainability into credit assessments and internal lending structures.

- Explore the role of covenants, pricing adjustments, and performance targets in sustainability-linked finance.
- Build clarity around project finance fundamentals in a way that feels accessible for individuals without a finance background.
- Recognise how public, private, and blended credit lines expand opportunities for sustainable development.
- Study how lending teams examine transition strategies, project readiness, and operational strength.
- Identify key risks associated with green lending and project finance and understand how financial structures absorb them.
- See how mitigation strategies strengthen borrower stability and lender confidence.
- Understand how sustainability frameworks influence lending behaviour at institutional and market levels.
- Build confidence in interpreting green loans, sustainability-linked loans, and project finance structures with clarity and balance.

Green Loans and Sustainability-Linked Loans: Foundations and Market Logic

Green loans and sustainability-linked loans sit at the heart of modern transition finance, shaped by two different logics that complement each other. Green loans work through a use-of-proceeds model.

The lender provides capital that directly supports categories aligned with environmental improvement-renewable energy systems, efficient buildings, clean transport, water stewardship, nature-positive initiatives, and other project-driven outcomes. Each category is chosen with clarity, backed by credible documentation, governance structures, and measurable expectations.

Their strength lies in directing money toward initiatives that create visible, trackable environmental progress.

Sustainability-linked loans take a different path. They allow borrowers from any sector to demonstrate ambition through performance-based commitments.

These commitments revolve around key performance indicators that represent long-term priorities: emission reduction, renewable energy adoption, energy-efficiency improvement, waste-cycle optimisation, or other metrics suited to the borrower's industry.

Because these KPIs influence pricing, companies develop structured improvement pathways, internal monitoring systems, and transparent methodologies that create discipline across their operations.

Both instruments strengthen the relationship between intention and action. Green loans emphasise where the capital goes; sustainability-linked loans highlight how an organisation evolves.

Together, they expand access for diverse industries-sectors with strong project pipelines and sectors undergoing deeper strategic transitions. This dual model allows lenders to support high-impact projects while motivating broad organisational progress.

Lenders study several dimensions when evaluating these instruments. They examine environmental strategies, governance quality, transition readiness, and how upcoming regulations may influence operations. For green loans, lenders evaluate the pipeline of eligible projects, technical relevance, implementation plans, and monitoring systems. For sustainability-linked loans, they examine KPI selection, baseline credibility, target calibration, and the borrower's ability to measure and report progress across multiple years.

A global milestone helped accelerate confidence. According to the Loan Market Association and BloombergNEF, **sustainability-linked loan issuance crossed USD 1.5 trillion cumulatively by 2023**-a significant indicator of how quickly borrowers embraced performance-linked financing[24].

[24] *Bank for International Settlements (BIS), Quarterly Review – December 2023, BIS, 2023,* ***section on sustainable finance and loan markets (Credit Markets)****, citing BloombergNEF data,* *https://www.bis.org/publ/qtrpdf/r_qt2312.htm, accessed 7 December 2025.*

This scale shows that companies across manufacturing, services, real estate, logistics, and energy have integrated sustainability targets into mainstream borrowing activity.

This evolution reflects a maturing financial system. As green priorities enter national strategies and corporate planning, debt instruments become pathways to operational resilience.

Borrowers receive the benefit of purpose-aligned capital or performance-linked pricing, while lenders gain visibility into long-term commitments. Lending no longer supports only assets; it supports behaviour, governance, and long-term transition discipline.

How Banks Integrate Sustainability into Credit Decisions

Once sustainability considerations enter credit processes, the lender's evaluation approach transforms. The objective remains financial soundness, yet the lens widens to include environmental resilience, transition planning, and long-term operational maturity. This integration happens through several layers inside the bank.

- Due diligence now evaluates environmental performance, compliance track record, and exposure to climate risks.
- Carbon-heavy companies are assessed for upgrade plans, long-term transition pathways, and technological feasibility.
- Resource-sensitive sectors undergo deeper review around water risk, supply-chain stability, and efficiency practices.
- These environmental insights sit alongside traditional financial analysis to shape the final lending decision.

Criteria	Green Loans	Sustainability-Linked Loans (SLLs)
Core Logic	Use-of-proceeds model; funds must finance eligible green activities	Performance-based model; any use of funds allowed if KPIs are met
What Lenders Evaluate	Project eligibility, environmental categories, implementation plans	KPI selection, baseline strength, target ambition, reporting capacity
Typical Use	Solar, wind, energy efficiency upgrades, clean transport, water systems	Emission-intensity reduction, renewable-energy adoption, waste optimisation
Driver of Discipline	Project-level reporting and tracking	KPI-linked pricing adjustments (step-ups/step-downs)
Reporting Style	Allocation + impact reporting for financed assets	Annual KPI performance verification with agreed methodologies
Who Uses It	Borrowers with clear green project pipelines	Borrowers across all sectors, even without project pipelines
Pricing Logic	Standard loan pricing, sometimes concessional or blended	Pricing linked to KPI achievement across defined timelines
Ideal Benefit	Direct environmental improvement through targeted financing	Broad organisational transition, governance discipline, operational upgrades

Banks increasingly use ESG scoring frameworks to support this process. ESG scoring evaluates governance strength, operational practices, emissions trajectory, resource efficiency, safety systems, and disclosures. Though the scoring tools vary across institutions, their purpose is the same-to help credit teams judge whether environmental performance supports long-term stability.

Transition-readiness assessments also play a growing role. These assessments evaluate the company's strategy, technology adoption plans, business-model alignment with national or sectoral transition pathways, and internal capacity to meet sustainability commitments.

When these elements align, lenders feel confident that the borrower can manage both operational risks and evolving regulatory expectations.

Banks rely on internal taxonomies to guide these evaluations. Internal taxonomies classify economic activities based on environmental alignment, resilience potential, and transition feasibility.

They create structure within the credit decision process, allowing teams to categorise exposures, prioritise sustainable sectors, and identify where additional mitigation measures may be needed. Internal taxonomies also help ensure consistency across departments-risk, credit, sustainability, legal, and lending operations.

Scenario analysis strengthens this evaluation further. Banks run forward-looking models to understand how environmental or regulatory changes may affect cash flows.

For sectors facing transition pressure-such as heavy industry, chemicals, transport, or utilities-scenario analysis helps quantify how evolving emission norms, renewable-energy integration, or efficiency requirements may influence financial outcomes.

Lenders also analyse data quality. Borrowers with strong internal systems-audited metrics, digital tracking, clear baselines-gain smoother approval pathways because their reporting inspires confidence. Where data systems are still maturing, banks may require additional governance commitments, monitoring arrangements, or strengthened covenants to ensure progress remains measurable.

Through these practices, sustainability becomes part of credit reasoning rather than an accessory. Lending integrates environmental understanding with financial logic, allowing banks to support projects and organisations that move steadily toward long-term strength. The process is practical: it supports risk management, enhances transparency, and encourages borrowers to align operations with durable environmental expectations.

Covenants, Pricing, and Performance Targets: How Incentives Shape Behaviour

Covenants sit at the centre of sustainability-linked lending because they define what the borrower commits to achieve. These covenants outline improvement pathways, timelines, and measurable expectations. They also include provisions for how progress will be reviewed, how data will be verified, and how underperformance will influence pricing.

Pricing adjustments reinforce these covenants. When a borrower meets or exceeds targets, the pricing curve shifts in their favour. When progress slows, the pricing mechanism applies a step-up.

This approach strengthens accountability and encourages internal alignment across teams-finance, sustainability, operations, and strategy all work together to meet commitments that influence financial outcomes.

In sustainability-linked loans, KPIs act as anchors. Each KPI must be material to the borrower's sector, measurable through audited or verifiable data, and ambitious enough to reflect meaningful progress. Banks evaluate whether the chosen KPI demonstrates clear transition pathways. For example, a manufacturing company may commit to energy-efficiency improvements, renewable energy sourcing, or emission-intensity reduction. A logistics company may focus on fleet electrification, route optimisation, or fuel-efficiency gains.

- Many sustainability-linked covenants include extra action-based requirements.
- Some require the borrower to adopt new technologies or implement certified systems.
- Others define clear reporting timelines, quarterly, semi-annual, or annual.
- The reporting rhythm depends on the KPI's complexity and the company's operational scale.
- These features strengthen discipline and ensure steady visibility on progress.

A simple narrative anchor helps illustrate this structure. Imagine a mid-sized industrial firm seeking a sustainability-linked loan. The company selects emission-intensity reduction as its core KPI.

It establishes a baseline from audited data, sets a multi-year target aligned with industry pathways, and develops an upgrade plan for machinery and energy sourcing. The covenant includes annual verification, and pricing is tied to performance bands.

The structure encourages the company to follow through on its improvement plan because operational gains translate into financial benefits.

In green loans, covenants focus more on project-level discipline-eligibility definitions, procurement requirements, environmental-management systems, and reporting commitments. Although the logic differs, the purpose remains the same: create a transparent pathway where financial incentives support environmental outcomes.

Banks design these structures with careful attention. Covenants protect the lender's interest, pricing aligns with performance, and targets encourage operational maturity. Borrowers gain credibility in the market and strengthen their internal systems. Lending thus becomes a partnership that supports both sustainability progress and financial resilience.

Seeing Project Finance Through a Green Lens

Project finance often feels technical from the outside, yet its core idea is simple: a project must stand on its own feet. The loan is repaid from the project's future cash flows. This structure is helpful for sustainable sectors because many green assets-solar parks, wind farms, water systems, energy-efficient infrastructure-are capital-intensive with long lifecycles. A well-designed project finance structure allows such assets to attract capital confidently and transparently.

At the heart of project finance lies the SPV, or Special Purpose Vehicle. The SPV acts as the home for the entire project. Contracts, revenues, risks, and obligations sit within this entity.

This keeps the project clean, clearly defined, and insulated from the wider operations of the sponsor. For banks, this clarity is essential. It lets them study project fundamentals without dilution from unrelated activities.

Risk allocation sits beside the SPV as the second pillar. In project finance, every risk is placed with the party best equipped to manage it. Construction firms handle completion risk through EPC contracts. Operators take responsibility for performance.

Off-takers demonstrate the capacity to purchase energy or services. Government authorities provide long-term licenses or concessions. When risks sit with the right party, the project gains structural stability.

Cash-flow design ties the system together. Revenue flows must be predictable, aligned with debt schedules, and supported by strong contractual arrangements.

Power purchase agreements, availability-based payments, and user-fee mechanisms help create dependable financial ecosystems. For green assets, cash-flow visibility is especially important because investors value stability alongside environmental outcomes.

As sustainability expectations grew, project finance expanded its assessments.

Environmental impact studies became more detailed. Technical due diligence started including lifecycle emissions, supply-chain sustainability, energy efficiency performance, and resilience to climate variability.

Bankability reviews began looking at long-term environmental compliance and alignment with national transition strategies. This shift encouraged project sponsors to adopt stronger governance systems, better monitoring tools, and more transparent documentation.

A notable fact reveals the scale of this transformation: **renewable energy accounted for more than 70% of all global project finance investment in the power sector by 2022** (IEA Global Investment Report[25]). This single trend shows how strongly the project finance world moved toward sustainable assets, driven by technological maturity, policy clarity, and lender confidence.

---

[25] *International Energy Agency (IEA), World Energy Investment 2023: Overview and Key Findings, IEA, 2023,* https://www.iea.org/reports/world-energy-investment-2023/overview-and-key-findings*, accessed 7 December 2025.*

Project finance, when viewed through a green lens, becomes more than a lending method.

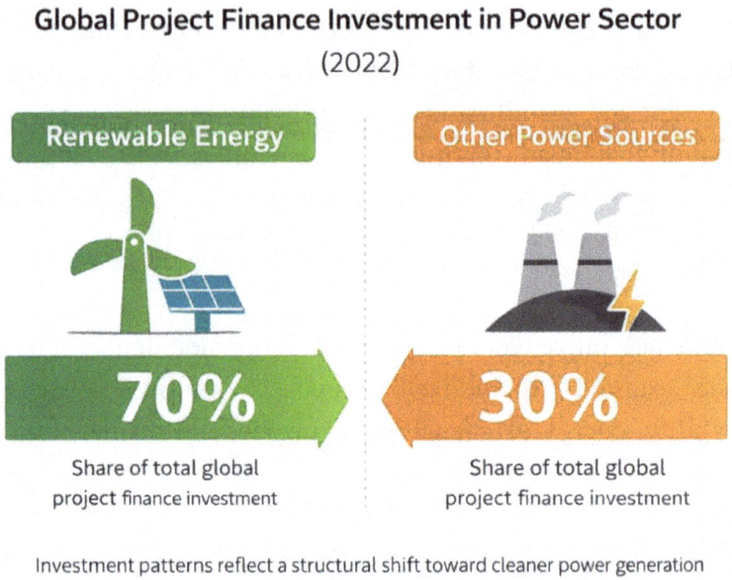

It is a discipline that shapes responsible development. It promotes high-quality preparation, strong contractual frameworks, and environmentally aligned design choices. These qualities help green projects earn trust, attract long-term capital, and demonstrate their value across decades of operation.

Public, Private, and Blended Credit Lines: Expanding Access to Sustainable Capital

Climate-aligned development grows fastest when multiple financial actors move together. Public institutions set direction, private lenders bring scale, and blended structures help bridge early-stage gaps. This ecosystem makes sustainability financing more accessible, flexible, and viable for a wider range of sectors.

Development finance institutions (DFIs) and multilateral development banks (MDBs) play a foundational role here. Their credit lines provide catalytic capital that lowers cost, extends tenures, and encourages sector-wide adoption.

These institutions support renewable energy corridors, water and sanitation systems, climate-smart agriculture, and efficient infrastructure. Their participation builds confidence because DFIs carry deep sector expertise, rigorous due diligence processes, and long-standing relationships across emerging markets.

Blended credit brings together concessional funds, commercial lending, guarantees, and risk-sharing mechanisms. Concessional capital can reduce interest costs or absorb early risks in innovative technologies.

Guarantees unlock private participation by buffering specific risk layers. Risk-sharing facilities encourage commercial banks to extend credit to sectors they previously viewed as unfamiliar or complex. Each tool contributes to a more inclusive financial ecosystem.

Public institutions add strength beyond capital. National green banks, government-backed sustainability facilities, and strategic programs provide direction for industries.

They help set standards, identify priority sectors, and coordinate policies that make long-term credit pipelines viable. When policy signals align with financing tools, transition pathways speed up.

Commercial banks build on this momentum. They partner with MDBs and DFIs to co-lend, participate in syndicated structures, or utilise dedicated on-lending credit lines for green projects. With this support, lenders become more comfortable financing new technologies, distributed solutions, and large-scale infrastructure upgrades. Commercial participation is vital because it determines how fast the sustainable finance market can grow.

Blended structures proved especially impactful in distributed renewable energy, green hydrogen pilots, electric mobility ecosystems, and energy-efficiency retrofits. These sectors require patient capital, flexible financing models, and a shared understanding of risk. Blended credit lines help meet these needs while opening the door for long-term expansion.

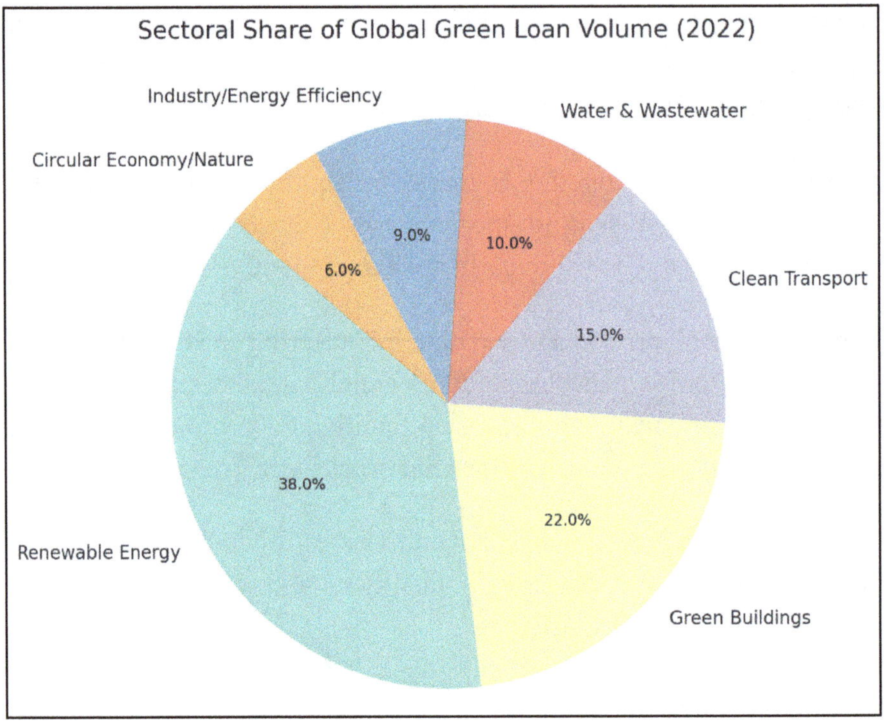

Source: Climate Bonds Initiative, 2023 Sector Report.

As sustainable finance expands, this public-private combination becomes a central building block.

It shapes new markets, strengthens institutional collaboration, and ensures that capital reaches both large developers and smaller enterprises. Through this lens, blended credit lines are financial mechanisms-and instruments of structural transformation.

Typical Risks in Green Lending and Project Finance: Structured Mitigation Approaches

Every lending structure carries risk, and green finance is no exception. What distinguishes sustainable lending is the discipline with which risks are identified, allocated, and managed. Strong mitigation frameworks improve bankability, attract long-term lenders, and help projects stay resilient across their lifecycle.

Technical risk emerges when project components are new, evolving, or sensitive to operational conditions. Lenders address this by requiring proven technologies, certified equipment, strong engineering partners, and detailed performance assessments. Independent technical advisors evaluate expected output, degradation curves, and system reliability.

Construction risk revolves around timelines, quality, and costs. Banks mitigate this through fixed-price EPC contracts, performance guarantees, and step-in rights. Contractors commit to clear obligations, while insurance structures cover unforeseen events.

This approach ensures that delays or overruns do not weaken financial stability.

Operational risk relates to long-term performance. For renewable assets, resource variability-such as changes in wind speed or solar irradiation-affects generation patterns.

Lenders address this through robust resource studies, conservative forecasting, and long-term operations and maintenance (O&M) contracts. Strong monitoring systems ensure that deviations are identified early.

Market risk becomes relevant when revenue depends on fluctuating demand, commodity prices, or tariff structures. Power purchase agreements, minimum offtake guarantees, and availability payments offer stability. In sectors where demand shifts more frequently, lenders prefer diversified revenue streams and long-term contracts.

Environmental and permitting risk gained importance as sustainability standards became stricter. Banks review compliance frameworks, restoration plans, biodiversity considerations, and community engagement processes. Independent environmental and social impact assessments (ESIAs) support transparency and strengthen planning.

For each category, the objective is consistent: design structures that guide projects toward long-term strength. Mitigation tools create a stable foundation for lenders and encourage borrowers to adopt disciplined practices. Over time, this strengthens the overall transition landscape and raises the quality of green investments.

Key Takeaways

- Green loans and sustainability-linked loans provide structured pathways for climate-aligned credit.
- Banks evaluate sustainability readiness, operational systems, and measurable outcomes while shaping loan terms.
- Covenants and pricing mechanisms reinforce discipline and improve long-term performance.
- Project finance structures help complex green assets achieve viability through strong cash-flow design.
- Public, private, and blended credit lines expand access to sustainable capital.
- Risk mitigation tools enhance bankability and support consistent performance across project stages.
- Sustainability-aligned lending builds resilient financial systems and accelerates national transition priorities.

6

Equity, Funds and Sustainable Investment Strategies

Equity markets have moved to the centre of global sustainability thinking. Earlier, investors analysed companies through financial ratios and growth expectations alone. Over time, long-horizon research, shifting consumer preferences, and the rise of responsible capital expanded the lens.

Equity investors now study how companies manage natural resources, innovate for resilience, strengthen governance, and contribute to broader societal outcomes.

This evolution transformed equities from simple ownership claims into instruments that reflect an organisation's long-term direction. Institutional investors, pension funds, sovereign wealth pools, and retail participants all shape this landscape through expectations that reward clarity, responsibility, and forward-looking strategy.

As this market matured, sustainability tools became more precise. ESG integration brought structured analysis into mainstream investing, helping investment teams evaluate risks and opportunities rooted in environmental, social, and governance practices.

Screening models refined decision-making by identifying the themes, behaviours, or exposures that align with purpose-driven investing. Thematic strategies encouraged targeted investment in areas such as clean energy, water stewardship, health systems, or circularity. Alongside these, impact-oriented frameworks strengthened the emphasis on measurable outcomes.

Public equity managers, private equity funds, and venture capital teams interpret these ideas through their own lenses, each category focusing on time horizon, data availability, operational insight, and transformation potential.

These shifts redefined the relationship between investors and companies. Stewardship practices encouraged long-term dialogue. Engagement helped shape strategic clarity. Voting behaviour conveyed expectations around governance, board composition, climate strategy, and capital allocation.

Fund-level due diligence sharpened the signals that guide corporate decision-making. Markets across India, the UAE, the GCC, and other emerging economies show this transition clearly, where sustainability-focused equity approaches influence how companies innovate, allocate capital, and strengthen resilience.

These patterns reveal that equity-based sustainable investing shapes real-world behaviour, often more quickly and consistently than regulatory mandates.

According to Global Sustainable Investment Alliance (GSIA), sustainability-aligned assets surpassed **USD 30 trillion globally by 2022**, reflecting how deeply sustainability priorities have shaped equity and fund strategies[26].

OBJECTIVES OF THE CHAPTER

This chapter will help individuals:

- Understand how ESG integration, screening, and thematic strategies influence equity selection.
- Learn how impact investing and outcome-oriented capital shape long-term value creation.
- Explore how public equity, private equity, and venture capital interpret sustainability through unique analytical lenses.
- Gain clarity on stewardship, engagement practices, and sustainability-aligned voting behaviour.

---

[26] *Global Sustainable Investment Alliance (GSIA), Global Sustainable Investment Review 2022, GSIA, 2023,* *https://www.gsi-alliance.org/wp-content/uploads/2023/11/GSIA-Report-2022-FINAL-Compressed.pdf, accessed 10 December 2025.*

- See how sustainable funds assess companies through structured metrics and forward-looking indicators.
- Understand how corporate strategy evolves when investors favour resilience, innovation, and sustainability alignment.
- Observe practical examples from India, the UAE, the GCC, and other emerging markets that illustrate how sustainable equity models operate.
- Build confidence in analysing sustainable investment approaches across fund types and geographies.
- Recognise the expanding influence of sustainability in shaping market behaviour, competitive advantage, and growth pathways.

How Integration, Screening Models and Thematic Strategies Shape Equity Decisions

Equity investing changed significantly once ESG considerations became part of mainstream analysis. Integration brought environmental stewardship, social wellbeing, and governance strength into the same analytical space that once focused only on cash flows, margins, and competitive positioning.

Today, sustainability signals help investors understand operational resilience, supply-chain reliability, regulatory exposure, and long-term innovation potential. Integration works as a layered approach, analysts study sustainability indicators alongside financial metrics and use this combination to form a clearer, more future-ready view of a company.

Screening models offer another set of tools. Each style sharpens decision-making by highlighting the values, priorities, or performance thresholds that align with fund strategy.

Positive screening identifies companies creating meaningful progress, leaders in renewable energy, biodiversity protection, digital inclusion, or workplace equity. Norms-based screening looks at alignment with international guidelines.

Best-in-class models identify companies that perform strongly within their sector. These methods help investors construct portfolios that reflect clarity, consistency, and a structured view of sustainability ambition. Thematic strategies deepen this focus by aligning capital with global shifts.

Clean energy, circular economy models, water systems, health technologies, sustainable transport, and innovation-driven development each represent opportunities shaped by scientific, demographic, and policy momentum. Thematic portfolios allow investors to participate in these transitions with precision.

These strategies grow stronger when backed by transparent methodologies, sector research, and clear outcome expectations.

An insight reflects this expansion: according to Morningstar's global sustainable funds database, **sustainable fund assets crossed USD 2.7 trillion by 2023**, driven largely by ESG integration and thematic interest. This growth confirms how structured sustainability methods have become part of mainstream equity research[27].

Across integration, screening, and thematic investing, one pattern stands out, these tools help translate a wide landscape of sustainability signals into organised analysis. They bring discipline to equity selection and encourage a forward-looking mindset that aligns with global development priorities.

---

[27] *Hong Kong Exchanges and Clearing Limited (HKEX), ETF Spotlight: Sustainable ETFs, July 2023, https://www.hkex.com.hk/-/media/HKEX-Market/Products/Securities/Exchange-Traded-Products/Launch/HKEX-ETF-Spotlight-July-2023_TH_EN_vF.pdf, accessed 10 December 2025.*

A few guiding questions often shape this process:

- Which sustainability attributes strengthen a company's long-term competitiveness?
- How consistent is its governance and disclosure quality?
- Does the business model align with long-horizon transition trends?
- How effectively can the company innovate within sustainability-linked value chains?

Such questions guide investment managers as they use ESG integration, screening, and thematic frameworks to build portfolios that reflect both financial and sustainability strength.

Impact Investing and Outcome-Oriented Capital

Impact investing operates on a wider canvas. It focuses on contributions that can be measured, observed, and linked to real outcomes. This style differs from ESG integration because its core purpose is intentional impact creation rather than risk-adjusted performance enhancement.

Impact funds anchor their decisions in a clear theory of change, they map how capital flows contribute to environmental restoration, community wellbeing, livelihood improvement, or climate resilience.

Outcome-oriented capital depends on measurable results. Investors track indicators such as emissions reduced, patients reached, hectares restored, or communities served.

These metrics help establish whether a company or project is aligning with its intended purpose. Depth, scale, and additionality sit at the centre of this thinking. Depth reflects the significance of the change. Scale reflects reach. Additionality reflects progress that emerges because capital was introduced.

Impact strategies operate across models. Finance-first funds integrate measurable outcomes into commercial strategies. Impact-first funds prioritise mission delivery while maintaining disciplined financial management. Both styles rely on structured frameworks, transparent methodologies, and continuous evaluation.

Global benchmarks such as GIIN's guidance and the IRIS+ system help
96 standardize impact measurement and improve comparability across markets.

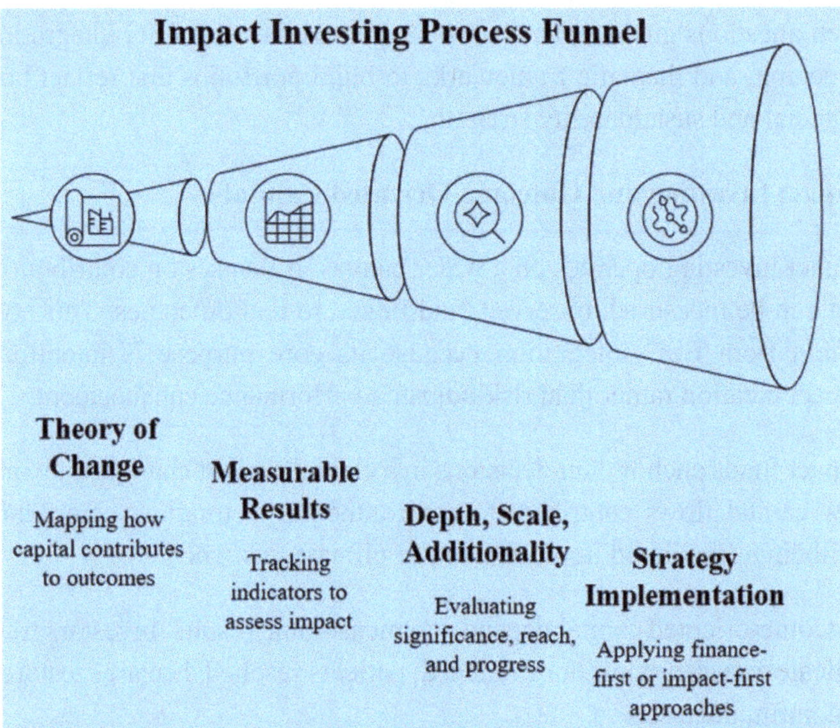

This approach encourages long-term resilience because it directs capital toward challenges that require persistent effort, clean water access, regenerative agriculture, public-health systems, waste-cycle transformation, climate adaptation technologies, or inclusion-based enterprises.

Impact investing also grows quickly in emerging markets where development priorities intersect with sustainability goals. Funds operating in these regions often combine operational insight with community-centred planning, making impact strategies highly responsive to regional needs.

Outcome-oriented capital strengthens market discipline because issuers learn to articulate measurable intentions, plan interventions clearly, and build credible reporting systems. As this thinking matures globally, impact investing increasingly serves as a bridge between finance and measurable progress.

Public Equity, Private Equity and Venture Capital Approaches

Sustainable investing looks different across public equity, private equity, and venture capital. Public equity managers interpret sustainability through disclosures, KPIs, governance structures, and forward-looking transition plans.

They study climate-aligned strategies, product-level innovation, workforce stability, board oversight, and supply-chain resilience. Public equity portfolios often focus on listed companies with extensive reporting requirements, which allows analysts to compare sustainability performance across geographies and peer groups.

Private equity teams operate with deeper involvement. They participate directly in operational improvement, supply-chain design, cost structure optimisation, and leadership development. This hands-on approach helps private equity funds influence sustainability practices at an organisational level.

Long holding periods create space for transformation, energy-efficient facilities, transparent governance systems, advanced digital tools, responsible sourcing, and nature-aligned processes. Private equity thus works as both investor and strategic partner.

Venture capital brings innovation to the centre. Venture teams identify early-stage companies developing technologies and models that support climate transitions, battery innovation, AI-driven resource optimisation, green mobility, water systems, agritech, sustainable materials, or circularity solutions.

These investments involve higher uncertainty yet offer significant long-term influence. Venture capital builds ecosystems where sustainability-driven innovation grows rapidly and attracts institutional partnerships.

Each investment style carries distinct risk appetites, time horizons, data expectations, and engagement depth. Public equity relies heavily on transparency and comparability. Private equity values operational detail and leadership strategy. Venture capital looks for visionary potential, scalable ideas, and emerging market opportunities.

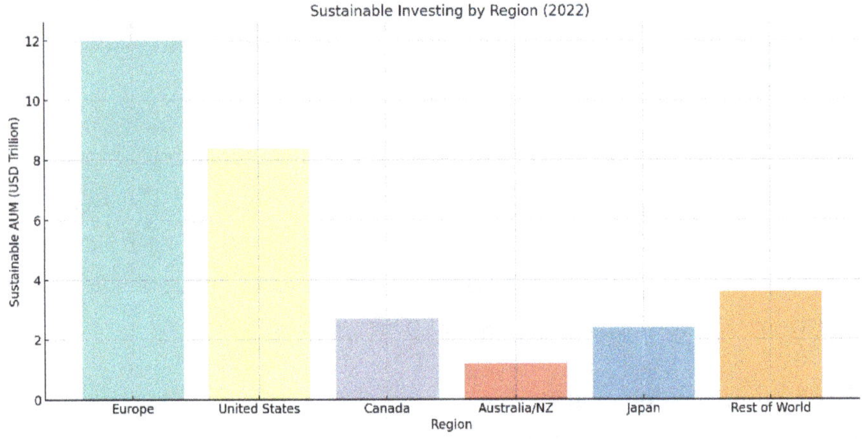

Source: Global Sustainable Investment Alliance (GSIA), 2022 Global Sustainable Investment Review - Regional AUM Breakdown.

Across these categories, sustainability signals help identify resilient business models, organisations capable of adapting to policy transitions, technological shifts, and evolving customer behaviour.

As more funds adopt structured sustainability tools, companies across regions, India, the UAE, GCC markets, Southeast Asia, Africa, and Latin America, strengthen governance, refine disclosure, and innovate across their value chains.

Public markets reward consistency and clarity. Private equity rewards transformation and execution strength. Venture capital rewards ingenuity and forward-looking ambition. Together, these investment approaches shape a diversified pathway for sustainability-aligned market evolution.

Stewardship, Engagement and Voting as Transformation Tools

Stewardship has become one of the strongest signals of maturity in sustainable investing. It reflects a shift from passive ownership to active participation, where investors use their influence to strengthen long-term resilience within companies.

Engagement is the core of this approach.

Through structured conversations, feedback cycles, and periodic reviews, funds encourage management teams to refine sustainability strategies, strengthen governance, and enhance transparency. Engagement frameworks focus on clarifying expectations, supporting improvement, and creating alignment between capital providers and leadership teams.

Voting elevates this dialogue into formal influence. Decisions related to board composition, climate strategies, executive compensation, and disclosure standards shape how organisations evolve across time. Asset managers and pension funds frequently publish their voting rationales, allowing markets to understand the principles guiding their decisions.

Voting records also serve as indicators of stewardship quality, because they reveal consistency between stated sustainability priorities and actual actions taken.

Escalation pathways operate when engagement requires stronger reinforcement. This can include intensified dialogue, collaborative investor action, changes in voting stance, or public communication of expectations. These steps maintain a constructive tone while signalling that certain themes, climate alignment, resource efficiency, human capital development, or governance clarity, are essential for long-term performance.

Asset owners increasingly evaluate stewardship as part of fund selection. They examine engagement themes, voting behaviour, transparency of processes, and documented outcomes. These assessments help distinguish between funds that simply track sustainability trends and those that play an active role in shaping corporate direction. **According to the PRI, more than USD 121 trillion in assets were managed by signatories committed to stewardship and responsible investment principles by 2023**, reflecting how widely stewardship practices have been embraced across the global investment landscape. [28]

Stewardship ultimately supports a market environment where dialogue, accountability, and shared responsibility encourage purposeful corporate growth.

How Sustainable Funds Assess Companies

Assessment frameworks guide how funds interpret a company's sustainability trajectory. Internal scoring systems help consolidate data from disclosures, third-party evaluations, and sector-specific indicators. These systems rest on materiality prioritisation, identifying which themes meaningfully shape a company's resilience and long-term value. Materiality varies across industries: emissions intensity may be central

---

[28] *Principles for Responsible Investment (PRI), Annual Report 2023, PRI Secretariat, London, 2023, https://public.unpri.org/download?ac=19741 , accessed 10 December 2025.*

to energy companies, while supply-chain practices may anchor manufacturing assessments.

Transition readiness forms a major part of this evaluation. Funds observe how companies allocate capital, position themselves in evolving markets, and plan long-term operational shifts. Clarity around technology adoption, climate risk management, and product innovation often signals strong transition alignment. Analysts also study whether a company's growth strategy mirrors global sustainability pathways, reinforcing confidence in its direction.

Governance quality adds depth to this assessment. Boards play a decisive role in sustainability oversight, risk management, executive accountability, and strategic integration. Funds consider how leadership teams incorporate sustainability into decision-making structures, incentive design, and performance measurement. Strong governance signals durability and strategic coherence.

Dimension	Public Equity	Private Equity	Venture Capital
Core Lens	Disclosures, KPIs, governance signals, climate strategy	Operational detail, supply chain, transformation potential	Innovation, scalability, technology readiness
Engagement Depth	Moderate: stewardship, voting, structured dialogue	High: direct involvement in operations and strategy	High but focused on product, market fit and scaling
Time Horizon	Medium to long	Long (multi-year, transformation-focused)	Long but uncertain; depends on innovation cycles

Data Dependence	Heavy reliance on formal reporting and comparability	Deep reliance on internal access, audits, operational metrics	Emerging metrics; depends on early-stage signals
Type of Sustainability Influence	Encourages disclosure quality, transition clarity, governance strength	Drives operational improvement, cost optimisation, sustainability systems	Catalyses new climate technologies and sustainable business models
Risk Appetite	Moderate	Moderate to high	High
Ideal Impact Zone	Listed companies improving governance and transition pathways	Mid to large companies needing structured transformation	Early-stage innovation shaping future sustainability markets

Sustainable funds also rely on specialised sources, environmental data providers, climate-scenario models, supply-chain traceability tools, biodiversity analyses, and workforce indicators.

These inputs strengthen their understanding of operational conditions, competitive positioning, and potential for future improvement. Analysts combine internal systems with external benchmarks to form a balanced view, allowing decision-makers to appreciate both current performance and long-range opportunity.

A focused set of analytical questions often guides this process:

- Does the company understand its material sustainability risks and opportunities?
- How effectively does it allocate capital toward long-term transition themes?

- Are disclosures consistent, comparable, and aligned with recognised frameworks?
- Is governance sufficiently equipped to oversee sustainability strategy?
- Does the company demonstrate innovation potential in areas central to its sector?

Assessment is both structured and dynamic. It supports disciplined investment decisions and fosters conversations that encourage strategic evolution across companies.

Corporate Strategy Implications + Short Case Snapshots (India, UAE, GCC, Emerging Markets)

Sustainability-aligned investing shapes corporate strategy in fundamental ways. Companies refine their product design, resource choices, and operational models to align with future expectations.

This often includes investment in cleaner technologies, upgrades to energy efficiency, responsible sourcing, digital systems that improve traceability, and expanded focus on human capital development. These adjustments strengthen resilience and position companies to thrive within evolving market conditions.

Supply chains evolve as well. Organisations partner with suppliers that demonstrate credible sustainability commitments, adopt circularity practices, or invest in low-carbon systems.

These decisions influence industries across manufacturing, logistics, consumer goods, and infrastructure. Capital allocation mirrors these priorities. Many companies shift budgets toward long-term innovation, transition technologies, or nature-aligned operations to reinforce their competitiveness.

Internal systems also strengthen. Sustainability teams collaborate with finance, strategy, and operations to build structured reporting practices and forward-looking risk models. Board committees deepen oversight, while leadership teams incorporate sustainability indicators into performance evaluation and organisational planning.

Short case snapshots illustrate these developments:

India

Indian corporates increasingly integrate renewable energy procurement, energy-efficient manufacturing, and digital financing tools. Several large companies align with national transition goals through green hydrogen pilots, circularity models, and electric-mobility investments. Equity markets recognise these shifts, rewarding firms that build clear, measurable transition pathways.

UAE and GCC

The region's sustainability ambitions reflect rapid diversification and innovation. Companies strengthen climate strategies in alignment with national goals around hydrogen, mobility, responsible water use, and carbon-efficient operations. Sustainability disclosures improve steadily, and equity investors look closely at governance clarity, transition readiness, and technological preparedness.

Other Emerging Markets

Southeast Asia, Africa, and Latin America showcase innovation in waste-resource models, biodiversity-linked finance, sustainable agriculture, and community-focused infrastructure. Companies refine operational frameworks to align with global expectations while building growth opportunities around environmental commitments.

Across all these regions, sustainability expectations influence capital access. Companies with transparent disclosures, strong governance, and clear transition strategies attract deeper investor support. This dynamic encourages organisations to strengthen long-term planning and helps align capital flows with global development priorities.

Key Takeaways

- Equity and fund strategies send strong, long-horizon sustainability signals across markets.
- ESG integration, screening approaches, and thematic models create clarity within investment decisions.
- Impact investing focuses on measurable outcomes and structured contribution logic.
- Public equity, private equity, and venture capital interpret sustainability through distinct lenses.
- Stewardship and voting encourage companies to align with long-term sustainability pathways.
- Sustainable funds evaluate companies through materiality, transition readiness, and governance strength.
- Corporate strategies evolve as investor expectations expand across disclosure, innovation, and operational systems.
- Sustainable investment practices support durable value creation and broaden global pathways for climate-aligned growth.

7

Climate and Environmental Risk in Finance

Climate and environmental risks now shape the core of financial decision-making. What once lived primarily in scientific and policy discussions has become central to how banks, insurers, investors, and regulators plan balance sheets and long-term strategy.

Institutions study how heatwaves, floods, storms, changing rainfall cycles, drought patterns, and rising sea levels influence asset quality and future value.

Alongside these physical pressures, transition dynamics-policy evolution, technological advancement, shifting consumer preference, and regulatory direction-guide how capital moves across sectors.

Climate considerations hold the same weight as credit, market, and liquidity assessments because they stretch across time horizons and asset classes. **A distinct signal of institutionalization emerged when more than 50 jurisdictions had either mandated or formally guided climate-related financial disclosures by 2023, embedding climate risk into supervisory and reporting frameworks across markets[29]**.

Understanding these risks requires structured, multidisciplinary tools. Scenario models reflect different warming pathways and policy outcomes. Stress-testing frameworks reveal how portfolios respond under varied physical or transition conditions. Sectoral mapping highlights exposure across energy, transport, agriculture, infrastructure, real estate, and manufacturing.

Technology pathways clarify which industries are positioned for future competitiveness and which need deeper adaptation. Institutions rely on

---

[29] *International Organization of Securities Commissions (IOSCO), ISSB Standards and Regulatory Adoption, IOSCO, 2023,* https://www.iosco.org/library/pubdocs/pdf/IOSCOPD747.pdf, *accessed 10 December 2025.*

hazard maps, carbon-intensity datasets, transition indicators, and asset-level tools to build clarity around evolving risk profiles and design strategies suited to long-term resilience.

It moves from physical and transition risk to sector and portfolio exposure, from scenario planning to stress-test models, and from stranded-asset dynamics to regulatory expectations. Concepts such as time-horizon planning, transition readiness, and structured data frameworks become practical tools for financial decision-making.

A lender structures a facility differently when climate exposure becomes visible. An investor refines capital allocation when transition pathways reshape value. A regulator strengthens supervision when system-wide patterns require coordinated insight.

By understanding the architecture behind climate-risk tools and frameworks, professionals gain the clarity needed to interpret disclosures, evaluate strategies, and make decisions aligned with emerging standards. This chapter sets the foundation for that analytical confidence and opens a structured window into one of finance's most influential transitions.

OBJECTIVES OF THE CHAPTER

This chapter supports a structured understanding of climate and environmental risk by guiding individuals to:

- Understand physical and transition risks within financial systems, and how they shape valuation, exposure, and resilience.
- Study how climate risk influences sector-level and portfolio-level decisions, highlighting how different industries experience unique pressures.

- Learn the logic of scenario analysis, stress testing, and long-term planning, and how these tools help institutions navigate uncertain pathways.
- Recognise the idea of stranded assets and how transition dynamics reshape valuations, useful life, and capital allocation.
- Identify tools, datasets, and frameworks used to measure climate and environmental exposure, including hazard maps, carbon metrics, and transition indicators.
- Explore how regulators shape climate-risk expectations, integrate them into supervisory frameworks, and strengthen market stability.
- Build clarity on why climate risk is treated as mainstream financial risk and how it influences portfolio construction and lending strategies.
- Gain confidence in interpreting climate-related disclosures, scenario pathways, and regulatory signals used across global markets.
- Strengthen understanding of how climate and environmental risks influence pricing, governance, operational design, and future market positioning.

1. Physical and Transition Risk: The Two Pillars of Climate Exposure

Climate and environmental risk reveal their full shape when viewed through two foundational pillars: physical risk and transition risk. Physical risk captures direct environmental pressures-heat intensity, storm frequency, floods, drought cycles, and wildfire patterns.

These forces influence asset durability, operational continuity, insurance models, and revenue stability. When a manufacturing facility experiences repeated heatwaves or a logistics corridor is exposed to urban flooding, lenders and investors incorporate these patterns into pricing, credit limits, and long-term planning because environmental volatility changes the financial profile of an asset.

Transition risk emerges through shifts in policy direction, technology preference, consumer behaviour, and market expectations. Clean-energy incentives reshape the economics of fuel-based industries, while mobility standards change the trajectory of automotive systems.

Digital innovation and circularity principles influence supply chains and production choices. These developments add new sensitivities across revenue models and cost structures.

This shift is reinforced by supervisory practice: a **Bank for International Settlements** survey found that a majority of central banks now treat climate-related risks as a source of financial stability concern, integrating them into monitoring, stress analysis, or supervisory dialogue[30].

Organisations study these risks through sector mapping, scenario dashboards, comparative vulnerability assessments, and forward-looking planning.

Physical risk models help them understand how event frequency influences asset downtime.

Transition models help them understand how regulatory timelines influence revenue direction. Viewed together, these two pillars create a complete framework for climate-risk understanding and strategic preparation.

---

[30] *Bank for International Settlements (BIS), Climate-related Risk and Financial Stability, BIS Quarterly Review, September 2021, https://www.bis.org/publ/qtrpdf/r_qt2109.htm, accessed 10 December 2025.*

2. Sector and Portfolio-Level Exposure: Mapping Vulnerability and Opportunity

Climate risk affects every sector differently, and this variation guides lending behaviour, investment strategy, and corporate planning. Energy systems experience high transition sensitivity as fuel-mix evolution, renewable competitiveness, and emission-reduction expectations influence valuations. Transport systems face both physical disruptions and electrification trends.

Agriculture responds to rainfall patterns, crop sensitivity to temperature shifts, and water-availability cycles. Real estate reflects coastal exposure, heat zones, and evolving building-efficiency standards. Manufacturing must manage efficiency requirements, technology upgrades, and global supply-chain pressure.

Finance integrates all these pressures through its portfolios.

Portfolio-level exposure is assessed using structured indicators such as carbon intensity, revenue sensitivity to policy change, geographic concentration, supply-chain dependency, and the degree of technology lock-in. These indicators help institutions evaluate their long-term resilience and design transition pathways that strengthen value creation.

Example: Multi-Sector Equity Mapping (Case Snapshot)

A diversified equity portfolio holding utilities, automotive firms, industrial manufacturers, and financial institutions shows four different climate sensitivities. Utilities face strong transition pressure because generation mix influences cost trajectories.

Automotive firms respond to electrification demand and innovation in battery ecosystems. Industrial firms respond to efficiency norms and material innovation. Financial institutions face indirect exposure through all the sectors they finance. This simple mapping helps institutions understand where strategic refinement strengthens long-term stability.

To bring structure to these exposures, the following table compares how sectors respond to climate pressures:

Table: Sector Sensitivities Across Physical and Transition Risk Dimensions

Sector	Physical Risk Sensitivity	Transition Risk Sensitivity	Primary Drivers
Energy	Medium	High	Fuel mix, policy pathways, technology upgrades
Transport	Medium-High	Medium-High	Electrification, logistics exposure
Agriculture	High	Medium	Rainfall, temperature cycles, soil patterns
Real Estate	High	Medium	Coastal exposure, heat zones, building standards
Manufacturing	Medium	Medium-High	Efficiency norms, material shifts, global supply chains

Finance	Indirect	Indirect	Lending and investment exposure

These variations help markets interpret vulnerability, adjust pricing, and identify opportunities that emerge as sectors move toward resilience and cleaner economic models.

3. Scenario Analysis & Stress Testing: Building Forward-Looking Resilience

Scenario analysis creates a forward-looking approach to climate understanding. Instead of relying on historical data, institutions examine multiple pathways-policy evolution, technology trajectories, physical-risk intensification, and global economic patterns. Scenarios developed by NGFS, the IEA, and the IPCC offer structured insights into temperature outcomes, emission pathways, and transition timelines.

Financial institutions test portfolios under various possibilities such as orderly transition, delayed transition, rapid policy tightening, or high-physical-intensity futures.

These exercises help them understand how cash flows shift, how asset values respond to policy trajectories, and how resilience strategies evolve. Stress testing deepens this view by evaluating performance under extreme assumptions-accelerated decarbonisation, rapid technology adoption, or intensified climate events.

Short Historical Anchor: Bank of England CBES (Case Reference)

The Bank of England's Climate Biennial Exploratory Scenario (CBES) illustrated how systemic climate-risk exercises guide financial governance.

The CBES encouraged banks and insurers to examine transition pathways, strengthen data systems, and incorporate climate exposure into mainstream risk dashboards. This exercise demonstrated how scenario thinking supports long-term financial stability.

Scenario tools guide refinements in sector allocations, credit policies, collateral standards, and valuation models.

They show how climate-aligned planning encourages capital to move toward resilient infrastructure, renewable energy, clean mobility, climate-smart agriculture, and efficient manufacturing. Institutions turn scenario outputs into dashboards, alignment plans, heat maps, and sector-specific strategies that strengthen long-term resilience.

- Scenario tools reveal long-term patterns across physical and transition pressures.
- Stress tests strengthen risk governance by examining performance under extreme pathways.
- Institutions use scenario results to refine pricing, capital planning, and allocation strategies.
- Scenario frameworks support transition planning and encourage investment in resilient sectors.

This underlines how climate-scenario logic transforms complexity into structured analysis and strategic clarity.

Stranded Assets and Time Horizons: Understanding Long-Term Transition Dynamics

Stranded assets represent one of the clearest signals of how climate and environmental realities reshape long-term financial thinking.

When an asset's economic potential declines due to regulatory shifts, technology transitions, or changing market preferences, its valuation begins to drift away from earlier expectations.

This adjustment can happen gradually or accelerate sharply when policy timelines tighten or cost curves change.

Coal plants, petrochemical units, and inefficient industrial systems reflect these dynamics, because their long-term competitiveness depends on a world that no longer aligns with their original economic assumptions.

Economic stranding occurs when operating costs rise or revenues weaken due to cleaner alternatives gaining scale.

Regulatory stranding arises when emission norms, carbon pricing, or performance benchmarks create new compliance expectations that shift operating economics.

Both forms influence credit assessments, equity valuations, and insurance calculations because time horizons determine whether a transition-aligned asset or a legacy asset strengthens a portfolio.

A clear anchor comes from the global coal transition. As renewable energy costs continued to fall across multiple markets, coal assets experienced significant pressure.

The International Energy Agency (IEA) noted that solar power became the cheapest source of electricity in many regions by 2020[31], a shift that altered cost assumptions across coal-based systems.

---

[31] *International Energy Agency (IEA), World Energy Outlook 2020, IEA, 2020,* *https://www.iea.org/reports/world-energy-outlook-2020, accessed 10 December 2025.*

This milestone changed long-term planning for lenders and investors because energy economics began tilting toward lower-carbon pathways with stronger cost predictability.

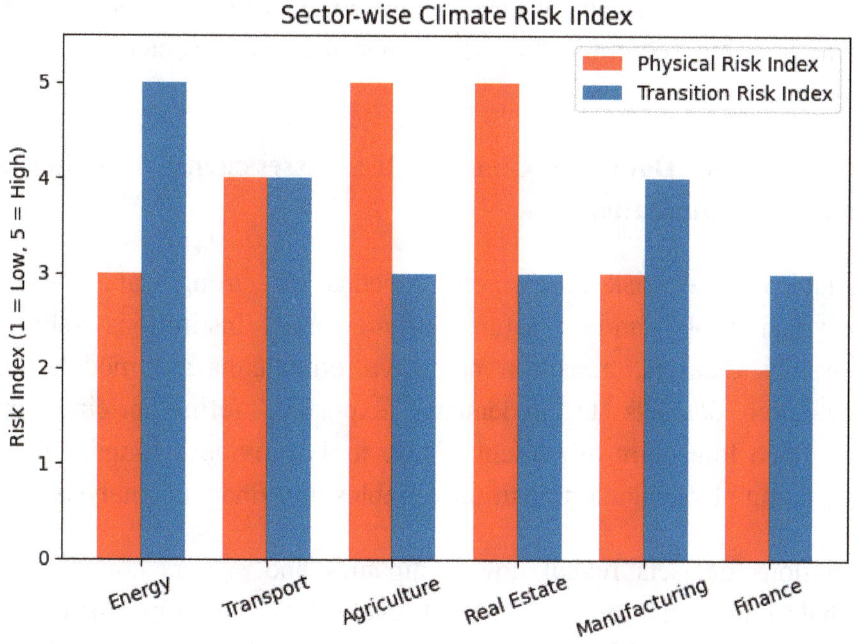

Data source: NGFS (2023-2025), IEA World Energy Outlook & Mobility Outlook (2024), IPCC Sixth Assessment Report (AR6, 2021-2023), OECD Transition Risk Framework (2022-2024), BIS Climate Risk Reports (2023-2025), and Global Disaster Risk Database (Munich Re & World Bank, 2024)

Time horizon thinking plays a central role in managing these dynamics. Banks examine whether a borrower's asset will remain viable throughout the loan tenor. Investors assess whether equity valuations reflect future policy direction.

Insurers study climate-adjusted loss models to understand whether asset durability aligns with long-term risk exposure. Pension funds and sovereign investors evaluate multi-decade pathways because shifts in asset performance influence their ability to preserve value.

Stranded-asset analysis encourages organisations to consider transition evolution as a continuous process rather than an abrupt shift. It brings clarity to capital-allocation decisions, strengthens portfolio resilience, and ensures that financial institutions align with systems that gain strength as markets move toward cleaner and more efficient economic structures.

2. Tools and Data for Climate Risk Assessment: Building an Analytical Foundation

Reliable climate-risk assessment depends on strong data systems, analytical tools, and structured frameworks. Institutions rely on emissions datasets, transition pathways, climate hazard models, and asset-level datasets to understand exposure, refine pricing, and strengthen long-term alignment. These tools provide a foundation for integrating physical and transition variables into financial analysis.

Emissions datasets reveal how companies and sectors contribute to global emissions profiles. Asset-level datasets help institutions understand geographic exposure and operational characteristics. Climate hazard maps identify vulnerabilities across temperature rise, rainfall variation, coastal sensitivity, and storm patterns. Transition pathways from NGFS, IEA, and IPCC offer structured guidance on how energy systems, industrial operations, and economic models evolve under different climate outcomes.

Several tools support this analytical discipline:

- **PCAF frameworks** help measure financed emissions across portfolios with clarity.
- **TCFD-style metrics** guide disclosure expectations around governance, strategy, risk management, and scenario thinking.
- **Geospatial risk tools** allow lenders and insurers to map assets against climate hazard zones.

- **Scenario platforms** help institutions stress-test portfolios under different transition and physical-risk assumptions.

These tools allow deeper evaluation through quantifiable insight rather than qualitative interpretation. Institutions integrate these datasets into credit assessments, valuation models, insurance pricing, and investment strategies. The goal is to combine scientific patterns with financial logic to understand how risks translate into economic consequences.

A global indicator of the scale of adoption is reflected in the Network for Greening the Financial System, which now brings together more than **135 central banks** and supervisors using common climate-scenario frameworks, strengthening the consistency of climate-risk evaluation across financial systems worldwide[32]. This widespread adoption brings structure, comparability, and forward-looking discipline into risk assessment.

In practice, institutions build layered analytical systems that integrate operational data, geographic sensitivity, policy direction, and technology trends. The combined view reveals patterns that influence collateral viability, sector resilience, long-term competitiveness, and strategic readiness. These insights guide capital flows toward systems that thrive in transition-aligned environments.

Bullet Summary Within This Section

- Climate-risk assessment requires strong data models, pathways, and geospatial tools.
- Emissions datasets and asset-level data strengthen sectoral analysis.

[32] *Network for Greening the Financial System (NGFS), About NGFS, https://www.ngfs.net/en/about-us, accessed 10 December 2025.*

- Scenario platforms provide forward-looking insight for credit, investment, and insurance decisions.
- Widespread adoption of NGFS frameworks enhances comparability and alignment across financial systems.

3. Why Climate Risk Is Now Mainstream Financial Risk

Climate risk is treated as mainstream financial risk because it shapes asset values, cash flows, capital planning, and long-term market stability. Regulatory frameworks across the world now integrate climate expectations into supervisory guidance, disclosure rules, and risk-management standards.

TCFD influenced global reporting direction, and ISSB standards created unified requirements for climate-related disclosures. NGFS guidance strengthened supervisory expectations, encouraging financial institutions to refine models, enhance data systems, and embed climate considerations into core planning.

Banks integrate climate factors into pricing by adjusting loan terms to reflect exposure patterns. They incorporate resilience considerations into provisioning standards, collateral frameworks, and sector-level policies.

Climate variables influence risk appetite statements, credit committee decisions, and portfolio steering strategies. These refinements strengthen system stability because they respond to long-term structural changes in the global economy.

Investors reflect climate signals in valuation logic, capital-allocation plans, and engagement strategies. Transition readiness, innovation strength, and emission trajectories influence equity valuations. Covenant design in private markets incorporates improvement pathways, operational resilience, and sustainability alignment.

Venture capital uses climate-tech innovation as a driver of future competitiveness. These patterns show how capital markets treat climate signals as integral to understanding growth potential.

Corporate strategy evolves as companies respond to market expectations. Strong sustainability positioning influences investor sentiment, cost of capital, customer behaviour, and long-term competitiveness.

Companies refine disclosure systems, design transition strategies, strengthen supply-chain performance, and allocate capital toward resilient technologies. This strategic evolution reinforces a cycle in which market expectations and financial discipline move together.

Climate variables no longer sit on the margins of financial planning. They influence credit policies, valuation logic, pricing frameworks, regulatory expectations, and investment trends. This alignment across stakeholders demonstrates why climate risk sits at the centre of financial-risk thinking today.

Key Takeaways

- Climate and environmental risks influence financial systems through physical forces and transition dynamics.
- Sector and portfolio exposure reveals how climate variables shape long-term performance and operational resilience.
- Scenario analysis strengthens planning by aligning financial models with scientific and policy-based pathways.
- Stranded-asset dynamics reshape valuations, transition expectations, and strategic allocation across markets.
- Analytical tools and datasets deepen clarity by combining emissions data, hazard maps, and transition pathways.
- Climate risk is treated as mainstream financial risk because it shapes pricing, supervision, governance, and capital strategy.
- Regulatory frameworks reinforce climate-risk management as a core element of financial stability.
- Institutions refine decision-making through forward-looking modelling, stronger disclosures, and enhanced monitoring systems.
- Market behaviour increasingly reflects climate alignment, encouraging companies and investors to strengthen long-term transition positioning.

8

Taxonomies, Disclosure Rules and Reporting

Taxonomies entered global finance at a moment when sustainability needed structure. As capital shifted toward climate-aligned growth, institutions required a shared way to identify which activities truly support environmental progress.

That need brought taxonomies into the mainstream. They help financial systems read sustainability with clarity, reduce uncertainty around definitions, and create a transparent foundation for long-term planning. Their rise mirrors the maturity of sustainable finance itself-moving from broad intention to organised, science-aligned classification.

Disclosure frameworks add another layer to this discipline. Markets now expect institutions to communicate climate strategy, governance, and resource decisions with precision. ISSB standards, TCFD recommendations, EU's CSRD rules, and several national systems guide this process by offering a consistent language for sustainability reporting.

This expectation has grown rapidly; by 2022, more than 2,600 organisations had expressed public support for TCFD-aligned reporting (Financial Stability Board[33]). Such momentum shows how deeply transparency has become part of financial culture.

This chapter explores how these systems transform behaviour across sustainable finance. It examines what makes a taxonomy effective, how leading global examples influence policy, and why disclosure rules shape issuer discipline and investor judgement.

It also looks at the expanding role of ratings, labels, and data providers, and how these elements affect banks, investors, and corporates. Together, they form a framework through which sustainable finance gains coherence, comparability, and long-term credibility.

OBJECTIVES OF THE CHAPTER

This chapter will help individuals:

- Understand what a green taxonomy is and why financial systems use it.
- Study the essential elements that make taxonomies credible and usable.
- Explore the design and purpose of major global taxonomy frameworks.
- Learn how disclosure systems support transparency, comparability, and trust.
- Understand the role of data providers, ratings, and labels in sustainable finance.

---

[33] *Financial Stability Board, "2022 TCFD Status Report: Task Force on Climate-related Financial Disclosures," 13 October 2022, https://www.fsb.org/2022/10/2022-tcfd-status-report-task-force-on-climate-related-financial-disclosures/ (accessed 12 December 2025).*

- Recognise how reporting expectations shape capital flows and organisational behaviour.
- Gain clarity on how issuers prepare structured sustainability information.
- Learn how investors interpret disclosures and integrate them into decisions.
- See how banks use taxonomies and reporting frameworks to refine internal lending policies.
- Build confidence in analysing sustainability classifications, ratings, and disclosures.

1. What a Green Taxonomy Does: Creating a Common Sustainability Language

A green taxonomy acts as a classification system that helps financial systems identify which economic activities support environmental progress.

It organises sectors, technologies, and practices into clearly defined categories so institutions know what counts as climate-aligned activity. This clarity matters because sustainable finance grows through shared understanding. When issuers, investors, and regulators speak the same language, capital moves with precision and policies guide markets effectively.

By classifying activities across energy, transport, land use, buildings, manufacturing, and enabling technologies, a taxonomy reduces interpretive uncertainty.

It gives issuers a structured reference for designing sustainability frameworks and identifying which projects fit long-term transition goals. It also clarifies eligibility criteria for instruments such as green bonds, sustainability-linked products, and transition frameworks.

For investors, a taxonomy is a decision-support tool. It signals alignment with environmental priorities, helps assess the depth of sustainability claims, and supports portfolio construction.

When investment funds compare issuers across markets, a taxonomy gives them the structure needed to evaluate consistency, sector readiness, and long-term resilience. This strengthens the quality of capital allocation and builds confidence across global portfolios.

A major early milestone came when the **EU released the first delegated act of its Green Taxonomy in 2021**, establishing detailed technical screening criteria for climate mitigation and adaptation. This event reshaped global thinking, as several jurisdictions later referenced or adapted elements of the EU approach while building their own systems[34].

The milestone illustrated a simple truth: classification creates coherence, and coherence strengthens sustainable finance.

2. Key Elements of Leading Taxonomies: Structure, Criteria and Purpose

Leading taxonomies share a structural logic that organizes information in a way that is both practical for financial institutions and aligned with scientific evidence. One of the strongest foundations is the use of **technical screening criteria**, which express the thresholds an activity must meet to qualify as climate-aligned.

These criteria reflect emissions pathways, resource efficiency expectations, ecosystem considerations, and long-term transition

---

34 *European Commission, Commission Delegated Regulation (EU) 2021/2139 of 4 June 2021 Supplementing Regulation (EU) 2020/852 by Establishing the Technical Screening Criteria for Climate Change Mitigation and Climate Change Adaptation, Official Journal of the European Union, 2021, https://eur-lex.europa.eu/legal-content/EN/TXT/?uri=CELEX:32021R2139, accessed 12 December 2025.*

requirements. They help markets differentiate between credible improvement and superficial change.

Another essential component is the **do-no-significant-harm (DNSH) principle**. This principle ensures that activities supporting one environmental goal do not undermine another. DNSH encourages balanced progress and avoids situations where a positive climate action inadvertently creates ecological stress elsewhere.

It strengthens the integrity of sustainability efforts.

Taxonomies also rely on **minimum safeguards**-standards around responsible business conduct, governance, human rights, and environmental management. These safeguards ensure that classification reflects holistic sustainability rather than environmental outcomes alone.

Combined with sector-wise granularity, they help users interpret sustainability within different industrial contexts.

A strong taxonomy aligns with **scientific pathways** that demonstrate how specific sectors transition over time. These pathways guide the pace of change, define ambition levels, and support long-term planning for capital-heavy industries such as energy, cement, steel, and mobility.

They give both issuers and investors a structured understanding of how the transition unfolds.

A useful comparative insight shows how regions take different approaches while following the same principles.

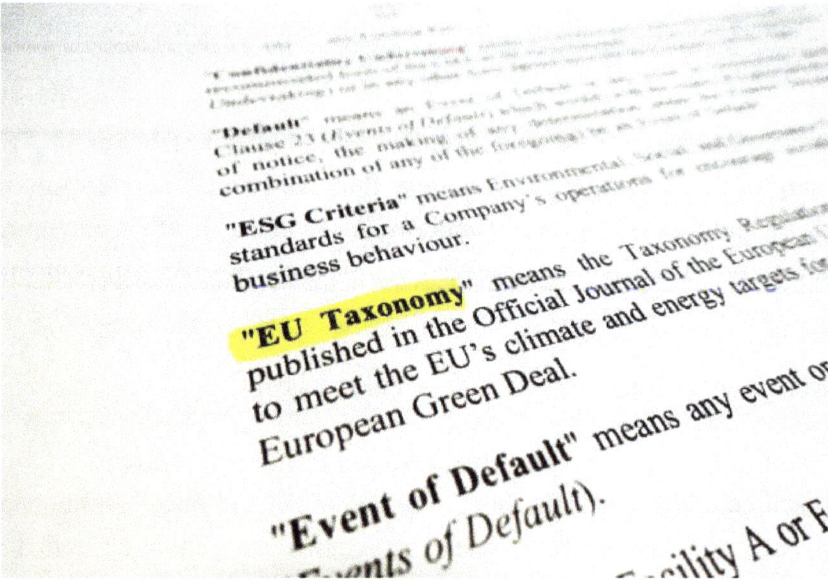

Source: istock.com

- **EU Taxonomy** emphasises detailed, science-driven thresholds.
- **China's Green Bond Endorsed Project Catalogue** focuses on large-scale, development-aligned activities with emphasis on rapid implementation.
- **ASEAN Taxonomy** combines science-based foundations with a traffic-light system, allowing flexibility for diverse emerging market circumstances.

This diversity highlights an important idea: every taxonomy adapts to local realities while still rooted in shared sustainability logic.

3. Disclosure Frameworks & Reporting Expectations: Strengthening Transparency

Disclosure frameworks give sustainability claims structure and allow financial institutions to evaluate long-term resilience with greater clarity.

They guide how organisations communicate governance practices, transition strategies, resource use, and climate-risk alignment.

Among these frameworks, the TCFD structure became widely recognised because it organised information around four pillars: **governance, strategy, risk management, and metrics**.

This format encourages organisations to show how climate priorities enter boardrooms, influence operations, and guide risk thinking.

The **ISSB** standards represent a global baseline designed to bring consistency across markets.

These standards unify multiple reporting lines, simplify expectations for cross-border investors, and help companies structure sustainability information in a coherent manner.

Their adoption across several jurisdictions demonstrates how global markets converge toward comparable reporting.

The **EU's CSRD and ESRS** frameworks create detailed guidance for companies operating in or interacting with European markets.

They introduce sector-specific standards, double materiality assessments, and granular disclosure requirements.

These rules elevate the expectations placed on organisations and strengthen confidence in sustainability information across supply chains and financial flows.

Feature	EU Taxonomy	China Green Catalogue	ASEAN Taxonomy
Technical Screening Criteria	Highly detailed, science-based	Broad sector-driven criteria	Tiered (traffic-light) approach
Do-No-Significant-Harm	Strongly embedded	Incorporated sectorally	Embedded with flexibility
Minimum Safeguards	Comprehensive	Governance-focused	Adapted for EM conditions
Sector Coverage	Extensive (energy, industry, buildings, transport)	Infrastructure-heavy focus	Broad with transition lens
Purpose	Precision + comparability	Rapid deployment + scale	Flexibility for diverse economies

National frameworks also play an important role. Countries adapt reporting expectations based on sectoral characteristics, economic priorities, and regulatory maturity. In several jurisdictions, climate disclosures have become part of mainstream corporate reporting, not an additional component.

A concise regulatory example comes from **the United Kingdom's adoption of mandatory TCFD-aligned reporting for large companies and financial institutions**, making it one of the first major markets to formalise climate disclosure in corporate law.

This shift demonstrated how reporting frameworks influence market behaviour and create incentives for stronger internal governance.

These disclosure systems encourage transparency, improve comparability, and help capital find credible sustainability pathways. They also strengthen organisational discipline by encouraging companies to refine data systems, clarify strategic commitments, and align with evolving global expectations.

1. Ratings, Labels and Data Providers: Influence on Market Behaviour

Ratings, labels, and data providers have become central actors in sustainable finance because they shape how markets interpret information. ESG rating agencies evaluate companies through multiple analytical lenses-environmental performance, governance structures, climate strategy, risk exposure, and transition readiness.

Their methodologies differ in weighting, data sources, sector relevance, and qualitative judgement, which makes each rating a distinct perspective rather than a universal score.

These differences actually enrich the overall landscape, as investors gain a multi-dimensional view of sustainability strength.

Data providers specialise in emissions inventories, climate-risk indicators, controversy tracking, and forward alignment metrics. Many institutions now rely on asset-level datasets, geospatial risk tools, and emission-pathway benchmarks to evaluate both present performance and future direction.

Labels such as green bond labels, sustainability-linked certifications, and taxonomy-aligned indicators increase visibility for issuers.

They help investors understand which financial instruments follow structured principles and which projects align with recognised standards.

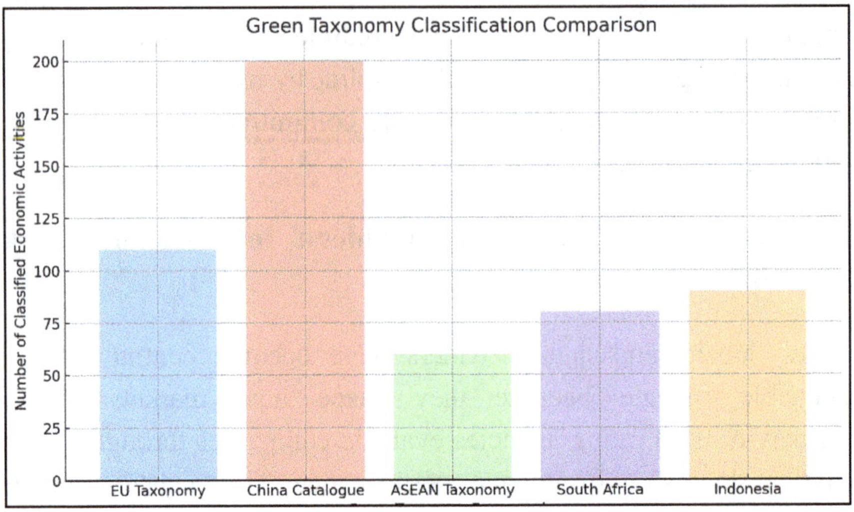

Sources: IMF Statistical Update (2023); EU Taxonomy Climate Delegated Act (2021); China Green Bond Catalogue (2015, revised 2021); ASEAN Taxonomy Board (2021); UK HM Treasury (2023 Draft); South Africa Green Taxonomy (2022); Indonesia Green Taxonomy (2022).

A notable reference comes from a **2022 OECD assessment**, which highlighted that ESG rating and data providers collectively influence trillions of dollars in capital allocation through their methodologies, coverage, and interpretation frameworks. This signals the growing importance of transparent data and structured evaluation tools in shaping investment flows[35].

Ratings, labels, and data models essentially create the informational backbone of modern sustainable finance. They direct attention, shape

[35] *Organisation for Economic Co-operation and Development (OECD), ESG Investing and Climate Transition: Market Practices, Issues and Policy Considerations, OECD Publishing, 2022, https://www.oecd.org/finance/esg-investing-and-climate-transition-6f64c3f7-en.htm, accessed 12 December 2025.*

perception, and strengthen market confidence by offering structured evidence behind sustainability claims.

2. Implications for Issuers, Investors and Banks: How Taxonomies Reshape Strategy

Taxonomies influence the strategic behaviour of every participant in the financial system. Issuers use them to determine which projects qualify for green financing, how bond frameworks should be structured, and how capital expenditure plans align with environmental pathways.

A taxonomy helps issuers design long-term transition strategies by showing which sectors evolve, how technologies are prioritised, and where innovation is expected. This clarity influences product planning, operational upgrades, and investment timelines.

Investors rely on taxonomies and disclosure frameworks when applying ESG integration, screening models, and stewardship practices. They interpret emissions data, risk exposure, and transition alignment to judge whether a company demonstrates a forward-looking strategy.

As reporting expectations become more structured, investors gain better visibility into governance strength, climate metrics, and capital allocation patterns. This helps them identify companies positioned to grow through the sustainability transition.

Banks use taxonomies to shape credit decisions, risk scoring, and portfolio alignment. They assess borrower activity against taxonomy criteria, analyse transition plans, and evaluate exposure to climate-sensitive sectors. This creates a stronger foundation for designing green loans, transition facilities, and sustainability-linked lending structures.

A well-designed taxonomy also supports internal models by providing concrete thresholds and evidence-based criteria.

A simple example illustrates the shift. When a bank aligns part of its portfolio with a national taxonomy, it often updates its sector policies, lending grids, and due-diligence templates.

Renewable energy projects may receive priority evaluation under clarified eligibility rules, while high-emission sectors undergo deeper transition assessment. This encourages institutions to refine governance systems and integrate sustainability more deeply into credit operations.

Through these mechanisms, taxonomies drive systematic improvements across issuers, investors, and financial intermediaries. They help market participants move in a coordinated direction, strengthening confidence and creating a clear pathway for capital alignment.

3. Practical Evaluation Lens: How to Assess Taxonomy & Reporting Quality

Evaluating the quality of a taxonomy or disclosure framework requires a structured lens that blends scientific clarity, financial logic, and operational transparency.

Criteria should be measurable, sector-specific, and consistent across time. Thresholds aligned with recognised environmental pathways create confidence that the taxonomy promotes long-term sustainability rather than short-term adjustments.

Consistent alignment with science strengthens credibility and guides investment decisions with greater precision.

One important dimension is the coherence between disclosures, targets, and capital allocation. Strong reporting demonstrates how commitments influence real-world decisions-technology choices, capacity expansions, resource use, and supply-chain development.

This alignment shows whether sustainability ambition enters strategic planning in a meaningful way. When companies disclose transparent metrics, investors and banks can understand progress pathways clearly.

External assurance provides further confidence. Independent verification helps confirm data quality, strengthens internal systems, and reinforces trust.

Data tools and scenario insights enrich analysis by illustrating how organisations handle transition risks and physical hazards. Institutions increasingly rely on forward-looking data, including climate alignment metrics, resilience indicators, and sectoral pathways.

A structured reporting approach contributes directly to market maturity. It enables institutions to compare performance, recognise credible strategies, and identify potential risks.

It supports better pricing decisions, stronger governance practices, and deeper alignment with sustainability priorities. The more coherent and transparent a taxonomy or disclosure system is, the stronger the financial ecosystem becomes.

Key Takeaways

- Taxonomies create a shared foundation for identifying sustainable activities and strengthening clarity across markets.
- Clear classification enables issuers to design frameworks aligned with recognised environmental pathways.
- Disclosure structures improve transparency around governance, strategy, and performance.
- ESG ratings, labels, and data providers shape investment decisions through structured insights.
- Strong reporting systems improve comparability and guide capital toward credible sustainability outcomes.
- Regulatory frameworks encourage deeper integration of sustainability within organisational planning.
- Taxonomy-aligned pathways support disciplined strategy design and long-term transition planning.
- Investors rely on verified metrics, disclosures, and external assessments for portfolio construction.
- Banks refine lending, risk scoring, and portfolio alignment by applying taxonomy criteria.
- Together, these elements strengthen accountability and accelerate sustainable finance momentum.

9

Policy, Regulation and the Role of Central Banks

Public policy now shapes the direction of sustainable finance in a very deliberate way. As governments announce transition plans, climate goals, and sectoral priorities, they set signals that influence how institutions position themselves for future opportunities. These signals guide credit, investment, technology adoption, and long-term planning.

With this shift, policy becomes a coordinating force that aligns national ambition with financial-market behaviour.

Central banks add strength to this landscape through supervision, scenario guidance, and expectations around climate resilience. They study how physical hazards and transition pathways influence system-wide stability and integrate these insights into prudential thinking. Their involvement highlights a fundamental shift: sustainability factors sit within the core framework of financial risk and resilience. Through direction-setting and analytical tools, central banks raise the standard of preparedness across institutions.

This chapter moves through that intersection of policy direction and regulatory design. It explores how public finance tools unlock new sectors, how guarantees support transition pathways, how carbon-pricing systems influence capital decisions, and how macroprudential approaches enhance long-term stability.

The aim is to bring clarity to how policies shape market behaviour, business strategy, and the broader financial ecosystem.

OBJECTIVES OF THE CHAPTER

- Understand how public policy influences green finance and market behaviour.
- Study how central banks guide climate-risk supervision and resilience expectations.
- Learn the prudential and macroprudential logic behind climate integration.
- Explore how public finance, guarantees, and blended structures support transition sectors.
- Examine how carbon pricing and market mechanisms redirect capital.
- Gain clarity on how institutions respond to regulatory signals.
- Recognise how policies strengthen stability, transparency, and long-term planning.
- Build confidence in interpreting policy frameworks through a financial lens.
- Understand how policy creates momentum for sustainable investment and innovation.
- Observe how regulatory ecosystems shape capital allocation across sectors.

1. Public Policy Signals and Green Finance: How Governments Shape Capital Direction

Public policy acts as a compass for financial markets. When governments outline climate commitments, set sectoral priorities, or introduce transition pathways, they create direction for long-term capital.

Investors observe these signals carefully because they influence future demand, cost structures, and competitive advantage.

Clear policy enhances confidence, aligns expectations, and reduces uncertainty around where the next wave of sustainable growth is emerging.

National climate roadmaps often become the first anchor point. They articulate emission-reduction milestones, renewable-energy targets, transport-sector transitions, and industry-wide efficiency plans. Each of these elements carries financial implications.

A country committing to large-scale renewable deployment, for instance, signals long-term opportunity in grids, storage, and clean-technology manufacturing.

A government prioritising water resilience or adaptation frameworks encourages investment across agriculture, natural ecosystems, and climate-smart infrastructure.

Green-industrial strategies deepen this relationship. They outline how industries evolve, which technologies receive support, and how supply chains strengthen over time.

These frameworks allow banks, investors, and corporates to map their plans with greater clarity.

Policies related to electric mobility, hydrogen corridors, carbon markets, and clean manufacturing create a structured environment where capital can flow confidently.

The more predictable the policy direction, the stronger the appetite for sustainable investment. An indicator of policy influence comes from the International Energy Agency: **more than 90% of global GDP is now covered by national or regional net-zero commitments (IEA Net Zero Tracker [36]).**

This demonstrates the scale at which policy signals have expanded and how deeply they shape financial planning.

When commitments reach this level of coverage, financial institutions begin embedding transition logic into pricing, credit allocation, and risk assessments across all sectors.

Public policies also influence how investors differentiate sectors. Clear incentives accelerate capital flow into renewables, EV ecosystems, efficiency technologies, and adaptation projects.

Regulatory constraints, such as emissions standards or phase-down schedules, reshape the economics of carbon-intensive activities.

Policy clarity creates opportunity; policy silence creates hesitation. For this reason, stable and forward-looking policies have become essential in mobilising both domestic and international capital.

---

[36] ***Net Zero Climate*** *(Oxford Net Zero, Energy & Climate Intelligence Unit, NewClimate Institute), Net Zero Stocktake 2024: Assessing the Status and Trends of Net Zero Target Setting, September 2024,* *https://netzeroclimate.org/wp-content/uploads/2024/09/Net_Zero_Stocktake_2024.pdf, accessed 12 December 2025; Global net-zero target coverage statistics from Net Zero Tracker.*

To distill the interaction between policy and finance, the table below outlines how policy signals influence capital direction:

Policy Signals and Their Influence on Financial Decisions

Policy Signal	Market Interpretation	Financial Effect
National climate targets	Predictable long-term direction	Increased capital flow to aligned sectors
Industrial transition plans	Sector evolution clarity	Stronger investment confidence
Carbon-pricing mechanisms	Clear cost trajectory	Reallocation toward low-carbon activities
Subsidies and incentives	Lower investment barriers	Scale-up of emerging technologies
Disclosure regulations	Higher transparency	Improved risk pricing and governance

These signals serve as catalysts that orient sustainable finance toward national and global priorities. The consistency of policy direction determines the pace and depth of financial engagement.

2. Central Bank Guidance, Supervision and Stress Tests: Anchoring Financial Stability

Central banks shape the sustainability landscape through supervisory expectations, analytical frameworks, and climate-risk guidance. Their influence extends across lending, investment, insurance, and payment systems because they define how institutions evaluate exposure, prepare for uncertainty, and strengthen resilience.

Supervisory expectations increasingly require institutions to incorporate climate considerations into governance, internal controls, scenario analysis, and risk management architecture.

This means boards examine climate exposure regularly, risk committees incorporate transition pathways into assessments, and internal teams integrate climate indicators into models.

Central-bank guidance frames these expectations and ensures that institutions treat climate dynamics with the seriousness given to credit, liquidity, or operational factors.

Climate-risk supervision includes thematic reviews, on-site examinations, horizontal comparisons, and structured assessments. Institutions assess exposure to physical hazards, evolving technologies, policy shifts, and changing consumer behaviour. The supervisory process looks at whether banks can identify vulnerabilities, respond through planning, and adjust portfolios to long-term transition pathways.

Scenario exercises strengthen this process further. They explore future conditions under various climate pathways-rapid transition, delayed action, disorderly adjustment, or high-warming outcomes. These exercises guide balance-sheet planning, provisioning, collateral valuation, and strategic alignment.

An important early milestone in this field came in **2021**, when the Bank of England launched its **Climate Biennial Exploratory Scenario (CBES),** one of the earliest system-wide climate stress-testing exercises to assess both physical and transition risks[37].

---

[37] *Bank for International Settlements (BIS), Climate-related Risk and Financial Stability, BIS Quarterly Review, 2021, https://www.bis.org/publ/qtrpdf/r_qt2109.htm, accessed 12 December 2025.*

It demonstrated how climate variables influence credit losses, insurance claims, and long-term business strategies across banks and insurers. Exercises like CBES set templates for other central banks worldwide.

Scenario-based supervision influences multiple layers of stability:

- Institutional resilience
- Sector-level vulnerability awareness
- System-wide forward planning
- Pricing and provisioning frameworks
- Transition-aligned portfolio strategies

As more central banks integrate climate factors, resilience becomes an integral part of financial-sector governance rather than an external expectation.

3. Prudential and Macroprudential Perspectives: Building System-Level Resilience

Prudential regulation examines how climate risk affects both institutions and markets. It operates at two layers: **microprudential**, which focuses on individual institutions, and **macroprudential**, which looks at stability across the entire system.

Microprudential guidance encourages banks to develop internal climate-risk models, integrate transition insights into pricing, and align governance practices with long-term exposure clarity. Additional capital buffers, enhanced risk reviews, and improved data systems support this evolution. The goal is to ensure that institutions remain resilient across multiple climate pathways.

Macroprudential perspectives focus on the interconnected nature of climate dynamics. Transition risk in one sector may affect supply chains, employment patterns, investment flows, and local economies. Physical hazards influence property markets, insurance capacity, migration patterns, and infrastructure resilience. Macroprudential tools, therefore, evaluate concentration risks, geographic vulnerabilities, correlation patterns, and systemic amplification effects.

These tools include:

- Sector concentration guidelines
- Portfolio-alignment indicators
- Countercyclical buffers linked to climate exposures
- Early-warning systems for regional climate stress
- Prudential reporting on vulnerable sectors

Central banks study how transition pathways influence financial stability. For example, as renewable energy gains scale, legacy energy systems evolve at different speeds. This requires forward-looking provisioning models and structured transition plans. Similarly, physical-risk-prone regions may require stronger appraisal practices or revised collateral frameworks.

Prudential authorities also refine early-warning indicators-tracking exposure trends, credit-quality shifts, insurance stress, and sector-level transition progress. The monitoring process guides policy dialogue, supervisory engagement, and strategic adjustments across institutions.

1. Public Finance, Guarantees and Blended Structures: Scaling Transition Capital

Public finance plays an essential role in expanding access to sustainable capital, especially in sectors where early-stage risk, long project horizons, or technology uncertainty create hesitation among commercial lenders. Governments, development finance institutions (DFIs), and sovereign entities step in as anchor partners to reduce risk and encourage private participation. Their involvement brings stability, lowers financing barriers, and allows projects with strong long-term value to move forward.

Guarantees are a central part of this toolkit. They allow public institutions to absorb portions of credit risk linked to construction delays, demand variation, technology maturity, or regulatory pacing.

Guarantees signal confidence in a sector's future trajectory, reducing the cost of capital for borrowers and making sustainable projects more feasible. Many renewable-energy, efficiency, and adaptation initiatives gained momentum because credit guarantees gave investors clearer visibility on long-term performance.

Blended finance builds on this logic by mixing concessional and commercial layers.

Concessional capital absorbs higher risk through lower interest rates, subordinated tranches, or extended tenors. This structure creates space for commercial lenders to participate without compromising their risk thresholds.

Co-financing arrangements encourage wider participation across banks, pension funds, sovereign funds, and corporate investors, creating stronger financial ecosystems around priority sectors.

Blended structures use several mechanisms:

- **First-loss tranches** that strengthen resilience in early years
- **Subordinated debt** that enhances creditworthiness
- **Concessional loans** that improve affordability
- **Risk-sharing agreements** between public and private lenders
- **Technical assistance** that supports data systems, governance, and financial modelling

These tools are especially valuable in areas such as clean mobility, distributed renewables, waste-to-value, sustainable agriculture, and adaptation infrastructure-sectors that require patient capital and strong institutional support.

An insight from the World Bank highlights the scale of blended finance: between 2015 and 2022, blended-finance structures mobilised more than USD 160 billion in private capital for climate-related investments (World Bank, Global Blended Finance Report) [38]. This demonstrates how powerful public-private structures have become in accelerating transition sectors globally.

Countries use blended structures in ways that align with their development priorities.

Some focus on large infrastructure such as transmission grids or desalination; others prioritise green MSME lending, efficiency upgrades, or nature-based solutions. Each approach shapes a unique capital

---

[38] *World Bank Group, Global Blended Finance Report 2023: Mobilizing Private Capital for Sustainable Development, World Bank, 2023, https://openknowledge.worldbank.org/handle/10986/39513, accessed 12 December 2025.*

ecosystem while maintaining the same principle: when risk is shared intelligently, more capital flows toward long-term sustainability.

2. Policy Signals Through Carbon Pricing and Market Mechanisms

Carbon pricing is one of the strongest tools available to align economic incentives with sustainability goals. It introduces a cost for emissions, encourages the adoption of cleaner technologies, and reshapes long-term planning.

Carbon pricing takes multiple forms: explicit carbon taxes, emissions trading systems (ETS), and internal or shadow pricing used by institutions for project evaluation.

A carbon tax sets a fixed price per tonne of emissions, creating predictability for industries planning investments. An ETS caps allowed emissions and enables companies to trade allowances, creating a flexible market-driven pathway for reducing emissions.

Shadow pricing is used internally by institutions to evaluate future competitiveness under tightening climate policies, even before regulatory pricing takes effect.

Carbon pricing influences several layers of financial behaviour:

- **Cost curves** shift in favour of low-carbon technologies
- **Investment decisions** reflect long-term emissions trajectories
- **Operational changes** accelerate to manage exposure
- **Technological innovation** receives stronger support
- **Capital allocation** shifts toward transition-resilient sectors

Institutions study carbon-price trajectories because they shape future profitability and asset valuation. A rising carbon price pushes companies to re-evaluate equipment, supply chains, and expansion plans.

Long-lived assets such as power plants, industrial facilities, and transport infrastructure face higher scrutiny as policy signals become clearer.

A strong example comes from the European Union's Emissions Trading System. As allowance prices strengthened over recent years, several energy utilities accelerated coal-plant retirements and expanded renewable portfolios.

The pricing signal influenced strategic decisions, portfolio shifts, and capital expenditure planning. This case shows how a market mechanism can align corporate behaviour with climate ambition.

Shadow pricing is now widely used in financial modelling. Institutions embed internal carbon prices to forecast future competitiveness, evaluate green-versus-conventional options, and assess transition risk.

This internal practice strengthens long-term planning and aligns investment decisions with policy expectations. Carbon-pricing mechanisms create a feedback loop: policy indicates direction; markets evaluate cost trajectories; institutions refine strategies; technology adoption accelerates; and policy frameworks evolve with improved clarity. This dynamic interaction supports a predictable pathway for transition finance.

3. Institutional Implications: How Banks, Investors and Firms Respond to Policy

Policy frameworks influence how institutions interpret risks, design strategies, and allocate capital. The shift begins with strategic planning and extends across governance systems, risk modelling, disclosure architecture, and resource allocation.

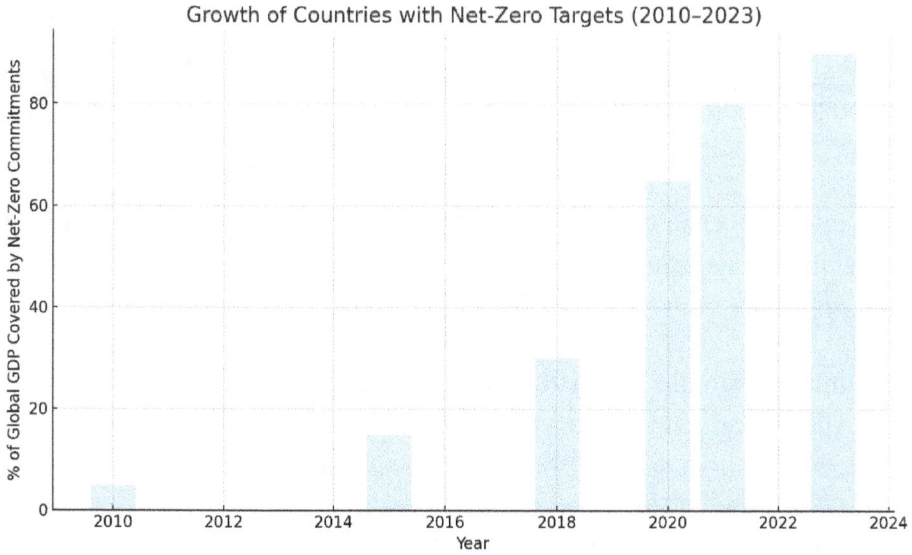

Source: IEA (2023); Net Zero Tracker (ECIU, Oxford University, NewClimate Institute, 2010-2023).

Banks integrate policy expectations into due-diligence practices and credit-evaluation models. They assess whether borrowers' business plans align with transition pathways, whether project economics withstand future carbon costs, and whether companies maintain readiness for policy upgrades or sector reforms. Lending portfolios evolve as banks identify sectors with stronger long-term resilience. Pricing logic incorporates transition dynamics, and internal controls monitor climate exposure more closely.

Investors respond by refining screening models, integrating forward-looking indicators, and aligning portfolios with national and global transition strategies.

Policies influence engagement priorities, stewardship dialogues, and thematic investing decisions. Institutional investors study how companies prepare for future policy changes, strengthen disclosures, and build adaptive capacity.

Firms adjust internal systems to match policy expectations. They strengthen governance structures around sustainability, enhance emissions and resource-use tracking, and refine capital-allocation strategies to support long-term competitiveness.

Policy clarity encourages companies to invest in efficiency technologies, diversify energy sources, redesign products, or explore circular-economy opportunities.

A simple example of institutional shift can be observed whenever a jurisdiction announces an upcoming carbon-pricing regulation. Banks update risk assessments; investors recalibrate valuations; companies reinforce internal measurement systems; and sectors pursue efficiency improvements.

This sequence demonstrates how policy signals cascade across the financial and corporate landscape.

Transition planning becomes more structured when regulatory direction is clear. Firms define milestones, establish transformation roadmaps, and develop investment plans aligned with future policy settings. Policies also encourage new partnerships across public and private sectors. As institutions advance, their governance systems and disclosure frameworks evolve in parallel.

Policy expectations influence capital flows by shaping the confidence of institutions. Clear, stable signals reduce uncertainty and support long-term investment.

As regulatory ecosystems mature, financial systems gain stronger capacity to respond to climate priorities with precision and scale.

Key Takeaways

- Public policy guides sustainable finance through structured direction and clear expectations.
- Central bank supervision integrates climate considerations into financial-stability frameworks.
- Prudential and macroprudential approaches strengthen resilience across institutions and markets.
- Guarantees and blended structures mobilise large volumes of capital for transition sectors.
- Carbon pricing influences investment logic by shifting long-term cost competitiveness.
- Market mechanisms shape innovation, technology adoption, and strategic planning.
- Regulatory clarity encourages institutions to refine lending models and risk architecture.
- Financial institutions strengthen governance, data systems, and scenario frameworks in response to policy.
- Corporate strategy evolves through well-defined transition signals and structured disclosures.
- Together, these tools align capital flows with sustainable development pathways across regions.

10

Energy Transition and Power Systems

The energy transition now stands at the centre of global strategy. Power systems that once depended on fossil plants are steadily shifting toward renewable corridors, distributed generation, and modern grid design.

This transformation shapes investment patterns, risk perspectives, and long-term planning, turning clean energy into a financial and systemic priority rather than a specialised theme.

Modern grids carry layered complexity. Utility-scale solar and wind expand rapidly, rooftop systems multiply, and storage becomes essential for balancing variability. Demand-side tools, digital controls, and flexible grid operations add new dimensions.

This blend makes the transition an economic redesign as much as a technological one, requiring coordination between engineering choices, policy signals, and financing structures.

Momentum continues to build across regions. Renewable energy additions accelerated sharply in recent years, and according to the International Energy Agency, **Global annual renewable capacity additions increased by almost 50% to nearly 510 gigawatts (GW) in 2023, the fastest growth rate in the past two decades**[39].

This scale sets the stage for deeper questions around system flexibility, storage economics, just-transition considerations, and the financing models that support large and distributed energy assets.

This chapter explores these dimensions through a practical lens. It walks through renewable integration, storage requirements, evolving grid designs, and transition pathways in fossil-fuel regions.

It studies risk allocation, financing structures, and selected sectoral examples from India, the UAE, the GCC, and other emerging markets. Together, these elements show how technology, policy, and finance shape resilient and adaptive power systems.

OBJECTIVES OF THE CHAPTER

This chapter will help individuals:

- Understand how utility-scale and distributed renewable systems reshape power markets.
- Study how storage, grid upgrades, and flexibility tools strengthen system stability.
- Explore the economic, social, and financial dimensions of a just transition.
- Examine financing models and risk-sharing structures for energy projects.

---

[39] *International Energy Agency (IEA), Renewables 2023: Analysis and Forecast to 2028, IEA, 2023,* *https://www.iea.org/reports/renewables-2023, accessed 15 December 2025.*

- Gain clarity on sector-level examples illustrating practical transition pathways.
- Recognise how technology, policy, and finance interact across power systems.
- Build insight into how institutions evaluate transition-readiness within the energy sector.
- Observe the shift from fossil-based systems toward cleaner, more adaptive power architectures.
- Strengthen analytical skills for interpreting energy-transition investments.
- Understand why the power sector anchors global sustainability commitments.

1. Utility-Scale Renewables and Distributed Energy Systems: Rewriting Power Architecture

The foundation of modern power systems rests on the rapid expansion of utility-scale renewable energy. Large solar parks, onshore and offshore wind farms, pumped hydro corridors, and hybrid renewable complexes demonstrate how scale influences grid design, financing logic, and generation planning.

Utility-scale projects deliver predictable output profiles over large geographies and encourage long-term power-purchase frameworks that give investors clarity. These assets have become central to national energy strategies because they accelerate decarbonisation while lowering levelised costs across regions.

Distributed energy systems add a complementary layer. Rooftop solar, behind-the-meter solutions, and commercial-and-industrial (C&I) adoption create a decentralised architecture that reduces transmission pressure and enhances local resilience.

Distributed systems also shift the role of consumers, turning households and businesses into active energy participants with the ability to generate, store, and manage their own electricity. This structural change supports greater adaptability and helps power systems absorb variability.

Operational characteristics shape how renewables interact with the grid. Solar and wind bring variability, so forecasting accuracy becomes a core requirement. Grid operators plan dispatch schedules, reserve margins, and balancing needs around expected fluctuations. Renewable portfolios also encourage diversification; a portfolio that blends solar, wind, hydro, and biomass naturally smooths output patterns.

These dynamics influence market design, pushing power systems toward mechanisms that value flexibility, time-of-day pricing, and ancillary services. **IRENA reported that renewable power capacity additions reached 473 GW in 2023-the highest annual increase ever recorded**[40]**.** This scale reshapes how institutions view long-term planning, because renewable supply growth now consistently outpaces fossil-fuel additions.

Forecasting models, grid-investment plans, storage decisions, and financing structures all evolve in response to this new growth trajectory.

As utility-scale and distributed systems expand, planning becomes more dynamic. Transmission corridors must accommodate renewable clusters, while distribution networks require upgrades for reverse power flows.

---

40 *International Renewable Energy Agency (IRENA), Renewable Energy Capacity Highlights 2024, IRENA, 2024,* https://www.irena.org/-/media/Files/IRENA/Agency/Publication/2024/Mar/IRENA_RE_Capacity_Highlights_2024.pdf*, accessed 15 December 2025.*

Market operators redesign mechanisms to reward flexibility and resource diversity. This architectural shift is not a technical adjustment; it is a complete redesign of how power is generated, transported, and managed.

2. Storage, Grids and System Flexibility: Building the Backbone of Modern Power Systems

Energy storage turns intermittent renewable supply into reliable power. Battery systems provide short-duration balancing, frequency response, and peak shaving. Pumped hydro delivers large-scale storage over longer intervals and continues to anchor reliability in many regions.

Long-duration technologies-flow batteries, compressed-air systems, and thermal storage-expand the toolbox for handling seasonal patterns and evening peaks. Together, these solutions create stability across daily and monthly cycles.

Grid expansion plays an equally important role. As renewable corridors grow, transmission networks must extend into new geographies, often connecting solar deserts, windy coastlines, and remote hydro basins to consumption centres. Distribution grids integrate rooftop assets, electric-vehicle charging, and localised storage.

Digital tools-advanced metering, SCADA controls, remote diagnostics, and predictive maintenance-give system operators granular visibility and real-time decision capability.

Flexibility defines the modern power system. Demand-side management encourages industrial users to shift consumption. Smart appliances and automated load controllers help households adapt their usage without inconvenience. Ancillary-services markets reward fast-responding assets, while capacity markets ensure long-term adequacy.

These elements create a multidimensional system where supply, demand, and grid infrastructure move as a coordinated whole.

Year	Global Renewable Additions (GW)
2019	176
2020	261
2021	295
2022	336
2023	473

A simple example clarifies this evolution: countries with high renewable penetration increasingly adopt **"duck-curve management"** strategies-using storage, flexible thermal units, and demand shifting to absorb midday solar peaks and meet evening load.

This pattern appears wherever solar deployment expands rapidly and demonstrates how flexibility planning becomes central to grid stability.

Institutions approach system flexibility through structured evaluation. They assess reserve requirements, study ramping capabilities, and evaluate locational constraints. They map out future scenarios that include electrification of industry, expansion of electric mobility, and new forms of distributed demand.

Flexibility is not seen as an add-on; it is a core design principle for every long-term energy plan.

3. Just Transition in Coal and Fossil Regions: Economic and Social Adjustments

The energy transition extends beyond technology-it reshapes regional economies and workforce structures. A just-transition approach acknowledges the need to support communities historically dependent on coal mining, lignite production, oil extraction, and fossil-fuel-based industries.

These regions carry deep economic and cultural ties to energy production, so transition planning must create meaningful economic alternatives.

A just transition includes structured workforce planning. Workers shift toward renewable-energy construction, grid operations, storage management, and electrical maintenance. Training programmes, certification pathways, and reskilling initiatives prepare local populations for emerging roles.

Institutions collaborate with industry groups to map future job requirements and match them with regional skill profiles.

Economic restructuring forms another layer. Coal regions often anchor industrial zones, logistics networks, and local markets. Transition programmes support new business development, clean-tech clusters, agrivoltaics, or service-sector expansion to replace lost revenue.

Public funds, development-finance institutions, and philanthropic programmes create blended structures to catalyse investment in these emerging economies.

Asset rehabilitation also plays a part. Decommissioned coal plants can host solar parks, battery hubs, or green-hydrogen facilities. Transmission corridors remain in use, reducing project-development time.

This approach preserves regional relevance while shifting the asset base toward cleaner systems.

A global anchor example illustrates the momentum: **the European Union's Just Transition Mechanism mobilised more than €55 billion for coal and carbon-intensive regions, supporting economic**

diversification and workforce programmes over the period 2021-2027[41] in the most affected regions, to alleviate the socio-economic impact of the transition.

This milestone shows how structured financial packages accelerate social and economic adaptation during energy transitions.

Governments and institutions weave these elements into comprehensive transition strategies. The goal is long-term resilience-strengthening regional economies, maintaining social stability, and aligning technological change with community needs. Energy transition becomes both a financial transformation and a social commitment, ensuring that progress is shared across industries, regions, and generations.

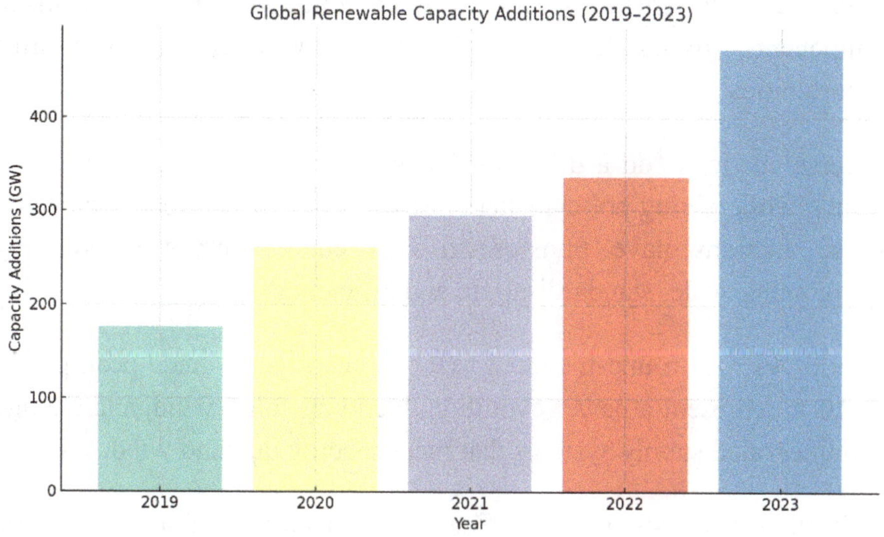

Source: IRENA, Renewable Capacity Statistics 2024.

[41] *European Commission, Just Transition Mechanism, European Union,* *https://commission.europa.eu/strategy-and-policy/priorities-2019-2024/european-green-deal/finance-and-green-deal/just-transition-mechanism_en, accessed 15 December 2025.*

1. Financing Models and Risk Allocation: Enabling Scalable Transition Projects

Energy-transition projects succeed when revenue certainty, risk-sharing structures, and policy alignment support long-term viability. Power-purchase agreements (PPAs) continue to anchor most renewable projects because they offer multi-year visibility on cash flows and establish clear obligations between developers and utilities.

Tariff design-whether fixed, escalable, or indexed-shapes the financial performance of each asset. Alongside PPAs, merchant models have grown in regions where wholesale markets mature and renewable assets can participate competitively without contractual protection.

Hybrid revenue structures combine fixed contracts with market-linked components, giving developers the flexibility to capture peak-price opportunities.

Reverse auctions add a different dynamic by encouraging competitive pricing while giving policymakers a structured tool to allocate capacity. These auctions have transformed cost curves across markets by encouraging scale, standardisation, and efficiency.

Hybrid PPAs, round-the-clock (RTC) contracts, and peak-power products represent a newer evolution, blending solar, wind, and storage into integrated supply systems that meet specific demand windows.

Risk allocation shapes the financial feasibility of each project. Developers typically manage construction timelines, technology choices, and performance optimisation. Utilities manage dispatch integration and system-level coordination.

Lenders focus on resource variability, curtailment probability, and regulatory continuity. Regulators influence the broader environment through tariff rules, grid-access frameworks, banking norms, and policy trajectories.

Construction risk reflects delays, cost overruns, equipment constraints, and contractor performance. Resource risk influences generation forecasts, especially for wind and solar assets where overestimation can weaken project cash flows. Curtailment risk emerges when grids face congestion or balancing constraints, and institutions assess this carefully during due diligence.

Grid-integration risk appears when renewable clusters grow faster than transmission expansion, requiring clear visibility on grid readiness.

Blended finance strengthens feasibility in markets that need catalytic support. Guarantees reduce perceived risk for private capital. Concessional funding lowers cost of capital for innovative technologies.

Public entities co-invest in early-stage assets to build confidence and encourage scale. Development banks support pilot technologies-green hydrogen, offshore wind, and long-duration storage-by absorbing early risk layers that commercial lenders assess conservatively.

The article states, "In 2021 it represented an aggregated financing of over $160 billion, with annual capital flows averaging approximately $9 billion since 2015[42]., expanding access to capital for countries and sectors transitioning to cleaner systems. This pattern shows how structured financing accelerates deployment and strengthens investor confidence.

---

42 *The article, titled "Blended finance can catalyze renewable energy investments in low-income countries" and published on* ***May 11, 2022****, explicitly states: https://blogs.worldbank.org/en/ppps/blended-finance-can-catalyze-renewable-energy-investments-low-income-countries*

Source: https://eninrac.com/horizon/the-c-suite-intelligence/advanced-material-in-hydrogen-storage-transport-unlocking-a-200b-global-opportunity-indias-strategic-role

Transition financing requires clarity, discipline, and continuous evaluation. Institutions examine tariff stability, policy durability, and operational readiness. Each project becomes a coordinated exercise across developers, policymakers, lenders, and system operators, shaping a financial ecosystem that can support scale.

2. Illustrative Energy Transition Snapshots: Sectoral Insights Across Regions

Short, sector-level snapshots show how transition pathways differ across geographies while sharing structural principles.

India - Large-scale solar ecosystems and integrated products

India's power system integrates expansive solar parks, hybrid wind-solar complexes, and green-energy corridors that deliver high-capacity transmission from renewable clusters to load centres. Round-the-clock renewable products combine multiple resources with storage, offering firm supply. These innovations create revenue stability and strengthen the commercial viability of renewable portfolios.

UAE - Hydrogen pilots, advanced solar, and grid modernisation

The UAE advances large-scale solar through projects that consistently achieve competitive tariffs while investing in hydrogen pilots linked with industrial decarbonisation. Grid modernisation improves load management, supports high-solar-penetration conditions, and prepares the system for new electrification demands.

GCC - Diversification and ultra-low-cost renewable models

The GCC region integrates renewables alongside established hydrocarbon economies, creating diversified energy portfolios. Auctions deliver some of the world's lowest solar tariffs, reflecting investor confidence, high-quality resources, and predictable regulatory structures. These markets explore storage pathways and flexible-grid programs to complement renewable supply.

Other Emerging Markets - Distributed and resource-specific transition models

Across Africa, Southeast Asia, and Latin America, mini-grids, geothermal systems, biomass plants, and distributed solar networks support energy access and reliability. Countries with geothermal potential use resource stability to balance variability from solar and wind. Markets with remote communities deploy mini-grids to achieve resilience, affordability, and local economic participation.

These snapshots demonstrate a shared theme: each region adapts its transition strategy to resource profiles, policy maturity, and system needs while following similar analytical logic-scalability, flexibility, and long-term competitiveness.

3. Practical Evaluation Lens for Energy-Transition Investments

Institutions evaluate transition investments through a structured lens that aligns technical, financial, and regulatory considerations. Resource quality forms the first layer-solar irradiation, wind speeds, hydrological stability, and geothermal potential guide generation forecasts and capacity-factor assumptions. Resource data supports modelling, technology selection, and design optimisation.

Policy stability gives projects directional confidence. Long-term national plans, tariff frameworks, renewable-purchase obligations, and grid-expansion roadmaps influence investment appetite. Institutions study the consistency of policy signals across multiple years, because clarity reduces uncertainty and strengthens valuation.

Tariff logic becomes a core financial filter. Analysts compare cost curves, revenue designs, auction outcomes, and market-linkage mechanisms. Hybrid contracts or RTC products require granular modelling to understand dispatch patterns, ramping requirements, and storage contributions. Clear tariff structures increase bankability and reduce negotiation cycles.

Technical-readiness checks follow a systematic approach:

- Grid-absorption capacity
- Substation readiness
- Transmission timelines
- Storage-pairing suitability
- Equipment reliability factors
- O&M planning frameworks

These checks help institutions evaluate whether a project can operate efficiently and integrate smoothly into the wider system.

Financial-readiness assessments examine revenue stability, contract structures, counterparty strength, exposure patterns, and liquidity cushions. Institutions use sensitivity analysis to test scenarios across resource variability, curtailment conditions, and grid-availability assumptions.

These evaluations deepen confidence in long-term performance.

Transition-readiness assessments look beyond immediate project economics. They reflect a forward lens-competitiveness over time, alignment with national transition goals, adaptability to policy evolution, and resilience as technology advances.

Institutions examine whether the asset fits into a future where electrification expands, storage costs fall, and flexible systems become universal.

A structured evaluation lens blends technical accuracy with strategic insight. It creates a consistent approach for understanding project feasibility, sectoral resilience, and long-term competitiveness.

This balanced evaluation approach prepares institutions to engage confidently with the evolving energy landscape.

Key Takeaways

- Power systems evolve through a coordinated expansion of renewables, distributed generation, storage, and flexible-grid tools.
- Utility-scale and decentralised systems reinforce each other by improving stability and enabling diversified supply.
- Storage, grid upgrades, and flexibility mechanisms anchor reliability across daily and seasonal cycles.
- Just-transition strategies support economic resilience and social well-being in fossil-dependent regions.
- Financing structures-PPAs, auctions, guarantees, and blended models-shape the scale and speed of deployment.
- Clear revenue design and balanced risk allocation strengthen project feasibility.
- Regional transition pathways reflect local resource profiles, policy maturity, and system conditions.
- Investment evaluation requires resource assessments, technical checks, financial clarity, and future-competitiveness insight.
- Institutions apply structured frameworks to identify risks and opportunities across energy portfolios.
- The power sector remains central to achieving global transition goals and long-term system resilience.

11

Buildings, Infrastructure and Cities

Cities now stand at the centre of global sustainability efforts because they carry most of the world's economic activity, infrastructure demand, and resource pressure.

As urban populations expand, the built environment-buildings, transport corridors, water systems, drainage networks, and waste-management pipelines-absorbs increasing responsibility for both emissions and resilience. Every decision about how a city grows, renovates, manages traffic, distributes water, or handles waste shapes long-term climate outcomes.

This makes urban systems a core focus for sustainable finance, since capital allocation choices determine how efficiently cities consume energy, how well they manage environmental stress, and how resilient their infrastructure becomes.

An estimate by UN-Habitat shows that **cities consume nearly 78 percent of global energy and account for more than 60 percent of**

greenhouse-gas emissions-a scale that highlights why urban assets influence national climate pathways. [43]

The built environment functions as an integrated ecosystem rather than a set of isolated assets.

A green building affects demand on the grid; efficient retrofits change how utilities plan capacity; electric-mobility systems influence air quality, traffic design, and energy load curves; water conservation reduces stress on treatment systems; and modern waste infrastructure strengthens circular-economy outcomes.

These interactions require coordination across engineering, architecture, policy, city planning, technology platforms, and financial structuring. A high-performing city is one where these elements reinforce each other: buildings that use less energy, transport systems that reduce congestion, water cycles that prevent scarcity, and waste channels that recover resources.

This interconnected view explains why sustainable urban finance demands both systemic thinking and granular project understanding.

A wide range of ideas unfold in this chapter: how green-building standards shape construction and operational choices; how retrofitting older structures delivers deep efficiency gains; how electric buses, metro corridors, and non-motorised transport are gradually redefining mobility; how water and waste systems evolve with circular principles; how municipal finance instruments help cities raise capital; how public-private partnership channels distribute risks; how sub-sovereign entities

---

[43] *UN-Habitat, Cities and Climate Change: Global Report on Human Settlements, United Nations Human Settlements Programme, 2011,* *https://unhabitat.org/sites/default/files/download-manager-files/Cities%20and%20Climate%20Change%20Global%20Report%20on%20Human%20Settlements%202011.pdf, accessed 15 December 2025.*

refine creditworthiness; and how city-level climate plans reveal funding gaps and transition priorities.

Regional snapshots from India, the UAE, and the GCC provide practical illustration of how different geographies handle growth, resilience, and decarbonisation. Together, these elements show how urban decision-making builds the long-term architecture of national sustainability.

OBJECTIVES OF THE CHAPTER

This chapter will help individuals:

- Understand how green buildings and retrofit programs influence energy use and operating efficiency.
- Study how urban transport, water, and waste systems shape climate pathways.
- Explore how city-level climate action plans highlight funding gaps and investment opportunities.
- Learn how municipal bonds, sub-sovereign tools, and blended instruments support urban projects.
- Examine public-private partnership models used for large infrastructure assets.
- Observe practical examples from India, the UAE, the GCC, and other regions.
- Gain clarity on how cities structure projects to attract investors and lenders.
- Identify what makes an urban project bankable, scalable, and resilient.
- Build insight into how integrated planning strengthens long-term urban transformation.
- Recognise why urban systems anchor national sustainability strategies.

1. Green Buildings and Efficiency Retrofits: Engineering the Built Environment

The modern building sector increasingly depends on structured sustainability pathways that combine design, technology, and operational discipline. Certification systems such as LEED, BREEAM, IGBC, and Estidama guide how projects optimise energy use, water performance, indoor-air quality, materials, and embodied carbon.

Source: *https://constructiondigital.com/sustainability-green-building/LEED-building-a-greener-future-for-construction*

These frameworks help project developers and asset owners evaluate building performance through measurable criteria, making it easier to align investments with long-term efficiency targets.

Architects and engineers now design around passive cooling, efficient HVAC systems, advanced insulation, adaptive lighting, and materials that carry lower lifecycle impact.

Retrofits form a parallel pathway, especially in cities with ageing infrastructure. Upgrading building envelopes, replacing inefficient systems, improving metering, and integrating automation transforms older structures into high-performing assets.

Performance data drives this shift. Financial institutions examine how retrofits reduce operating costs, stabilise demand, and enhance asset value over time. Portfolios with strong energy-performance indicators often show better lease outcomes, higher occupancy stability, and stronger resilience to regulatory tightening. Across many markets, retrofitting is treated as a strategic investment rather than a maintenance expenditure.

A key insight comes from the International Energy Agency: **improving building efficiency could reduce global energy demand by roughly 25 percent by 2050**[44], highlighting the scale of opportunity that structured retrofits create.

This single figure illustrates how building-level action influences national sustainability commitments and long-term energy planning. It also reinforces why city-level strategies prioritise building upgrades before pursuing larger infrastructure shifts.

Urban planners and financiers frequently evaluate green-building portfolios as part of broader climate-aligned development.

When buildings consume less energy and manage water effectively, cities gain room to integrate distributed systems, support electric mobility, and stabilise grid stress.

These interactions position green buildings as foundational elements in urban transition pathways.

[44] *International Energy Agency (IEA), Net Zero by 2050: A Roadmap for the Global Energy Sector, IEA, 2021,* https://www.iea.org/reports/net-zero-by-2050.

2. Urban Transport, Water and Waste Systems: Designing Resilient Urban Flows

Transport, water, and waste infrastructure shape how cities function every day. Their performance influences air quality, economic productivity, public health, and the investment appeal of urban corridors. As cities expand, these systems require redesign grounded in efficiency,

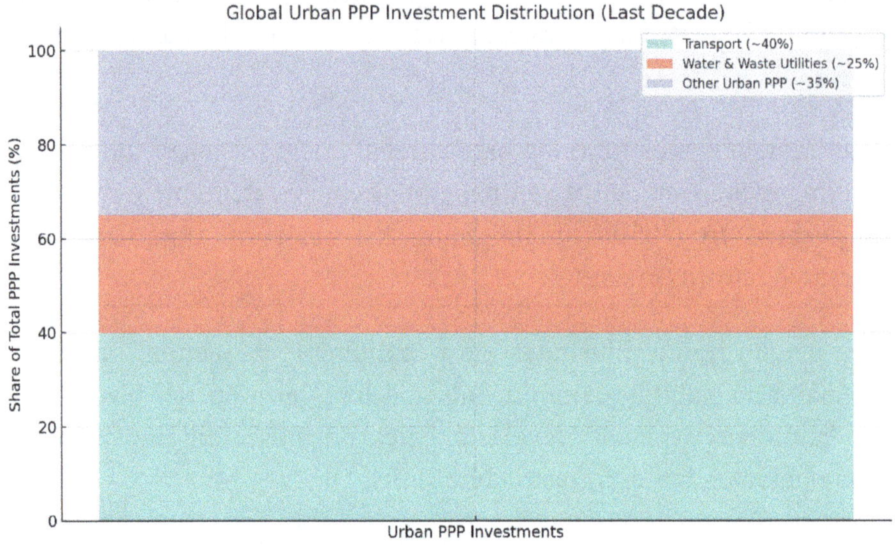

circularity, and long-term resilience.

Source: World Bank, Private Participation in Infrastructure (PPI) Database 2023 - sectoral distribution of urban PPP investments over the last decade.

Urban mobility now evolves around electric buses, metro expansions, BRT corridors, feeder services, and walkable public spaces. Electric mobility reduces operating costs and enhances air quality, while metro systems and dedicated bus lanes improve passenger throughput and reliability.

Streets redesigned for pedestrians and cyclists ease congestion and extend the lifespan of existing transport assets. Many cities adopt integrated mobility plans where electrification, digital ticketing, last-mile connectivity, and clean fleets support cohesive movement patterns.

Water networks follow a similar need for structural renewal. Non-revenue water (NRW) control through leak detection, district metering, and pressure management helps cities conserve a scarce resource. Wastewater treatment upgrades enable nutrient recovery, biogas generation, and safe reuse.

Circular-water systems strengthen resilience during droughts and reduce the operational load on supply networks. These improvements influence financial models as utilities assess tariff stability, operating margins, and long-term asset health.

Waste infrastructure now carries a more circular approach. Segregation at source, material recovery facilities, composting, and waste-to-energy plants shift cities away from landfill dependency.

Digital tracking of waste flows helps municipal bodies optimise routing, reduce emissions, and extend landfill life.

Material-recovery channels also create employment opportunities and strengthen informal-sector integration.

Across these systems, urban assets behave as interconnected flows rather than isolated components. A shift in mobility influences emissions and energy demand.

Water efficiency influences city planning and fiscal stability. Waste infrastructure influences carbon baselines. These linkages guide how institutions analyse risk, allocate capital, and plan future projects.

3. City-Level Climate Action Plans and Finance Gaps: Understanding the Urban Funding Challenge

City-level climate action plans operate as structured blueprints for long-term transformation. They identify emissions sources, outline sectoral interventions, provide cost estimates, and map expected benefits. These plans help municipalities demonstrate seriousness to lenders, clarify financing needs, and prioritise investments.

A strong climate action plan links governance, engineering, and economics into a unified roadmap that allows institutions to evaluate feasibility and readiness.

Funding needs often exceed municipal balance-sheet capacity. Cities face demands for renewable integration, smart mobility, water resilience, drainage upgrades, waste-processing facilities, and retrofitting pipelines-each requiring specialised financing.

The gap arises not only from limited debt capacity but also from the absence of structured risk-sharing models, inadequate project preparation, and evolving regulatory environments.

A clean illustrative example is how many medium-sized cities note that climate-action plans identify capital needs several times larger than annual municipal budgets.

Illustrative estimates from multilateral urban-finance studies suggest that a medium-sized city may require **several billion dollars** over a decade to upgrade mobility, water, and waste systems, while its annual capital expenditure often remains below a **few hundred million dollars**. [45] This

---

[45] *World Bank, Financing Sustainable Cities: How We're Helping Cities Raise Their Ambitions, World Bank Group, 2018,* *https://www.worldbank.org/en/news/press-release/2022/11/14/india-s-urban-infrastructure-needs-to-cross-840-billion-over-next-15-years-new-world-bank-report* *; 15 December 2025.*

gap highlights the scale of mobilised finance required for comprehensive urban transformation.

Municipal finance tools-such as sub-sovereign bonds, pooled-finance facilities, viability-gap instruments, and blended structures-attempt to bridge this gap.

They allow cities to leverage external capital without compromising governance or operational autonomy. As urban systems mature, project-preparation facilities and specialised advisory programs help municipalities structure bankable proposals and attract institutional investors.

To support analytical clarity, the table below shows an illustrative snapshot of **typical climate-infrastructure investment needs across key urban sectors**, aligned with common patterns observed in global studies.

Urban Sector	Typical Investment Need over 10 Years (USD Billion)	Key Drivers
Urban Transport (EV buses, metro, BRT)	1.2 - 3.0	Electrification, congestion relief, low-emission mobility
Water Supply & Wastewater	0.8 - 2.0	NRW reduction, reuse systems, treatment upgrades
Solid Waste & Circular Systems	0.4 - 1.0	Segregation, MRFs, waste-to-energy

Green Buildings & Retrofits	0.5 - 1.5	Efficiency improvements, operational savings
Urban Resilience & Drainage	0.3 - 1.0	Flood protection, climate-resilient design

1. Municipal and Sub-Sovereign Instruments: Expanding Urban Finance Capacity

Cities increasingly rely on structured financial instruments that allow them to access external capital without overwhelming municipal budgets. Municipal bonds, pooled-finance structures, guarantees, and credit-enhancement mechanisms help urban bodies raise long-term funds for transport corridors, water networks, waste-processing plants, and large-scale retrofitting programs.

These instruments operate on a simple logic: strengthen governance, stabilise cash flows, demonstrate financial discipline, and build investor confidence through transparent reporting.

Municipal bonds have gained momentum in markets that prioritise sub-sovereign autonomy. They allow cities to raise capital for climate-aligned projects while developing a track record in financial management. Credit enhancements-such as state guarantees, structured reserves, and escrow mechanisms-support issuances from cities that have not yet reached full investment-grade strength. Pooled-financing models help smaller cities combine their needs into a single bond, reducing transaction costs while improving access.

A research reinforces the growing relevance of this pathway: **India crossed USD 2 billion in cumulative municipal bond issuances by**

2023 (SEBI & NIUA data), signalling that sub-sovereign financing is steadily entering mainstream sustainable-finance conversations. [46]

Similar trends emerge in markets across the UAE and GCC, where municipal entities increasingly explore structured financing to support mobility corridors, efficient buildings, and water-waste systems.

Cities that aspire to unlock large-scale funding often begin with internal reform. Property-tax efficiency, user-charge rationalisation, predictable cash flows, audited accounts, and mature procurement systems help create the stability required for long-term instruments.

Once these elements align, external investors gain confidence, and credit agencies build clearer profiles of municipal performance. This combination of reforms and instruments forms the backbone of scalable urban finance.

2. Public-Private Partnership Models: Structuring Urban Infrastructure

Public-private partnerships (PPPs) help cities execute complex projects by combining public-sector vision with private-sector engineering, operations, and capital discipline. PPPs operate through structured contracts such as design-build-operate models, long-term concessions, annuity frameworks, and hybrid arrangements that match incentives across the lifecycle of an asset.

These structures allocate construction risk, performance risk, demand risk, and payment certainty among the involved parties.

For transport projects, PPP models often rely on annuity-based payments or revenue-sharing mechanisms that stabilise long-term returns. Water

---

[46] *Securities and Exchange Board of India (SEBI) and National Institute of Urban Affairs (NIUA), Status of Municipal Bond Market in India, Government of India, 2023, https://mohua.gov.in/, accessed 15 December 2025.*

and waste systems frequently use concession models where private operators manage treatment plants, pipelines, or recovery facilities under performance-linked contracts.

Urban building retrofits sometimes adopt energy-service company (ESCO) models, where contractors guarantee efficiency savings.

The feasibility of a PPP depends on how clearly responsibilities are distributed. When engineering, procurement, risk coverage, and service expectations are structured coherently, cities attract strong developers, lenders, and investors.

When these elements align with transparent governance, PPPs accelerate transformation by bringing innovation, operational experience, and timely delivery.

Regional snapshots show how this model adapts:

India - Indore Integrated Solid Waste Management PPP

A landmark concession model that achieved high segregation rates, efficient processing, and stable revenue recovery. It demonstrated how integrated waste-systems can scale with contractual discipline.

UAE - Dubai's Solar Parks through PPP structures

The Mohammed bin Rashid Al Maktoum Solar Park uses Independent Power Producer (IPP) models that secure competitive tariffs and global investor participation. These structures influence how cities evaluate utility-scale clean-energy projects.

GCC - Riyadh Metro PPP Components

Although largely public funded, selected system components follow PPP-style contracts for operations, signalling how mixed-model approaches strengthen delivery capacity.

These examples highlight how PPPs combine public oversight with private innovation, making them critical for city-level decarbonisation.

An anchor strengthens this perspective: **the World Bank's PPP database reports that more than USD 100 billion of urban-sector PPP projects were recorded globally in the last decade**[47], reflecting how infrastructure transition depends on shared risk and structured contract design.

3. What Makes a City-Level Project Bankable: Evaluation Lens for Urban Assets

Bankability in urban projects relies on clarity, stability, and structured decision-making. Lenders and investors examine whether a project aligns with long-term planning, carries predictable revenue potential, and maintains transparent governance. City-level projects gain traction when demand patterns are clear, tariffs are rational, and operational responsibilities are well defined.

Policy stability is the first signal. Urban infrastructure requires decades of service life, so financial institutions assess whether regulatory frameworks, urban plans, and institutional mandates remain consistent. When policy direction is coherent, risk models become simpler and capital flows grow.

Revenue models form the next layer. Mobility corridors evaluate fare structures, viability-gap mechanisms, or rolling subsidies. Water systems assess user charges, bulk-supply contracts, and treatment-plant service payments. Waste systems examine tipping fees, material-recovery revenues, and long-term processing obligations.

---

[47] *World Bank Group, Private Participation in Infrastructure (PPI) Database, World Bank, accessed 15 December 2025, https://ppi.worldbank.org/.*

Buildings and retrofit programs evaluate savings-linked repayment pathways.

Governance structures add significant weight to the evaluation lens. Cities with strong project-management units, transparent procurement, digital monitoring, and audited accounts often secure preferential financing terms.

Technical readiness also matters-resource assessments, engineering studies, grid integration logic, and environmental clearances shape the credibility of project design.

A smooth institutional example helps clarify this lens:

Case: Pune River Rejuvenation (India)

The project advanced through a combination of multilateral funding, state-level guarantees, and structured tendering. Its readiness came from clear feasibility studies, phased execution, and predictable revenue mechanisms-all of which positioned it as a bankable urban intervention.

As sustainable infrastructure becomes central to city planning, institutions evaluate transition readiness alongside financial feasibility. Long-term competitiveness, resilience measures, carbon-footprint reduction, and adaptive system design influence how capital allocators view the project.

According to the OECD, nearly USD 6 trillion per year is required globally for sustainable urban infrastructure through 2030[48], underlining how bankability frameworks guide trillions in future allocations.

---

[48] *Organisation for Economic Co-operation and Development (OECD), Global Infrastructure Outlook: Infrastructure Investment Needs 2016–2030, OECD Publishing, 2017, https://www.oecd.org/investment/global-infrastructure-outlook/, accessed 15 December 2025.*

Key Takeaways

- Municipal and sub-sovereign tools expand a city's ability to finance long-term climate infrastructure.
- Credit enhancements and financial discipline help cities build investor confidence.
- PPP frameworks align public vision with private innovation and operational depth.
- Clear risk allocation strengthens feasibility across transport, water, waste, and building assets.
- Regional cases reveal how cities customise PPP structures to local contexts.
- Bankable projects combine stable policy, predictable revenue, and strong governance systems.
- Technical readiness and transparent procurement elevate the credibility of urban proposals.
- Financing structures shape the scale and pace of urban transformation.
- Cities rely on structured evaluation lenses to attract lenders and institutional investors.
- Urban infrastructure plays a defining role in national sustainability and economic pathways.

12

Industry, Manufacturing and Hard-to-Abate Sectors

Industrial systems form the backbone of modern economies. Steel mills, cement plants, chemical facilities, refineries, aluminium smelters, and manufacturing corridors transform raw materials into products that build cities, enable mobility, and support daily life. These sectors also carry substantial emissions profiles, making them central to every national climate strategy.

The transition of industry represents one of the most complex and consequential chapters in global decarbonisation, one that requires technological innovation, financial creativity, and coordinated policy support.

Unlike power systems where renewable alternatives matured rapidly, industrial decarbonisation follows a different logic. High-temperature processes, chemical reactions intrinsic to production, and capital-intensive infrastructure with decades-long lifecycles create unique challenges.

Yet progress accelerates. Breakthrough technologies emerge, financing models adapt, and companies design credible transition pathways that balance operational continuity with environmental ambition. The International Energy Agency notes that **industry accounts for approximately 30% of global CO_2 emissions, with steel, cement, and chemicals representing the largest contributors**[49].

This scale underscores why industrial transition sits at the heart of climate finance.

Financial institutions increasingly view industrial transition as an opportunity rather than a constraint.

Transition finance instruments, performance-linked facilities, and technology-focused credit lines help companies navigate the pathway from carbon-intensive operations toward cleaner production systems. Investors study how companies allocate capital, adopt emerging technologies, and align strategies with science-based targets.

Banks refine lending frameworks to support gradual improvement while maintaining credit discipline. Policymakers create enabling conditions through carbon pricing, technology subsidies, and regulatory clarity.

This chapter explores how industry approaches decarbonisation through structured transition planning. It examines emissions profiles across sectors, cleaner production pathways, technology deployment strategies, and the financing models that support transformation.

It studies company-level transition plans, evaluates sector-specific examples, and presents case studies from India, the UAE, and the GCC that illustrate practical pathways.

---

[49] *International Energy Agency (IEA), Industry - Energy System, IEA,* https://www.iea.org/energy-system/industry, accessed 18 December 2024

Together, these elements show how industrial systems evolve toward resilience, efficiency, and long-term sustainability.

OBJECTIVES OF THE CHAPTER

This chapter will help individuals:

- Understand emissions profiles across major industrial sectors and how they shape transition priorities.
- Study cleaner production methods, process innovations, and efficiency upgrades that reduce carbon intensity.
- Explore transition finance structures designed for carbon-intensive sectors with long asset lifecycles.
- Examine how technology risk influences investment decisions and how policy support strengthens deployment confidence.
- Learn how companies design transition plans that align operational strategy with climate commitments.
- Observe sector-specific examples that demonstrate practical decarbonisation pathways.
- Analyse case studies from India, the UAE, and the GCC that show regional approaches to industrial transition.
- Build confidence in evaluating industrial transition strategies from financial and operational perspectives.
- Recognise how structured planning, technology adoption, and financing coordination accelerate sectoral transformation.
- Understand why industrial decarbonisation requires patient capital, innovation support, and multi-stakeholder collaboration.

1. Emissions Profiles in Industry: Understanding Sectoral Complexity

Industrial emissions emerge from diverse sources, combustion processes, chemical reactions, electricity consumption, and fugitive releases. Each sector carries distinct characteristics that influence decarbonisation approaches.

Steel production relies on blast furnaces that use metallurgical coal for iron reduction, creating process emissions difficult to eliminate through fuel switching alone. Cement manufacturing produces emissions through calcination, a chemical transformation of limestone, alongside energy-intensive heating processes. Chemical plants generate emissions across feedstock processing, reaction pathways, and thermal operations.

Aluminium smelting requires enormous electrical input, making emissions profiles dependent on grid carbon intensity. Refineries process crude oil through energy-intensive distillation and conversion units. Pulp and paper operations combine biomass combustion with chemical processing. ach pathway presents unique technical characteristics that shape transition strategies and influence financing requirements.

A clear sectoral breakdown helps institutions understand where emissions concentrate and how different industries approach reduction:

Sector	Primary Emission Sources	Decarbonisation Complexity	Key Transition Pathways
Steel	Blast furnace coal use, process emissions	High, chemical reaction intrinsic	Hydrogen DRI, electric arc furnaces, scrap utilisation

Cement	Limestone calcination, fuel combustion	High, process emissions dominant	Alternative fuels, clinker substitution, carbon capture
Chemicals	Feedstock processing, steam cracking, reactions	Medium-High, varies by product	Electrification, bio-feedstocks, process efficiency
Aluminium	Electricity-intensive smelting	Medium, depends on grid	Clean electricity, recycling expansion
Refining	Distillation, conversion units, hydrogen production	Medium-High, integrated operations	Efficiency upgrades, renewable hydrogen, electrification

This sectoral diversity explains why industrial transition requires customised approaches rather than universal solutions. Financial institutions study these profiles to understand technical feasibility, capital requirements, and timeline expectations when evaluating transition plans.

According to the World Economic Forum, **heavy industry sectors face cumulative investment needs exceeding USD 15 trillion through 2050 to achieve net-zero aligned pathways**[50]. This magnitude reflects both

[50] *World Economic Forum, Net-Zero Industry Tracker 2024, World Economic Forum, 2024, https://www.weforum.org/publications/net-zero-industry-tracker-2024/, accessed 18 December 2024.*

the challenge and the opportunity, industrial decarbonisation creates demand for technology deployment, infrastructure development, and innovation financing at unprecedented scale.

Emissions intensity varies significantly even within sectors. Integrated steel mills using blast furnaces carry higher intensity than electric arc furnace operations. Cement plants with modern precalciner systems perform better than older wet-process kilns. Chemical facilities producing different product mixes show varied emission profiles.

This granularity matters because lenders and investors evaluate performance against peer benchmarks and sector trajectories rather than absolute emissions alone.

Understanding these profiles helps institutions design appropriate financing structures, set realistic performance targets, and appreciate the time horizons required for meaningful transformation. It also clarifies why industrial transition demands both incremental efficiency gains and breakthrough technology deployment working in parallel.

2. Cleaner Production and Process Upgrades: Building Efficiency into Operations

Cleaner production begins with efficiency, using less energy, reducing waste streams, optimising material flows, and improving process control. Many industrial facilities achieve significant emissions reductions through operational discipline before requiring major capital investments.

Energy management systems, waste heat recovery, advanced process controls, and maintenance optimisation deliver measurable results while strengthening profitability.

Steel plants recover waste gases, upgrade reheating furnaces, and improve casting efficiency. Cement facilities adopt co-processing of alternative fuels, optimise grinding operations, and reduce clinker ratios through blended cements. Chemical plants enhance catalyst performance, integrate heat exchange networks, and implement real-time process monitoring. These improvements reduce emissions intensity while lowering operating costs, a combination that strengthens financial viability and makes efficiency investments attractive to lenders.

Process upgrades represent the next layer of transformation. They involve capital expenditure to replace or modernise core equipment with more efficient alternatives. Examples include transitioning from open-hearth to electric arc furnaces in steel, installing modern precalciner systems in cement, or adopting energy-efficient membrane technologies in chemical separation.

These upgrades carry higher capital requirements but deliver step-change improvements in emissions performance.

Material efficiency also plays a central role. Steel producers expand scrap utilisation, cement manufacturers increase supplementary cementitious materials, and chemical companies explore circular feedstock options. These strategies reduce primary production intensity and align operations with circular economy principles.

They also create new supply chains, partnerships, and business models that support long-term resilience.

A notable example comes from India's steel sector: **Tata Steel has committed to reducing carbon emissions intensity by 30% by 2030 through a combination of energy efficiency, renewable energy integration, and technology deployment**[51]. This commitment demonstrates how large industrial players structure transition strategies

---

[51] *Tata Steel, Sustainability Report 2023-24, Tata Steel Limited, 2024, https://www.tatasteel.com/sustainability/, accessed 18 December 2024.*

around measurable targets supported by operational and capital-investment programmes.

Source: *https://www.deccanherald.com/business/companies/tata-steel-reports-rs-759-crore-net-profit-in-q2-3264805*

Cleaner production extends to supply-chain optimisation. Companies reduce transportation emissions, source low-carbon materials, and collaborate with suppliers to lower embedded carbon in inputs.

These efforts create ripple effects across industrial ecosystems and encourage broader sectoral transformation.

Financial institutions evaluate cleaner production initiatives by examining baseline data quality, monitoring systems, capital allocation plans, and performance tracking mechanisms.

Projects with clear measurement frameworks, transparent reporting, and credible savings projections receive more favourable financing terms because they demonstrate management discipline and transition readiness.

3. Transition Finance for Carbon-Intensive Sectors: Designing Structured Pathways

Transition finance emerged specifically to support sectors where immediate decarbonisation proves technically or economically unfeasible. These instruments recognise that heavy industry requires time, capital, and technology maturity to achieve deep emissions reductions. Rather than excluding carbon-intensive sectors from sustainable finance, transition frameworks encourage gradual, measurable progress aligned with science-based trajectories.

Sustainability-linked loans anchor much of this activity. Companies commit to key performance indicators, emissions intensity reduction, renewable energy adoption, energy efficiency improvement, and link financing costs to achievement. These structures encourage disciplined planning because underperformance triggers pricing adjustments.

They also create transparency because regular reporting requirements ensure investors and lenders track progress consistently.

Transition bonds represent another pathway. Unlike green bonds that finance specific eligible projects, transition bonds support broader capital expenditure programmes aimed at reducing portfolio emissions. Issuers articulate transition strategies, set interim targets, and demonstrate alignment with sectoral decarbonisation pathways. External reviews assess credibility, ambition, and measurement methodologies.

Blended finance structures help de-risk early-stage technology deployment. Development finance institutions provide subordinated capital or guarantees that reduce commercial lender exposure. Concessional funding lowers interest costs for pilot projects. Risk-sharing mechanisms encourage banks to extend credit to innovative processes before they reach full commercial scale. These tools proved essential for technologies like hydrogen-based steelmaking, carbon capture systems, and alternative cement formulations.

A meaningful development illustrates growing market acceptance: **Japan issued the world's first sovereign transition bonds in 2024, raising JPY 1.6 trillion (approximately USD 10 billion) to support industrial decarbonisation and clean energy infrastructure**[52]. This landmark issuance demonstrated how national governments use transition finance to catalyse sectoral transformation while maintaining fiscal discipline.

Policy support strengthens transition finance by creating predictable frameworks. Carbon pricing signals long-term cost trajectories. Technology subsidies reduce early-stage investment risk.

Regulatory roadmaps provide clarity on future performance expectations. When these elements align, financial institutions gain confidence that transition investments will preserve value across extended time horizons.

Transition finance also requires robust governance.

Companies establish board-level oversight, integrate climate considerations into strategy, and build internal capabilities around emissions measurement and target setting. Investors evaluate governance strength alongside financial metrics because credible transition planning depends on organisational commitment and execution capacity.

4. Technology Risk and Policy Support: Navigating Innovation Pathways

Industrial decarbonisation depends heavily on technologies at varying maturity stages. Some, like electric arc furnaces and high-efficiency motors, operate commercially at scale. Others, such as hydrogen direct

---

[52] *Japan Ministry of Finance, Japan's Transition Finance Framework, Government of Japan, 2024, https://www.meti.go.jp/english/policy/energy_environment/transition_finance/index.htmlaccessed 18 December 2024.*

reduction for steel or carbon capture for cement, remain in demonstration or early commercial phases. Technology risk influences how financial institutions structure investments, price credit, and evaluate long-term viability.

Early-stage technologies carry higher uncertainty around performance, cost, and scalability. Lenders address this through phased financing, performance guarantees, technology insurance, and off-take agreements. Developers mitigate risk by partnering with established equipment suppliers, conducting extended pilot periods, and securing policy support that buffers market uncertainty.

Policy frameworks reduce technology risk by creating demand visibility, providing deployment incentives, and supporting research and development. Carbon contracts for difference guarantee minimum carbon prices, making low-carbon production economically viable even if market prices fluctuate.

Production tax credits reward clean output directly. Capital grants support demonstration projects. These mechanisms allow companies to invest in emerging technologies with greater confidence.

International collaboration accelerates technology deployment. Knowledge-sharing platforms, joint research initiatives, and cross-border pilot projects reduce duplication and spread learning.

Multilateral institutions coordinate funding, technical assistance, and policy dialogue across regions. This collaborative ecosystem helps emerging technologies move faster from concept to commercial readiness.

A clear example of policy-technology integration comes from the UAE: **ADNOC announced plans to invest USD 15 billion in low-carbon**

solutions by 2030, including carbon capture, clean hydrogen, and sustainable aviation fuel production[53].

This commitment demonstrates how strategic policy direction combined with substantial capital allocation accelerates technology deployment in traditionally carbon-intensive sectors.

The UAE's approach creates confidence for technology providers, engineering firms, and financial institutions to participate in industrial transformation at scale.

Investors study technology risk through multiple lenses, technical readiness levels, commercial track records, supply chain maturity, regulatory support, and long-term cost competitiveness.

Projects with proven technologies receive more favourable terms than those deploying first-of-a-kind systems.

However, structured risk-sharing mechanisms allow breakthrough technologies to access capital when backed by credible partners and supportive policies.

Technology deployment also creates learning effects. Each successive project reduces costs, improves performance, and builds operational experience.

Financial institutions value these learning trajectories because they indicate strengthening commercial viability and growing competitive advantage for early adopters.

---

[53] *ADNOC, ADNOC Announces Ambition to Achieve Net Zero by 2045, Abu Dhabi National Oil Company, 2023, https://www.adnoc.ae/en/2030-sustainability-strategy accessed 18 December 2024.*

5. Company-Level Transition Plans and Their Financing: Strategic Alignment in Practice

Credible transition planning begins with comprehensive emissions inventories, Scope 1, Scope 2, and increasingly Scope 3 across value chains. Companies establish baselines, identify reduction opportunities, prioritise interventions, and set interim targets aligned with long-term net-zero commitments. These plans integrate operational improvements, capital investments, technology adoption, and supply-chain engagement into coherent strategies.

Financial institutions evaluate transition plans through structured criteria. They assess whether targets align with science-based pathways, whether capital allocation matches stated ambitions, whether governance systems support implementation, and whether measurement systems enable transparent tracking. Strong plans demonstrate clear accountability, realistic timelines, and recognition of technological and market constraints.

Capital expenditure programmes reflect transition commitment. Companies allocate budgets toward energy efficiency, renewable energy procurement, low-carbon process technologies, and carbon capture infrastructure.

These investments compete with traditional expansion projects, so board-level prioritisation signals strategic seriousness. Lenders and investors study capex plans to understand how sustainability integration influences long-term growth and competitiveness.

Sustainability-linked financing increasingly anchors transition plans by creating external accountability. Performance targets become contractual obligations that influence borrowing costs. Regular reporting requirements ensure transparency. Independent verification strengthens credibility. These mechanisms transform transition plans from aspirational documents into operational commitments with financial consequences.

A structured example illustrates this integration: **ArcelorMittal, one of the world's largest steel producers, committed to reducing carbon emissions intensity by 25% by 2030 across its global operations, backed by EUR 10 billion in transition capital expenditure**[54]. The company secured sustainability-linked financing facilities that tie interest rates to emissions reduction targets, demonstrating how transition plans translate into structured financial arrangements.

Transition financing also supports research and development. Companies invest in pilot technologies, demonstration facilities, and partnership programmes with universities and research institutions. These investments carry higher risk but create long-term optionality. Development finance institutions and government innovation funds often co-invest to share risk and accelerate learning.

As transition plans mature, companies increasingly link executive compensation to climate targets. This governance evolution strengthens internal alignment and signals commitment to external stakeholders.

It also influences how investors evaluate management quality and strategic execution capability.

6. Sector Examples and Lessons: Practical Pathways Across Industries

Different sectors approach transition through distinct technological and financial pathways. Steel demonstrates multiple routes, hydrogen direct reduction replaces coal-based blast furnaces, electric arc furnaces expand

---

[54]*ArcelorMittal, Climate Action Report 3, ArcelorMittal, 2022,* *https://corporate.arcelormittal.com/media/press-releases/arcelormittal-publishes-second-group-climate-action-report* *, accessed 18 December 2024.*

using renewable electricity, and scrap utilisation increases through improved collection systems.

Each pathway requires different capital structures, partnership models, and policy support. Leading producers pursue parallel strategies, reducing risk by diversifying technology portfolios while building operational experience across multiple options.

Cement faces unique challenges because calcination emissions arise from chemical transformation rather than fuel combustion alone. The sector advances through clinker substitution using supplementary materials, alternative fuel adoption, carbon capture deployment, and novel cement chemistries. Financing structures often combine equipment loans for efficiency upgrades with project finance for carbon capture systems.

Policy support through carbon pricing and green procurement standards strengthens commercial viability.

The chemical sector pursues electrification of processes traditionally powered by fossil fuels, explores bio-based feedstocks as alternatives to petroleum derivatives, and improves energy integration across production complexes.

Transition finance supports modular investments that reduce intensity progressively rather than requiring complete facility replacement. Partnerships with renewable energy developers and waste-to-chemical technology providers create integrated value chains.

Aluminium's pathway centres on clean electricity access. Producers secure long-term renewable energy contracts, invest in smelter efficiency upgrades, and expand recycling capacity. Green aluminium premiums create market incentives for low-carbon production. Financing structures often link facility loans to renewable energy procurement commitments, creating coordinated pathways that reduce emissions while maintaining cost competitiveness.

A valuable lesson emerges from these sectoral patterns: **successful industrial transition combines incremental efficiency gains with transformational technology deployment, supported by financing structures that recognise different risk profiles and time horizons**. No single approach works universally, each sector, geography, and company requires customised strategies that balance technical feasibility, economic viability, and strategic ambition.

Regional cooperation strengthens sectoral transformation. Industrial clusters develop shared infrastructure, hydrogen networks, carbon capture pipelines, renewable energy corridors, that reduce individual project costs.

Governments coordinate policies across related industries to create systemic momentum. Financial institutions develop sector expertise that allows them to evaluate projects with greater precision and confidence.

7. Case Studies: Industrial Transition from India, the UAE, and the GCC

India: Tata Steel's Transition Roadmap

The company's strategy combines energy efficiency programmes, renewable energy procurement exceeding 500 MW, waste heat recovery systems, and pilot projects for hydrogen-based steelmaking. Tata Steel secured sustainability-linked financing facilities where interest rates adjust based on emissions performance.

The company also partnered with technology providers to test hydrogen injection in blast furnaces, a bridging technology toward full hydrogen-based direct reduction. This case demonstrates how integrated steel producers in emerging markets structure transition plans that balance operational continuity, technology risk, and financial viability.

UAE: ADNOC's Industrial Decarbonisation Programme

Abu Dhabi National Oil Company (ADNOC) exemplifies how resource-based economies approach industrial transition through strategic investment and technology leadership. ADNOC committed USD 15 billion toward low-carbon solutions including carbon capture capacity expansion to 10 million tonnes annually by 2030[55], green hydrogen production facilities, and sustainable aviation fuel development.

Source: *https://globalcompetitionreview.com/regions/united-arab-emirates*

The company secured project financing for carbon capture infrastructure while establishing partnerships with international technology leaders. ADNOC's approach demonstrates how traditionally carbon-intensive industries can lead transition efforts through substantial capital allocation, clear targets, and partnership-driven innovation.

[55] *ADNOC, Sustainability Report 2023, Abu Dhabi National Oil Company, 2024, https://corporate.arcelormittal.com/media/3fwar2wu/2024-sustainability-report.pdfy, accessed 18 December 2024.*

The programme strengthens the UAE's position as a regional hub for industrial decarbonisation technologies.

GCC: SABIC's Circular Carbon Programme

Saudi Basic Industries Corporation (SABIC), one of the world's largest chemical manufacturers, launched comprehensive circular carbon initiatives including renewable feedstock adoption, chemical recycling technologies, and carbon capture utilisation.

Source: https://www.sabic.com/en/news/17356-saudi-basic-industries-corporation-sabic-announces-the-opening-of-the-board-of-director-nomination-for-the-next-term

SABIC's Trucircle portfolio offers products with certified recycled content, creating market differentiation while reducing virgin fossil feedstock dependence.

The company invested in advanced recycling technologies that convert mixed plastic waste back into chemical feedstocks, a breakthrough addressing both circularity and emissions. SABIC secured green financing facilities to support these initiatives and established partnerships across the value chain from waste collectors to brand owners.

This case illustrates how chemical companies in the GCC integrate circular economy principles into transition strategies, creating business opportunities while advancing environmental goals[56].

These case studies reveal common elements: clear targets aligned with science-based pathways, substantial capital commitment, technology partnerships, structured financing arrangements, and governance systems that ensure accountability.

They also show regional diversity, India emphasises efficiency and bridging technologies, the UAE focuses on large-scale infrastructure and hydrogen, and the GCC leverages chemical expertise toward circularity. Together they demonstrate that industrial transition advances through multiple pathways shaped by regional strengths, market structures, and policy frameworks.

---

[56] *SABIC, Sustainability Report 2023, Saudi Basic Industries Corporation, 2024,* *https://www.sabic.com/en/sustainability, accessed 18 December 2024.*

Key Takeaways

- Industrial sectors account for approximately 30% of global emissions, making their transition central to climate goals.
- Emissions profiles vary significantly across steel, cement, chemicals, aluminium, and refining, each requiring customised decarbonisation strategies.
- Cleaner production through efficiency upgrades, process optimisation, and waste reduction delivers immediate emissions reductions while strengthening profitability.
- Transition finance structures, sustainability-linked loans, transition bonds, and blended facilities, support gradual, measurable progress in carbon-intensive sectors.
- Technology risk influences investment decisions, with policy support reducing uncertainty and accelerating deployment of emerging solutions.
- Company-level transition plans integrate emissions measurement, capital allocation, target setting, and governance into coherent strategies.
- Successful sectoral transformation combines incremental improvements with breakthrough technology deployment across varied time horizons.
- Regional case studies from India, the UAE, and the GCC demonstrate diverse approaches, efficiency focus, infrastructure scale, and circular innovation, all advancing industrial decarbonisation.
- Financial institutions evaluate transition readiness through baseline quality, governance strength, capital commitment, and alignment with science-based pathways.

- Industrial transition requires patient capital, multi-stakeholder collaboration, and recognition that meaningful transformation unfolds across decades rather than years.

13

Agriculture, Land Use and Nature-Based Solutions

Agriculture and land systems hold a unique position in climate finance. They function simultaneously as emissions sources, carbon sinks, biodiversity reservoirs, and livelihood foundations for billions of people.

This dual nature creates both urgency and opportunity, land-use decisions shape atmospheric carbon levels while agricultural practices determine food security, water availability, and rural prosperity.

Nature-based solutions offer pathways that align economic activity with ecological restoration. Reforestation, sustainable farming, wetland conservation, and regenerative land management create measurable climate benefits while strengthening natural systems. These approaches gained prominence as scientific understanding deepened around how intact ecosystems regulate climate, protect watersheds, and support biodiversity.

Financial institutions increasingly recognise agriculture and nature as investment frontiers rather than peripheral concerns. The Food and

Agriculture Organization estimates that **agriculture, forestry, and land use contribute approximately 24% of global greenhouse gas emissions**[57]. This scale positions land systems at the centre of transition finance, requiring capital flows that support farmers, protect ecosystems, and build resilience across rural landscapes.

The complexity lies in integration, agricultural finance must balance productivity with sustainability, economic returns with ecological outcomes, and immediate needs with long-term stewardship. Rural credit systems, insurance products, value-chain financing, and conservation funds each play distinct roles in this transformation. When these elements align, they create comprehensive support structures that encourage sustainable land management at scale.

This chapter explores how finance shapes agricultural transition and nature-based solutions. It examines climate risks in food systems, sustainable production practices, forestry initiatives, rural finance mechanisms, and the social dimensions that ensure inclusive progress. Case studies from the UAE, GCC, and global contexts illustrate practical pathways where capital meets conservation.

OBJECTIVES OF THE CHAPTER

This chapter will help individuals:

- Understand climate and nature risks affecting agricultural systems and land-use decisions.

- Study sustainable agriculture practices and how they integrate into value chains.

- Explore forestry, restoration, and conservation projects from financial and ecological perspectives.

---

[57] *Food and Agriculture Organization (FAO), Emissions from Agriculture and Forest Land, FAO,* https://www.fao.org/faostat/en/ *, accessed 20 December 2024.*

- Learn how rural credit, insurance, and resilience finance support farmer adaptation.
- Examine nature-based solutions and their integration into green finance structures.
- Recognise social dimensions and inclusion considerations in land-use finance.
- Analyse case studies from the UAE, GCC, and other regions demonstrating agricultural innovation.
- Build confidence in evaluating nature-aligned investments and sustainable agriculture projects.
- Understand how finance channels support both climate mitigation and ecosystem restoration.
- Appreciate why agricultural transition requires patient capital and community engagement.

1. Climate and Nature Risks in Agriculture and Land Use: Understanding Systemic Vulnerabilities

Agricultural systems face mounting pressures from shifting rainfall patterns, temperature extremes, water scarcity, soil degradation, and biodiversity loss. These stresses influence crop yields, livestock productivity, and the viability of farming communities. Climate variability creates uncertainty around planting seasons, harvest outcomes, and market stability, dynamics that ripple through entire food systems.

Water availability sits at the core of agricultural risk. Regions dependent on monsoon patterns face increased variability. Groundwater depletion threatens irrigation-based systems. Droughts reduce productivity while floods damage infrastructure and crops. These water stresses create financial risks for lenders, reduce farmer income stability, and influence national food security planning.

Soil health determines long-term agricultural viability. Industrial farming practices sometimes deplete organic matter, reduce microbial diversity, and increase erosion vulnerability. Degraded soils require more inputs while delivering lower yields, a pattern that weakens farm economics and increases environmental pressure. Regenerative practices that rebuild soil health offer both climate benefits and improved productivity over time.

Biodiversity loss affects agricultural resilience. Pollinator decline impacts crop production. Loss of crop diversity increases vulnerability to pests and diseases. Ecosystem degradation reduces natural pest control and water regulation services. These interconnections mean agricultural finance increasingly considers ecosystem health alongside traditional productivity metrics.

The World Bank reports that **climate change could push an additional 132 million people into poverty by 2030, with agricultural disruption being a primary driver**[58]. This statistic underscores how climate risks in farming systems carry profound social and economic consequences that extend far beyond individual farm boundaries.

Financial institutions assess these risks through multiple lenses, crop insurance data, water availability projections, soil quality indicators, and climate scenario models. They evaluate whether farming operations demonstrate adaptive capacity through diversified cropping, water-efficient technologies, soil conservation practices, and market linkages that absorb production variability.

---

[58] *World Bank, Poverty and Shared Prosperity 2020: Reversals of Fortune, World Bank Group, 2020, https://openknowledge.worldbank.org/handle/10986/34496, accessed 20 December 2024.*

Risk Category	Agricultural Impact	Financial Consequence	Adaptation Pathway
Water Stress	Irrigation constraints, yield reduction	Lower revenue, higher input costs	Drip systems, drought-resistant varieties, water storage
Temperature	Heat stress, growing season shifts	Production variability, crop failure risk	Climate-adapted seeds, shading systems, timing adjustments
Soil Degradation	Declining fertility, erosion	Rising input costs, yield decline	Cover cropping, organic matter, conservation tillage
Biodiversity Loss	Pollinator decline, pest pressure	Yield reduction, higher pest management costs	Habitat corridors, integrated pest management, diversity

This table clarifies how climate and nature risks translate into financial considerations that shape lending decisions, insurance pricing, and investment strategies in agricultural sectors.

2. Sustainable Agriculture and Value Chains: Building Resilient Food Systems

Sustainable agriculture integrates environmental stewardship with economic viability. Practices include precision farming that optimises input use, integrated pest management that reduces chemical dependence, crop rotation that maintains soil health, and agroforestry that combines trees with crops or livestock. These approaches improve resource efficiency while reducing environmental footprint.

Organic farming gains traction where market premiums justify certification costs and transition periods. Regenerative agriculture rebuilds soil carbon, enhances water retention, and strengthens biodiversity. These methods often require initial investment in knowledge, equipment, and market access before delivering financial returns, a pattern that influences how finance structures support adoption.

Value chains determine whether sustainable practices reach scale. When buyers, processors, retailers, food service companies, commit to sourcing sustainably produced commodities, they create stable demand that encourages farmer adoption. Certification systems verify practices, premium pricing rewards sustainability, and long-term contracts reduce market uncertainty.

Finance flows through value chains via multiple mechanisms. Input suppliers offer credit for seeds and equipment. Processors provide advance payments against future harvests. Banks structure loans secured by off-take agreements. Development finance institutions support aggregator models that collect production from smallholders and connect them to premium markets.

A clear example demonstrates this integration: **Nestlé committed to sourcing 50% of its key ingredients through regenerative agriculture by 2030, backed by farmer support programmes and sustainability-linked financing arrangements**[59]. This corporate commitment creates pull-thro ugh effects, farmers gain market access, financial

[59] *Nestlé, Regenerative Agriculture: Scaling Up Nature-Positive Food, Nestlé S.A., 2023, https://www.nestle.com/sustainability/climate-change/regenerative-agriculture, accessed 20 December 2024.*

institutions develop specialised credit products, and technology providers scale sustainable farming solutions.

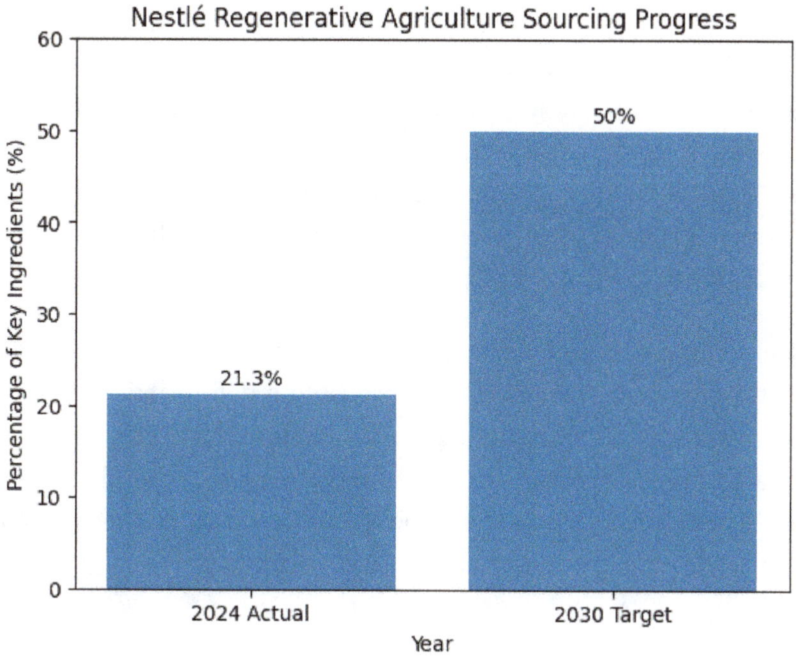

Traceability technologies strengthen value chains by providing transparent information from farm to consumer. Blockchain systems, satellite monitoring, and digital payment platforms reduce information asymmetry and build trust. This transparency improves credit access because lenders gain better visibility into production practices, volumes, and quality.

Cooperatives and farmer producer organisations play essential roles in sustainable value chains. They aggregate production to achieve scale, negotiate better prices, access technical assistance, and qualify for formal financing. These collective structures reduce transaction costs and strengthen farmer bargaining power, both critical for smallholder participation in sustainable agriculture.

3. Forestry, Restoration and Conservation Projects: Nature as Climatc Infrastructure

Forestry initiatives serve multiple functions, carbon sequestration, biodiversity conservation, watershed protection, and community livelihoods. Reforestation restores degraded lands, afforestation establishes forests in previously non-forested areas, and sustainable forest management maintains timber production while preserving ecosystem services. Each approach requires distinct financing models that match time horizons, risk profiles, and benefit streams.

Carbon markets create financial incentives for forest conservation. Projects generate carbon credits by preventing deforestation, improving forest management, or planting new forests. These credits trade on voluntary and compliance markets, providing revenue that supports project operations and community benefits. Verification standards ensure additionality and permanence, critical elements for carbon credit integrity.

Restoration projects extend beyond forests to include grasslands, mangroves, peatlands, and degraded agricultural lands. Mangrove restoration protects coastlines from storm surges while supporting fisheries and sequestering carbon. Grassland restoration maintains pastoralist livelihoods while improving soil carbon storage. These diverse ecosystems offer varied co-benefits that strengthen project attractiveness to impact investors.

Blended finance structures support restoration initiatives by combining grant funding, concessional loans, and commercial investment. Grants cover establishment costs and community engagement.

Concessional capital extends tenors to match long forest growth cycles. Commercial investment participates once revenue streams from timber, non-timber products, or carbon credits achieve predictability.

The UN Decade on Ecosystem Restoration highlights ambition: **global restoration efforts aim to restore 350 million hectares of degraded land by 2030, creating ecosystem benefits valued at over USD 9 trillion**[60]. This scale demonstrates how restoration moves from conservation projects to mainstream economic strategy with substantial capital requirements and measurable returns.

Protected area financing represents another model. Conservation finance combines tourism revenue, payments for ecosystem services, biodiversity credits, and philanthropic capital.

These mechanisms ensure protected areas maintain ecological integrity while supporting surrounding communities through employment and sustainable resource use.

Financial evaluation of forestry and restoration projects considers multiple factors, land tenure clarity, community participation, biodiversity baselines, carbon accounting methodologies, and market access for sustainable products.

Strong projects demonstrate clear governance, transparent benefit-sharing, and monitoring systems that track ecological and social outcomes.

4. Rural Credit, Insurance and Resilience Finance: Supporting Farmer Adaptation

Rural credit systems determine whether smallholders can invest in sustainable practices, adopt climate-resilient technologies, or recover from production shocks. Traditional banking often views smallholder agriculture as high-risk due to income variability, limited collateral, and

---

[60] *UN Environment Programme (UNEP), UN Decade on Ecosystem Restoration 2021-2030, UNEP, https://www.decadeonrestoration.org/, accessed 20 December 2024.*

exposure to climate events. Specialised rural finance institutions address these barriers through tailored products and risk-mitigation mechanisms.

Microfinance institutions provide small loans for inputs, equipment, and working capital. They use group lending models, alternative collateral arrangements, and mobile banking to reach remote farmers. Success depends on understanding agricultural cycles, building relationships in farming communities, and structuring repayment schedules around harvest timing.

Agricultural insurance protects farmers against weather risks, pest outbreaks, and price volatility. Index-based insurance pays out when weather parameters, rainfall, temperature, wind speed, cross predetermined thresholds, eliminating lengthy claims assessments. This automation reduces costs and accelerates payments, making insurance viable for smallholders.

Resilience finance goes beyond credit and insurance to include savings products, weather derivatives, and social protection linkages. It recognises that climate adaptation requires diverse financial tools that work together, credit for investments, insurance for shocks, savings for smoothing income, and social programmes for extreme events.

The Global Index Insurance Facility reports that **index insurance reached over 60 million farmers globally by 2023, protecting more than USD 18 billion in agricultural assets**[61]. This growth reflects how innovative products expand financial inclusion while supporting climate resilience in vulnerable farming communities.

Digital platforms transform rural finance delivery. Mobile money enables instant payments and reduces transaction costs. Remote sensing

[61] *World Bank, Global Index Insurance Facility (GIIF) Annual Report, World Bank Group, 2023, https://www.worldbank.org/en/topic/financialsector/brief/global-index-insurance-facility, accessed 20 December 2024.*

provides crop monitoring data that improvcs risk assessment. Digital credit scoring uses alternative data, mobile usage, input purchases, weather patterns, to evaluate creditworthiness without traditional collateral.

Development finance institutions catalyse rural finance markets by providing wholesale funding to local banks, offering credit guarantees that share risk, and supporting capacity building for financial institutions entering agricultural lending. These interventions create enabling conditions for commercial capital to follow.

5. Nature-Based Solutions in Green Finance Structures: Mainstreaming Natural Capital

Nature-based solutions generate multiple benefits, climate mitigation, adaptation strengthening, biodiversity conservation, water regulation, and community wellbeing. This multi-benefit character makes them attractive to blended finance structures that combine climate funds, biodiversity finance, adaptation capital, and community development resources.

Payment for ecosystem services creates direct financial flows from beneficiaries to land stewards. Downstream water users pay upstream communities for watershed protection. Carbon credits reward forest conservation. Biodiversity credits compensate landowners for habitat preservation. These mechanisms align economic incentives with ecological outcomes.

Green bonds increasingly include nature-based projects within their use-of-proceeds frameworks. Reforestation, wetland restoration, sustainable agriculture, and coastal ecosystem protection qualify as eligible categories. This inclusion expands capital availability for nature-based solutions while allowing issuers to diversify environmental impact portfolios.

Blue bonds specifically target marine and coastal ecosystems. Seychelles issued the world's first sovereign blue bond to finance sustainable fisheries and marine protected area expansion. This innovation created a template that other island nations and coastal countries adapt to their contexts.

Natural capital accounting strengthens nature-based finance by quantifying ecosystem service values, carbon storage, water purification, pollination, flood protection.

When these values become measurable, they integrate into financial decision-making, corporate reporting, and national economic planning. Institutions increasingly use natural capital assessments to evaluate project impacts and dependencies.

A milestone demonstrates market evolution: **the Taskforce on Nature-related Financial Disclosures (TNFD) released its final recommendations in 2023, providing a framework for organisations to report nature-related risks and opportunities**[62]. This development parallels TCFD's influence on climate disclosure and signals growing recognition that nature considerations belong in mainstream financial reporting.

Conservation finance vehicles pool capital from multiple sources, impact investors, philanthropic foundations, development agencies, into funds that support ecosystem restoration at landscape scale.

These funds employ diverse instruments, grants, concessional debt, equity stakes in sustainable enterprises, results-based payments, to match different project needs and investor preferences.

---

[62] *Taskforce on Nature-related Financial Disclosures (TNFD), Recommendations of the Taskforce on Nature-related Financial Disclosures, TNFD, September 2023, https://tnfd.global/recommendations/, accessed 20 December 2024.*

6. Social Dimensions and Inclusion: Ensuring Equitable Transitions

Agricultural and land-use transitions carry profound social implications. Smallholder farmers comprise the majority of global agricultural producers but often lack access to capital, markets, and technology. Transition finance must actively include these populations rather than concentrating benefits among large commercial operations.

Land tenure security influences investment decisions. Farmers with clear property rights invest more in soil conservation, tree planting, and infrastructure because they capture long-term benefits. Tenure insecurity discourages sustainable land management and limits access to formal finance.

Programmes that strengthen tenure clarity enable broader participation in green agriculture initiatives.

Women play central roles in agriculture yet face systematic barriers to credit, land ownership, and decision-making. Gender-responsive finance products, flexible collateral requirements, group lending models, financial literacy programmes, improve access and strengthen household resilience.

Evidence shows women invest agricultural income in nutrition, education, and community wellbeing at higher rates than men.

Indigenous communities steward much of the world's remaining intact ecosystems. Their traditional knowledge guides sustainable resource management, yet they often lack formal recognition and financial support. Conservation finance increasingly partners with indigenous organisations, ensuring that carbon credit revenues, tourism income, and ecosystem service payments flow directly to communities.

Youth engagement determines long-term agricultural sustainability. Young people perceive farming as economically unattractive when lacking modern tools, market access, and adequate returns.

Programmes that support agripreneurship, digital agriculture, and value-addition activities make farming viable for new generations and drive innovation.

Labour considerations matter in agricultural transitions. Shifts toward mechanisation, precision agriculture, or new crop varieties affect employment patterns. Just transition approaches ensure training programmes, alternative livelihood options, and social protection mechanisms support affected workers during agricultural transformation.

7. Case Studies: Agricultural Innovation in the UAE, GCC, and Beyond

UAE: Jabal Ali Hydro-Agriculture Initiative

The Jabal Ali area in Dubai demonstrates how arid regions advance sustainable agriculture through innovation and investment.

Projects integrate advanced hydroponics, vertical farming technologies, and precision irrigation systems that dramatically reduce water use while maintaining productivity. These facilities use renewable energy to power climate-controlled environments, creating closed-loop systems that minimise resource inputs.

Dubai's government supports these initiatives through infrastructure investment, research partnerships, and preferential procurement programmes that favour locally grown produce. Financial institutions provide specialised credit facilities recognising the unique capital intensity and operational characteristics of controlled-environment agriculture.

Source: https://www.nationalgeographic.com/environment/article/desalination-plants-produce-twice-as-much-waste-brine-as-thought/

The success at Jabal Ali positions the UAE as a regional hub for agricultural technology innovation, demonstrating how water-scarce regions can achieve food security goals through strategic investment in sustainable production systems[63].

GCC: Saudi Arabia's National Center for Palms and Dates Development

Saudi Arabia's date palm sector represents a successful integration of tradition, sustainability, and commercial viability. The National Center supports farmers through improved varieties, pest management technologies, and quality certification programmes. Date production uses minimal water compared to alternative crops while generating substantial export value.

---

[63] *Dubai Municipality, Sustainable Agriculture in Dubai, Government of Dubai, 2023, https://www.dm.gov.ae/environment-and-sustainability/sustainable-agriculture/, accessed 20 December 2024.*

The government facilitates access to finance through specialised agricultural lending programmes that recognise date palms' long production cycles and high establishment costs. Sustainability practices include organic certification, integrated pest management, and water-efficient irrigation.

Export markets in Europe, Asia, and North America pay premiums for quality dates, creating economic incentives that align with resource conservation. This model shows how traditional agricultural systems can modernise while maintaining sustainability and cultural significance[64].

Global: The Livelihoods Carbon Funds

The Livelihoods Funds represent innovative blended finance vehicles supporting smallholder agriculture and ecosystem restoration globally.

---

[64] *Ministry of Environment, Water and Agriculture, National Center for Palms and Dates, Kingdom of Saudi Arabia, https://www.mewa.gov.sa/en/Pages/default.aspx, accessed 20 December 2024*

Danone, Mars, and other companies invest in projects that improve farmer livelihoods while generating carbon credits and securing sustainable supply chains. Projects include agroforestry in Kenya, mangrove restoration in Indonesia, and regenerative agriculture in India.

These funds demonstrate how corporations integrate carbon offsetting, supply chain resilience, and community development into unified strategies. Financial structures combine company capital with development finance, creating patient funding that matches long project timelines. Rigorous monitoring tracks both carbon sequestration and social outcomes, income improvements, food security, and ecosystem health.

This approach creates replicable models for nature-positive finance that deliver measurable benefits across environmental and social dimensions[65].

---

[65] *Livelihoods Funds, Combining Business with Carbon Sequestration and Community Development, https://livelihoods.eu/, accessed 20 December 2024.*

Key Takeaways

- Agriculture and land systems contribute approximately 24% of global emissions while supporting billions of livelihoods, positioning them centrally in climate finance.
- Climate and nature risks create systemic vulnerabilities that financial institutions assess through water availability, soil health, biodiversity indicators, and adaptive capacity.
- Sustainable agriculture practices integrate into value chains through certification systems, premium pricing, and long-term sourcing commitments from buyers.
- Forestry, restoration, and conservation projects function as climate infrastructure generating carbon sequestration, biodiversity protection, and community benefits.
- Rural credit, insurance, and resilience finance products enable smallholder farmers to adopt climate-resilient practices and recover from production shocks.
- Nature-based solutions gain prominence in green finance structures through carbon markets, payment for ecosystem services, and natural capital accounting.
- Social dimensions require explicit attention to land tenure, gender inclusion, indigenous rights, youth engagement, and just transition considerations.
- Case studies from the UAE, GCC, and global contexts demonstrate diverse approaches, controlled-environment agriculture, traditional crop modernisation, and blended finance vehicles, all advancing sustainable land use.
- Successful agricultural transition finance combines patient capital, technical assistance, community engagement, and market linkages into comprehensive support systems.

- Nature-aligned investments require rigorous measurement of both environmental outcomes and social benefits to ensure credibility and long-term effectiveness.

14

Digital, Health and Social Infrastructure in a Green Transition

The transition toward sustainability extends far beyond energy systems and industrial processes, it reshapes the fundamental infrastructure that societies depend upon for health, education, connectivity, and wellbeing.

Digital technologies, healthcare facilities, educational institutions, and social support systems all play essential roles in building climate-resilient communities while advancing environmental goals. These sectors represent the human dimension of green finance, where capital flows strengthen both planetary health and human prosperity.

Digital systems have emerged as powerful enablers of sustainable development. They provide the data architecture, monitoring capabilities, and verification frameworks that give green finance its credibility and precision.

Advanced analytics, satellite imagery, blockchain verification, and artificial intelligence transform how institutions measure impact, track progress, and ensure accountability across environmental commitments. This digital backbone makes sustainability claims measurable, comparable, and trustworthy.

Healthcare and education infrastructure faces mounting pressures from climate change, rising temperatures affect public health outcomes, extreme weather events damage facilities, and shifting disease patterns require adaptive responses. Yet these same systems, when designed with sustainability principles, become catalysts for broader transformation. Green hospitals reduce emissions while improving patient outcomes.

Climate-smart schools educate the next generation while demonstrating sustainable practices. These examples show how social infrastructure and environmental progress reinforce each other.

The convergence of digital innovation, health resilience, and educational advancement creates opportunities for finance to support inclusive transitions. **The World Economic Forum estimates that digital technologies could enable a 20% reduction in global carbon emissions by 2050 through optimization, efficiency gains, and system-level transformation[66]**. This potential positions digital infrastructure as essential climate infrastructure, worthy of the same strategic attention and capital allocation as renewable energy or sustainable transport.

This chapter explores how digital systems, health facilities, educational institutions, and social programs integrate sustainability into their core operations. It examines data-driven impact verification, climate-resilient health systems, inclusive transition planning, and examples where environmental and social objectives align seamlessly. The focus remains

---

[66] *World Economic Forum, Harnessing Artificial Intelligence for the Earth, World Economic Forum, 2022, https://www.weforum.org/accessed 20 December 2024.*

on practical pathways that demonstrate how finance supports human wellbeing and planetary health simultaneously.

OBJECTIVES OF THE CHAPTER

This chapter will help individuals:

- Understand how digital systems enable transparency, efficiency, and accountability in green finance.
- Study data architecture, monitoring frameworks, and verification mechanisms that strengthen sustainability claims.
- Explore how health and education infrastructure adapts to climate realities while supporting environmental goals.
- Learn how inclusive transition planning ensures benefits reach vulnerable populations and marginalized communities.
- Examine examples where social and environmental objectives reinforce each other through integrated design.
- Recognize the role of technology in scaling sustainable solutions across health, education, and social sectors.
- Build confidence in evaluating digital-enabled sustainability projects and social infrastructure investments.
- Appreciate how green finance supports human development alongside environmental protection.
- Understand why social infrastructure represents a critical frontier for climate-aligned investment.
- Identify opportunities where digital innovation accelerates both social equity and environmental progress.

Digital Systems That Support Green Finance: Building the Data Foundation

Digital technologies have fundamentally transformed how green finance operates, bringing unprecedented transparency, efficiency, and scalability to sustainability efforts. These systems create the infrastructure through which environmental claims become verifiable, impact becomes measurable, and progress becomes trackable across time and geography. Without this digital backbone, modern sustainable finance would struggle to achieve the scale and credibility it has developed in recent years.

Blockchain technology offers immutable record-keeping that strengthens trust in environmental markets. Carbon credit registries built on blockchain ensure that credits cannot be double-counted or fraudulently issued. Supply-chain traceability platforms verify sustainable sourcing claims from farm to consumer.

Smart contracts automate payments when pre-defined sustainability targets are met, reducing administrative burden while ensuring compliance. These applications demonstrate how distributed ledger technology addresses longstanding challenges around transparency and verification.

Satellite monitoring and remote sensing provide real-time visibility into environmental changes that would be impossible to track through ground-based observation alone. Deforestation monitoring systems alert authorities to illegal logging within hours. Crop health assessments guide precision agriculture interventions.

Methane leak detection identifies emissions sources across energy infrastructure. Solar and wind resource mapping optimizes renewable energy project siting. These capabilities transform environmental management from periodic assessments to continuous monitoring.

Artificial intelligence and machine learning enhance decision-making across sustainable finance. Credit scoring models incorporate environmental performance data to predict long-term viability. Portfolio optimization algorithms balance financial returns with impact objectives. Predictive analytics forecast climate risks at asset level.

Natural language processing analyzes corporate disclosures for greenwashing signals. These applications show how AI transforms vast data streams into actionable insights that strengthen both financial and environmental outcomes.

The Global IoT market for environmental monitoring is projected to reach USD 23.4 billion by 2028, reflecting how rapidly digital sensing technologies are being deployed across sustainability applications[67]. This growth indicates strong market recognition that digital infrastructure serves as essential architecture for effective environmental management and credible green finance.

Digital platforms democratize access to green finance by reducing transaction costs and information barriers. Mobile banking enables smallholder farmers to access climate-smart agricultural loans.

Peer-to-peer renewable energy trading platforms allow households to monetize rooftop solar generation. Crowdfunding portals connect impact investors with local sustainability projects. Digital carbon marketplaces streamline credit trading. These platforms expand participation beyond traditional institutional channels, creating more inclusive sustainable finance ecosystems.

Cloud computing and edge computing infrastructure support the processing power required for sophisticated environmental modeling.

---

[67] *Fortune Business Insights, IoT in Environmental Monitoring Market Size, Share & Industry Analysis, Fortune Business Insights, 2023, https://www.fortunebusinessinsights.com/environmental-monitoring-market-111995?, accessed 20 December 2024.*

Climate scenario analysis, resource optimization, and real-time operational adjustments all depend on computational capabilities that cloud platforms provide.

Edge computing enables processing at the data source, on wind turbines, in smart buildings, or across transportation networks, improving response times and reducing bandwidth requirements.

This distributed computing architecture makes intelligent sustainability solutions viable at scale.

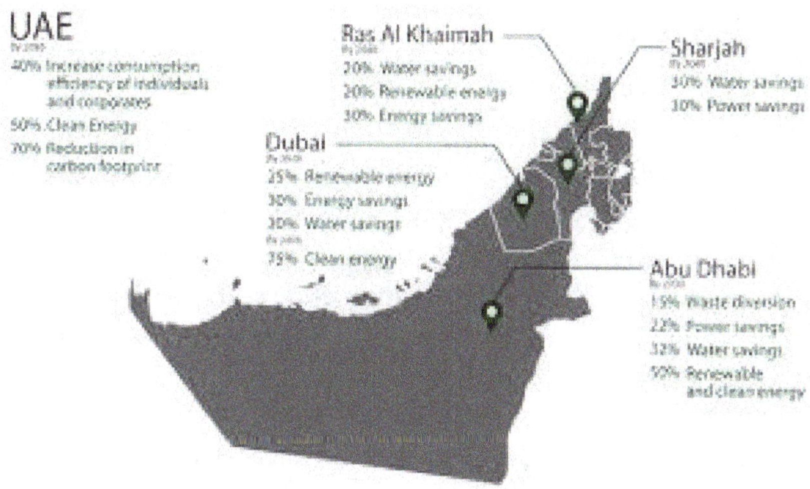

Source: EmiratesGBC [8]

The UAE has emerged as a regional leader in deploying digital infrastructure for sustainability purposes. Smart city initiatives in Dubai and Abu Dhabi integrate IoT sensors, AI-powered management systems, and real-time analytics to optimize energy use, water consumption, and waste management across urban systems. These implementations demonstrate how digital technologies enable resource efficiency at city scale while improving quality of life for residents.

Data, Monitoring and Verification of Impact: Ensuring Credibility Through Measurement

Credible green finance depends fundamentally on accurate measurement, consistent monitoring, and independent verification of environmental and social impacts. The evolution from aspirational sustainability claims to data-driven accountability represents one of the most significant developments in modern finance.

Stakeholders increasingly demand evidence that capital deployed toward environmental goals delivers measurable outcomes rather than merely supporting activities with environmental labels.

Impact measurement frameworks provide structured approaches for quantifying outcomes across diverse project types. The Impact Management Project's five dimensions, what, who, how much, contribution, and risk, guide comprehensive impact assessment. Global Reporting Initiative standards enable consistent disclosure. The IRIS+ system from GIIN offers standardized metrics across sectors. These frameworks create comparability that allows investors to evaluate projects using common reference points rather than idiosyncratic methodologies.

Environmental monitoring systems track physical changes resulting from green investments. Air quality sensors measure pollution reduction near clean transportation corridors. Water quality probes assess improvement from wastewater treatment upgrades.

Soil carbon monitoring verifies sequestration from regenerative agriculture. Energy meters track consumption reductions from efficiency retrofits. These direct measurements provide objective evidence of environmental performance that complements financial metrics.

Verification processes ensure independence and credibility in impact reporting. Third-party assessors examine project methodologies, validate data collection processes, and confirm alignment with standards.

Remote sensing technologies complement ground-truth verification, providing independent data sources that reduce reliance on self-reporting. Continuous monitoring replaces periodic assessment, enabling real-time transparency that strengthens accountability.

The market for ESG data and analytics reached approximately USD 1.4 billion in 2023, with double-digit annual growth driven by regulatory requirements and investor demand for verified sustainability information[68]. This expansion reflects how seriously financial markets now treat impact measurement as essential infrastructure rather than optional reporting.

Digital twins, virtual replicas of physical assets, enable sophisticated performance analysis and optimization. A digital twin of a building models energy flows, predicts maintenance needs, and tests efficiency improvements virtually before physical implementation. Wind farm digital twins optimize turbine positioning and predict component failures. Industrial facility twins identify process inefficiencies and test decarbonization scenarios.

These virtual models improve both performance and verification accuracy. Materiality assessments identify which environmental and social factors most significantly affect long-term value creation in specific contexts. Financial materiality considers how sustainability factors influence enterprise value. Impact materiality evaluates how business activities affect society and environment.

---

[68] *Opimas, ESG Data Market Sizing Report 2023, Opimas LLC, 2023,* *https://www.grandviewresearch.com/industry-analysis/esg-investing-market-report/*, *accessed 20 December 2024.*

Double materiality frameworks examine both dimensions, recognizing that material issues flow in both directions. This analytical discipline focuses measurement efforts on factors that matter most rather than creating exhaustive but unfocused reporting.

The table below illustrates how different digital technologies support impact verification across key dimensions:

Technology	Verification Application	Key Advantage	Example Use Case
Blockchain	Carbon credit tracking, supply chain transparency	Immutability, transparency	Renewable energy certificate trading
Satellite Imagery	Deforestation monitoring, land use verification	Wide coverage, independence	Forest conservation project verification
IoT Sensors	Real-time emissions tracking, resource consumption	Continuous measurement, automation	Smart building energy performance
AI Analytics	Pattern detection, anomaly identification	Scale, sophistication	Greenwashing detection in corporate disclosures

Digital Twins	Performance modeling, scenario testing	Precision, predictive capability	Industrial facility decarbonization planning

This technological toolkit transforms impact verification from periodic audits to continuous, multi-source validation that strengthens confidence across all stakeholders.

Health and Education Infrastructure in a Changing Climate: Building Adaptive Capacity

Healthcare systems face mounting pressures from climate change that reshape disease patterns, strain emergency response capabilities, and challenge infrastructure resilience.

Rising temperatures expand the geographic range of vector-borne diseases like malaria and dengue. Extreme heat events increase cardiovascular and respiratory illnesses.

Air pollution from wildfires and industrial sources exacerbates asthma and chronic conditions. These health impacts create economic costs alongside human suffering, influencing labor productivity, healthcare expenditure, and community wellbeing.

Green hospital initiatives demonstrate how healthcare facilities can advance environmental goals while improving patient outcomes. Energy-efficient HVAC systems maintain therapeutic environments while reducing operational costs.

Renewable energy installation ensures power reliability during grid disruptions. Water recycling systems conserve resources in water-stressed regions.

Waste segregation and treatment reduce environmental contamination while meeting infection control standards.

These operational improvements typically generate financial savings that justify initial investments while advancing sustainability.

The global green healthcare market is growing rapidly as institutions recognize alignment between environmental performance and health mission.

LED lighting improves visibility while cutting electricity use. Non-toxic cleaning products protect

patient and staff health. Sustainable food procurement reduces supply chain emissions while improving nutrition.

Telehealth platforms reduce patient travel emissions while expanding access. These examples show how environmental considerations integrate throughout healthcare operations rather than representing isolated initiatives.

Green hospitals can reduce energy consumption by 30-50% compared to conventional facilities while achieving better patient outcomes through improved air quality, natural lighting, and healing environments[69].

This dual benefit, environmental performance and improved care quality, makes green healthcare infrastructure increasingly attractive to investors seeking impact alongside financial returns.

---

[69] *Practice Greenhealth, Sustainability Benchmark Report 2023, Practice Greenhealth,* https://igbc.in/frontend-assets/html_pdfs/Green%20Hospitals.pdf *accessed 20 December 2024.*

Source: *https://www.engineeringnews.co.za/article/potsdam-wastewater-works-upgrade-breaks-ground-2023-08-02*

Educational infrastructure plays a pivotal role in building climate-resilient communities through both facility design and curriculum integration. Green schools demonstrate sustainable practices while educating students who will shape future decisions. Solar panels provide hands-on learning about renewable energy.

Rainwater harvesting teaches water conservation. School gardens connect students with food systems. These experiential learning opportunities create environmental awareness that extends into homes and communities.

Climate-resilient school design protects students and maintains educational continuity during extreme weather. Heat-resistant building materials and passive cooling strategies ensure comfortable learning environments without excessive energy use. Flood-resistant construction and elevated infrastructure protect against water damage. Backup power systems maintain operations during grid disruptions. Storm shelters provide community refuge during emergencies. These design features recognize that schools serve as critical community infrastructure beyond their primary educational function.

These facilities achieve high environmental performance while serving as community demonstration projects that influence broader adoption of sustainable practices. Teacher training programs ensure sustainability concepts integrate throughout curricula rather than remaining isolated topics.

Digital education platforms expanded dramatically during recent global disruptions, demonstrating how technology can maintain learning continuity while reducing infrastructure requirements and travel-related emissions. Hybrid models that blend in-person and remote learning offer flexibility while optimizing resource use.

Open educational resources reduce material consumption. Virtual laboratories enable scientific education without chemical waste. These innovations show how education systems can advance both learning outcomes and environmental goals through thoughtful technology integration.

Inclusive and Just Transition Considerations: Ensuring Equitable Progress

Climate transition carries profound social implications that require explicit attention to ensure benefits reach all communities rather than concentrating among those already advantaged. Inclusive transition planning recognizes that environmental progress must advance alongside social equity, otherwise, sustainability efforts risk widening existing inequalities rather than bridging them.

Energy access represents a fundamental justice consideration. While advanced economies focus on decarbonization, billions of people still lack reliable electricity or clean cooking fuels. Green finance must support both transition toward clean energy in developed contexts and expansion of clean energy access in developing contexts. Off-grid renewable systems provide electricity to remote communities. Clean cookstoves reduce indoor air pollution and deforestation. Mini-grids enable economic development in previously unserved areas. These interventions demonstrate how green finance can advance energy access and climate goals simultaneously.

Employment transitions require careful management as economies shift toward sustainable sectors. Workers in fossil fuel industries, carbon-intensive manufacturing, and other transitioning sectors need retraining programs, income support, and alternative employment pathways. Just transition frameworks ensure affected workers participate in designing transition plans rather than having changes imposed upon them. Skills development programs prepare workers for roles in renewable energy, circular economy, and green infrastructure sectors. These social investments create political support for climate action while ensuring fair treatment of affected communities.

Gender considerations influence how effectively green finance reaches intended beneficiaries. Women often manage household water and energy resources yet face barriers accessing credit, technology, and decision-making processes. Gender-responsive finance products, flexible collateral requirements, group lending models, targeted training, improve access and strengthen outcomes. Evidence consistently shows women invest income in nutrition, education, and community wellbeing at higher rates than men, amplifying social benefits from green finance interventions.

The International Labour Organization estimates that climate action could create 24 million new jobs globally by 2030, while requiring transitions for approximately 6 million workers in fossil fuel and carbon-intensive sectors[70]. This net positive employment impact depends on proactive transition planning that ensures workers and communities share benefits rather than bearing disproportionate costs.

---

[70] *International Labour Organization, World Employment and Social Outlook 2018: Greening with Jobs, ILO, 2018, https://webapps.ilo.org/weso-greening/? , accessed 20 December 2024.*

Youth engagement shapes long-term sustainability trajectories. Young people will experience the most severe climate impacts yet often lack voice in decisions that determine their futures.

Youth-focused green finance products support entrepreneurship in sustainable sectors. Educational programs build technical skills for green economy participation. Internship and mentorship initiatives create career pathways.

These investments recognize that engaging youth determines whether sustainability transitions achieve durable momentum.

Indigenous communities steward significant portions of remaining intact ecosystems and possess invaluable traditional knowledge about sustainable resource management.

Yet they frequently face marginalization in both conservation and development decisions. Rights-based approaches ensure indigenous peoples maintain control over ancestral lands and receive direct benefits from conservation finance.

Free, prior, and informed consent processes respect indigenous sovereignty. Benefit-sharing agreements channel carbon credit revenues, tourism income, and ecosystem service payments to indigenous organizations. These mechanisms recognize that conservation succeeds when respecting human rights and supporting community wellbeing.

Geographic equity matters as climate impacts and transition opportunities distribute unevenly. Small island states face existential threats from sea-level rise despite minimal historical emissions.

Sub-Saharan African nations experience severe climate impacts while holding negligible carbon debt.

Climate finance architecture must channel resources toward vulnerable regions rather than merely rewarding

profitable opportunities in already-developed contexts. Adaptation finance, loss and damage mechanisms, and capacity building support represent essential elements of global climate justice.

The GCC region demonstrates thoughtful attention to inclusive transition through strategic investments in workforce development, educational transformation, and social infrastructure that ensures citizens participate fully in emerging green economy opportunities. National strategies emphasize skill development, technology transfer, and entrepreneurship support that broaden economic participation while advancing sustainability goals.

Examples Where Social and Environmental Goals Align: Integrated Success Stories

The most powerful green finance initiatives demonstrate clear alignment between social and environmental objectives, creating mutual reinforcement rather than tradeoffs. These examples illustrate how thoughtful design produces solutions that serve multiple goals simultaneously, building political support and stakeholder engagement that accelerates implementation.

UAE: Mohammed bin Rashid Al Maktoum Solar Park Community Programme

The Mohammed bin Rashid Al Maktoum Solar Park represents more than clean energy generation, it embodies comprehensive community development aligned with environmental goals. The project includes educational visitor centers that teach renewable energy principles to students and tourists.

Source: https://www.worldatlas.com/

Training programs prepare Emirati citizens for careers in solar technology, operations, and maintenance. Local procurement requirements stimulate domestic green technology sectors. Community engagement initiatives ensure neighboring populations benefit directly from the park's presence through employment, educational opportunities, and infrastructure improvements.

The solar park's digital innovation hub develops and tests emerging clean energy technologies, creating an ecosystem that attracts research institutions, technology companies, and skilled professionals. This clustering effect builds long-term capabilities that extend far beyond the immediate project, positioning Dubai as a regional hub for clean energy innovation. The integrated approach demonstrates how large infrastructure projects can catalyze broader social and economic transformation when designed with community development as an explicit objective[71].

[71] *Dubai Electricity and Water Authority (DEWA), Mohammed bin Rashid Al Maktoum Solar Park, DEWA,*

GCC: Saudi Arabia's Green Riyadh Initiative

Green Riyadh aims to plant 7.5 million trees across the capital city, creating one of the largest urban forestry programs globally. Beyond carbon sequestration and air quality improvement, the initiative addresses social wellbeing through expanded green spaces, pedestrian pathways, and recreational facilities. Urban heat island reduction improves outdoor comfort and reduces cooling energy demand. Biodiversity corridors support native species while creating educational opportunities for environmental awareness.

The program integrates water sustainability through greywater recycling systems and drought-resistant species selection. Smart irrigation technologies optimize water use through sensors and AI-powered management. These features demonstrate how urban greening projects can advance multiple environmental objectives, carbon storage, biodiversity, water conservation, while simultaneously improving quality of life, public health, and community cohesion.

Employment generation represents another key dimension, with thousands of jobs created in nursery operations, planting activities, irrigation system installation, and ongoing maintenance. Skills development programs prepare Saudi citizens for green jobs while building domestic capabilities in urban forestry management.

This integrated approach shows how environmental megaprojects can drive inclusive economic development when designed with deliberate attention to social outcomes[72].

---

https://en.wikipedia.org/wiki/Mohammed_bin_Rashid_Al_Maktoum_Solar_Park? , accessed 20 December 2024.

[72] *Royal Commission for Riyadh City, Green Riyadh Project, Government of Saudi Arabia, https://www.rcrc.gov.sa/en/projects/green-riyadh, accessed 20 December 2024.*

Global: Remote Healthcare Through Clean Energy

Organizations like SELCO Foundation demonstrate how renewable energy enables essential health services in remote regions while advancing environmental goals.

Solar-powered health clinics maintain vaccine cold chains, enable night operations, and power medical equipment in communities lacking grid electricity.

Clean energy ensures reliable operations while eliminating diesel generator emissions and fuel costs.

These interventions produce cascading benefits, improved health outcomes, reduced healthcare costs, employment for local solar technicians, and demonstration effects that accelerate broader renewable adoption.

Mobile health clinics powered by solar arrays expand service reach while minimizing environmental footprint.

Telemedicine connections enable specialist consultations in remote facilities. These examples show how access to clean energy removes barriers to essential services while avoiding fossil fuel dependencies.

The model has been replicated across South Asia, Sub-Saharan Africa, and remote Pacific islands, demonstrating scalability and adaptability to diverse contexts.

Blended finance structures, combining philanthropic grants, concessional debt, and revenue from health service payments, create sustainable operations that neither depend on indefinite subsidy nor compromise service quality.

This financial innovation enables social and environmental impact at scale.

The table below summarizes key dimensions of alignment in integrated projects:

Project Type	Environmental Benefit	Social Benefit	Financial Mechanism	Region
Green Schools	Energy efficiency, renewable generation, environmental education	Improved learning environments, skill development, community engagement	Municipal bonds, green loans, public budget	UAE, Saudi Arabia, Global
Community Solar	Clean energy, emissions reduction	Local ownership, energy cost savings, employment	Community investment, green bonds, grants	USA, India, Kenya
Sustainable Healthcare	Operational efficiency, waste reduction	Improved patient outcomes, service reliability	Green healthcare bonds, impact investment	UAE, UK, Rwanda
Urban Forestry	Carbon sequestration, air quality, biodiversity	Public health, recreation,	Sovereign green bonds,	Saudi Arabia, Singapore

		heat mitigation	municipal finance	
Clean Cooking Programs	Deforestation prevention, emissions reduction	Health improvement, time savings, indoor air quality	Microfinance, carbon credits, grants	Sub-Saharan Africa, South Asia

These examples collectively demonstrate that the most successful sustainability initiatives intentionally design for co-benefits rather than viewing social and environmental goals as competing priorities requiring compromise.

Key Takeaways

- Digital technologies enable transparency, efficiency, and verification that strengthen credibility across green finance operations and environmental claims.
- Data architecture, monitoring systems, and impact measurement frameworks transform sustainability from aspiration to accountable, measurable progress.
- Healthcare infrastructure adapts to climate realities while reducing emissions through green building standards, renewable energy, and resource efficiency.
- Educational facilities demonstrate sustainable practices while preparing students for green economy participation through integrated curriculum and experiential learning.
- Inclusive transition planning ensures vulnerable populations, workers in transitioning industries, women, youth, and indigenous communities participate in and benefit from sustainability transformation.
- Digital platforms democratize access to green finance while sophisticated analytics improve decision-making and risk assessment across sustainability investments.
- Social and environmental objectives reinforce each other when projects deliberately design for multiple benefits rather than treating them as competing priorities.
- The UAE and GCC demonstrate leadership in integrating community development, education, and environmental stewardship within large-scale sustainability initiatives.
- Employment creation, skill development, and equitable benefit distribution determine whether climate action achieves lasting political support and social legitimacy.

- Green finance for social infrastructure, health, education, digital connectivity, represents a critical frontier where capital flows strengthen both human wellbeing and planetary resilience.

15

Banks, Investors and Financial Intermediaries

Financial intermediaries stand at the centre of sustainable finance transformation. Banks, asset managers, pension funds, insurance companies, and development finance institutions shape capital flows through lending decisions, investment strategies, product innovation, and risk assessment frameworks. Their internal systems, governance structures, incentive mechanisms, capacity-building programmes, and collaboration models, determine how quickly and effectively sustainability considerations integrate into mainstream financial operations.

This transformation extends beyond adding green products to existing portfolios. It requires fundamental shifts in how institutions evaluate risk, measure performance, engage with clients, and align business models with long-term environmental priorities. Banks redesign credit policies to incorporate climate considerations. Investors refine due diligence processes to assess transition readiness. Insurance companies recalibrate underwriting models to reflect physical and transition risks.

The scale of institutional influence becomes clear through market indicators. The Global Sustainable Investment Alliance reports that **sustainable investment assets under management reached USD 30.3 trillion globally in 2022, representing significant integration of environmental, social, and governance factors into investment decision-making**[73]. This figure demonstrates how deeply sustainability considerations have permeated institutional finance across equity, fixed income, and alternative asset classes.

Yet implementation carries practical complexities. Data availability varies across markets. Measurement methodologies evolve continuously. Regulatory expectations differ by jurisdiction. Talent pools with combined financial and sustainability expertise remain limited. These constraints shape how institutions build capacity, develop products, and coordinate across the financial ecosystem.

This chapter explores how financial intermediaries navigate this transformation. It examines internal strategy development, product innovation processes, governance evolution, cross-institutional collaboration, and practical responses to implementation challenges. Together, these elements reveal how the financial system itself transforms to support sustainable economic development.

OBJECTIVES OF THE CHAPTER

This chapter will help individuals:

- Understand how financial institutions develop internal strategies that embed sustainability across operations.

---

[73] *Global Sustainable Investment Alliance (GSIA), Global Sustainable Investment Review 2022, GSIA, 2023, https://www.gsi-alliance.org/members-resources/gsir2022/? , accessed 22 December 2024.*

- Study product development processes and pipeline-building approaches that create sustainable finance offerings.
- Examine governance structures, incentive systems, and capacity-building programmes that support green finance integration.
- Explore collaboration models across banks, investors, and other financial intermediaries that strengthen market development.
- Recognise practical constraints institutions face and how they design responses that maintain momentum.
- Build insight into how internal transformation enables external market leadership in sustainable finance.
- Learn how institutions balance commercial objectives with sustainability commitments through structured frameworks.
- Observe regional approaches to green finance strategy across developed and emerging markets.
- Develop confidence in evaluating institutional sustainability strategies and their operational effectiveness.
- Appreciate why systemic financial transformation requires coordinated action across multiple institutions and markets.

1. Internal Strategies for Green Finance: Building Organisational Foundations

Financial institutions approach green finance strategy through multiple layers, board-level commitment, executive sponsorship, cross-functional integration, and operational implementation. Strong strategies begin with clear articulation of sustainability ambition aligned with institutional mission, market position, and stakeholder expectations. This articulation guides subsequent decisions around portfolio composition, client engagement, and resource allocation.

Strategic frameworks typically establish quantitative targets, emissions reduction across portfolios, percentage of lending or assets under management aligned with sustainability themes, and growth trajectories for green products.

These targets create accountability and allow institutions to track progress systematically. Leading institutions increasingly align targets with science-based pathways, ensuring ambition matches climate imperatives rather than reflecting incremental improvements alone.

Portfolio analysis forms a critical early step. Institutions map existing exposures across sectors, geographies, and asset classes to understand current sustainability profiles. This analysis identifies concentration risks in carbon-intensive sectors, opportunities in transition-ready industries, and gaps where sustainable alternatives could expand. The mapping exercise also reveals where enhanced due diligence, client engagement, or strategic repositioning delivers the most impact.

Risk management integration represents another foundational element. Climate considerations enter credit risk models, investment risk frameworks, and insurance underwriting processes.

Institutions develop scenario analysis capabilities to understand how different climate and transition pathways affect portfolio performance. These scenarios inform capital allocation decisions, provisioning requirements, and long-term strategic planning.

A notable development demonstrates institutional commitment: **the Partnership for Carbon Accounting Financials (PCAF) grew to over 400 financial institutions globally by 2024, collectively representing more than USD 90 trillion in assets committed to measuring and disclosing financed emissions**[74]. This collaborative initiative shows how

---

[74] *Partnership for Carbon Accounting Financials (PCAF), Global GHG Accounting and Reporting Standard for the Financial Industry, PCAF, 2024, https://carbonaccountingfinancials.com/, accessed 22 December 2024.*

institutions recognise that credible sustainability strategies require transparent emissions accounting and standardised methodologies.

Internal strategies also address organizational culture. Institutions invest in employee education, leadership development, and cross-functional collaboration that breaks down silos between sustainability teams, risk departments, and business lines. When sustainability expertise distributes across the organization rather than concentrating in specialist units, implementation becomes more robust and integrated.

Target-setting exercises consider multiple dimensions, absolute emissions reductions, intensity improvements, renewable energy financing growth, green bond issuance volumes, and sustainable asset accumulation. This multi-dimensional approach recognises that transformation occurs through diverse pathways rather than single metrics alone.

2. Product Development and Pipeline Building: Creating Market Offerings

Product development translates institutional sustainability strategies into concrete market offerings. Banks design green loans, sustainability-linked credit facilities, transition finance structures, and blended finance vehicles. Asset managers launch thematic funds, impact investment vehicles, and ESG-integrated strategies. Insurance companies develop parametric products, resilience-focused coverage, and sustainability-linked underwriting.

Pipeline development determines whether product offerings achieve scale. Institutions identify client segments most receptive to sustainable finance, renewable energy developers, green building owners, sustainable agriculture operators, circular economy enterprises. They engage proactively with these clients to understand financing needs, technical requirements, and timeline expectations.

Structured pipeline approaches often begin with awareness-building, educating clients about sustainable finance options, eligibility criteria, and documentation requirements. This education phase reduces transaction friction and helps clients prepare stronger proposals. Some institutions establish dedicated advisory teams that work with clients through framework development, external review coordination, and ongoing reporting.

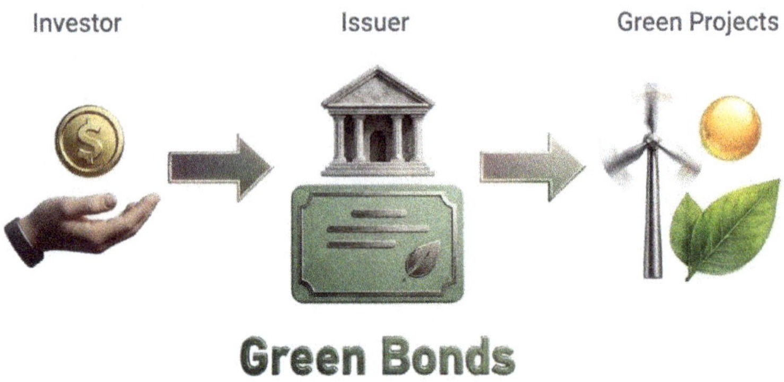

Product innovation responds to evolving market needs. Early green finance focused primarily on renewable energy project finance. Portfolios now encompass energy efficiency retrofits, electric mobility infrastructure, water systems, waste management, sustainable agriculture, and nature-based solutions. This diversification strengthens resilience and broadens market participation.

Standardisation supports scale. Institutions adopt common frameworks, Green Loan Principles, Sustainability-Linked Loan Principles, Green Bond Principles, that reduce customisation needs and accelerate transaction execution. Standardised documentation, eligibility criteria, and reporting templates allow institutions to process larger volumes while maintaining quality control.

The Loan Market Association reports that **sustainability-linked loan market volumes exceeded USD 1.5 trillion cumulatively by 2023, demonstrating rapid adoption of performance-based sustainable finance structures**[75]. This growth reflects how standardised products gain market acceptance when they offer clear value propositions, linking pricing to measurable sustainability improvements while maintaining operational flexibility.

Digital platforms increasingly support pipeline development. Online portals allow clients to check eligibility, upload documentation, track application status, and access educational resources. These platforms reduce administrative burden, improve transparency, and create data trails that support continuous improvement in product design.

Cross-selling opportunities emerge as institutions build sustainable finance capabilities. A bank providing green mortgages can offer solar financing, electric vehicle loans, and energy efficiency credit lines to the same customers. An asset manager launching green bond funds can develop complementary equity strategies and private debt vehicles that serve diverse investor preferences.

3. Governance, Incentives and Capacity Building: Enabling Institutional Transformation

Governance structures determine how sustainability considerations flow through institutional decision-making. Board committees oversee climate risk, sustainability strategy, and transition plan implementation. Executive leadership holds accountability for meeting targets and integrating sustainability across business lines. Management structures

---

[75] *Loan Market Association (LMA), Sustainability-Linked Loan Principles, LMA, 2023, https://www.lma.eu.com/sustainable-lending? , accessed 22 December 2024.*

ensure coordination between front-office teams, risk functions, and sustainability specialists.

Many institutions appoint Chief Sustainability Officers or similar roles with direct reporting lines to CEOs or boards. These positions signal organisational commitment and create focal points for strategy development, stakeholder engagement, and performance monitoring. Strong CSO mandates include authority to influence business decisions, access resources, and drive cultural change.

Incentive alignment translates sustainability commitments into individual accountability. Institutions incorporate ESG metrics into executive compensation, link bonuses to green finance portfolio growth, and recognise teams that innovate sustainable products. These mechanisms ensure sustainability considerations influence career advancement and resource allocation decisions.

Risk appetite statements increasingly embed sustainability limits. Institutions define maximum exposures to high-emission sectors, establish minimum thresholds for transition finance, and create exclusion lists for activities incompatible with climate goals. These statements guide lending officers, investment managers, and underwriters in daily decision-making.

Capacity building addresses knowledge gaps that constrain implementation. Training programmes educate relationship managers about sustainable finance products, teach credit officers climate risk assessment methodologies, and develop investment analysts' ESG integration skills. These programmes often combine classroom learning, case studies, and practical exercises that build confidence in applying new frameworks.

The UAE provides a strong regional example: **the Dubai International Financial Centre (DIFC) established the DIFC Academy's Sustainable Finance Programme, training financial professionals**

across the region on green finance principles, product structures, and regulatory frameworks[76]. This initiative demonstrates how financial centres support market development through systematic capacity building that strengthens institutional capabilities.

Source: https://www.arabianbusiness.com/

Knowledge management systems capture and share learning across organizations. Internal databases document transaction structures, store external reviews, archive client engagement best practices, and maintain research on sectoral transitions. These systems prevent knowledge loss when personnel change and accelerate onboarding for new team members.

Performance measurement systems track multiple dimensions, portfolio emissions intensity, green finance origination volumes, client engagement frequency, product innovation rate, and staff capability

[76] *Dubai International Financial Centre (DIFC), DIFC Academy Sustainable Finance Programme, DIFC Authority, 2023 https://academy.difc.ae/ /, accessed 22 December 2024.*

development. Regular reporting to senior leadership and boards ensures visibility and maintains strategic focus on sustainability integration.

4. Collaboration Across Institutions: Building Ecosystem Strength

Sustainable finance development requires coordination across banks, investors, insurers, multilateral institutions, and regulators. No single institution can build necessary infrastructure, set standards, or create market liquidity alone. Collaborative initiatives strengthen the ecosystem by pooling expertise, aligning methodologies, and creating common frameworks.

Industry associations facilitate this collaboration. The Net-Zero Banking Alliance brings together banks committed to aligning portfolios with net-zero pathways. The Glasgow Financial Alliance for Net Zero coordinates action across banking, insurance, asset management, and asset ownership. These platforms create peer accountability, share implementation experiences, and coordinate engagement with policymakers.

Working groups address specific technical challenges, financed emissions accounting, scenario analysis methodologies, sector transition pathways, and nature-related risk assessment. Participants contribute expertise, test approaches in their institutions, and refine frameworks through iterative feedback. This collaborative development ensures methodologies reflect practical realities rather than purely theoretical constructs.

Co-financing arrangements allow institutions to share large transaction risks while building expertise. A development bank might provide subordinated capital that enables commercial banks to participate in innovative green projects. Multiple investors syndicate green bonds or sustainability-linked loans, distributing exposure and increasing market liquidity.

Knowledge sharing accelerates market development. Banks publish case studies describing successful transactions, investors release research on sectoral transition strategies, and insurers share climate risk modeling approaches. This transparency reduces duplication, raises quality standards, and helps smaller institutions build capabilities more quickly.

The Network for Greening the Financial System exemplifies central bank collaboration: **NGFS membership expanded to over 135 central banks and supervisors by 2024, coordinating climate risk supervision and developing common scenario frameworks**[77]. This network demonstrates how regulatory coordination strengthens system-wide resilience and creates consistent expectations across jurisdictions.

Public-private partnerships bridge gaps between development objectives and commercial requirements.

Blended finance vehicles combine concessional funding from development institutions with commercial capital from banks and investors.

These structures enable sustainable infrastructure projects that might not proceed on purely commercial terms while building institutional comfort with new asset classes.

Regional collaboration responds to geographic priorities. Middle Eastern financial institutions coordinate around solar project finance and green hydrogen infrastructure.

Asian institutions focus on transition finance for manufacturing and coal phase-down. African institutions emphasise adaptation finance and

---

[77] *Network for Greening the Financial System (NGFS), NGFS Membership, NGFS, 2024, https://www.ngfs.net/en/about-us/membership, accessed 22 December 2024.*

nature-based solutions. This regional tailoring ensures collaboration addresses locally relevant challenges.

5. Practical Constraints and Institutional Responses: Navigating Implementation Realities

Data availability represents a persistent challenge. Many companies lack comprehensive emissions data, especially across Scope 3 value chains. SMEs often operate without formal sustainability reporting.

This data scarcity complicates portfolio emissions measurement, client engagement, and performance tracking. Institutions respond by investing in estimation methodologies, partnering with data providers, and supporting client capacity building that improves disclosure quality over time.

Methodological evolution creates uncertainty. Emissions accounting standards continue developing. Scenario analysis approaches vary across institutions. Transition pathway definitions differ by sector and geography.

These variations complicate peer comparisons and create implementation burden as methodologies update. Institutions respond by participating in standard-setting initiatives, adopting flexible systems that accommodate updates, and maintaining transparency about methodological choices.

Regulatory fragmentation affects cross-border operations. Taxonomies differ between jurisdictions. Disclosure requirements vary in scope and timing.

Prudential expectations around climate risk diverge across supervisors. Financial institutions with international operations must navigate multiple frameworks simultaneously, creating compliance complexity.

Responses include establishing regional teams with local expertise, advocating for international alignment, and building flexible systems that accommodate diverse requirements.

Talent constraints limit implementation speed. Professionals with combined finance and sustainability expertise remain scarce, particularly in emerging markets. Institutions compete for qualified personnel, driving compensation increases and creating retention challenges.

Responses include internal training programmes, partnerships with universities, secondment arrangements with sustainability organisations, and gradual capability building that develops existing staff rather than relying solely on external hiring.

Client readiness varies significantly. Large corporations often have dedicated sustainability teams and robust data systems.

SMEs typically lack resources for comprehensive sustainability management. This variation requires differentiated approaches, sophisticated frameworks for advanced clients, simplified tools for smaller enterprises, and educational support that builds capacity across client bases.

Short-term performance pressures sometimes conflict with long-term sustainability objectives.

Quarterly earnings expectations, annual bonus cycles, and market sentiment create incentives favouring immediate returns over patient capital deployment.

Institutions address this tension through governance structures that empower long-term perspectives, stakeholder engagement that builds understanding of sustainability value creation, and performance metrics that balance multiple time horizons.

Constraint Category	Specific Challenge	Institutional Response	Collaborative Solution
Data Availability	Scope 3 emissions gaps, SME disclosure	Estimation methodologies, client support	Industry data platforms, standardised templates
Methodology Evolution	Changing standards, scenario uncertainty	Flexible systems, standard participation	Working groups, peer learning
Regulatory Divergence	Multiple taxonomies, varied disclosure	Regional teams, flexible compliance	Advocacy for international alignment
Talent Scarcity	Limited sustainability expertise	Training programmes, university partnerships	Shared learning platforms, secondments
Client Readiness	Variable capacity, resource constraints	Tiered approaches, simplified tools	Collective education initiatives

This table illustrates how practical constraints receive responses at both individual institutional and collaborative levels, demonstrating that sustainable finance implementation requires coordinated problem-solving.

6. Case Study: Emirates NBD's Sustainable Finance Framework

Emirates NBD, one of the UAE's largest banking groups, developed a comprehensive sustainable finance strategy that demonstrates institutional transformation in practice.

The bank established a USD 50 billion sustainable finance target for 2021-2025, covering green and social finance across corporate and retail segments. This commitment signals board-level strategic priority and creates accountability for business-line leaders.

The bank structured its approach through multiple pillars, developing green product offerings including green loans, sustainability-linked facilities, and green bonds; integrating ESG considerations into credit risk assessment and investment decisions; building staff capacity through training programmes and cross-functional collaboration; and engaging clients through advisory services that support their sustainability journeys. Emirates NBD launched sector-specific sustainable finance frameworks tailored to real estate, manufacturing, and infrastructure clients. These frameworks provide clear eligibility criteria, streamlined documentation, and performance-tracking mechanisms.

Source: https://www.gdnonline.com/

The bank's green building finance programme offers preferential terms for LEED or Estidama certified projects, creating financial incentives aligned with environmental outcomes.

The institution invested in technology platforms that support sustainable finance operations, digital portals for client applications, automated eligibility checking, and portfolio monitoring dashboards. These systems reduce processing time while maintaining quality standards, enabling scale.

External recognition validates the approach, Emirates NBD received multiple awards for sustainable finance leadership and maintains strong sustainability ratings from ESG assessment agencies. The bank's bond issuances include green and social instruments that demonstrate its own commitment to sustainable funding.

This case illustrates how large regional institutions build comprehensive sustainable finance capabilities through strategic clarity, product innovation, capacity building, and technology investment, creating models that other financial institutions can adapt to their contexts[78].

7. Case Study: Mubadala Investment Company's ESG Integration

Mubadala Investment Company, Abu Dhabi's strategic investment vehicle managing over USD 280 billion in assets, exemplifies how sovereign investors integrate sustainability across diverse portfolios.

The institution adopted comprehensive ESG frameworks that guide investment decisions across sectors, energy, healthcare, aerospace, technology, and real estate.

---

[78] *Emirates NBD, Sustainability Report 2023, Emirates NBD Bank PJSC, 2024, https://www.emiratesnbd.com/en/about-emirates-nbd/sustainability/esg-and-integrated-reports, accessed 22 December 2024.*

Source: https://www.thearabtoday.com/

Mubadala's approach includes setting portfolio-level sustainability targets, conducting ESG due diligence on all new investments, engaging portfolio companies on sustainability improvement, and measuring impact across environmental and social dimensions. The institution established dedicated ESG teams that work alongside investment professionals, ensuring sustainability considerations receive appropriate weight in decision-making.

The company launched sustainability-themed investment vehicles including clean energy funds, sustainable infrastructure platforms, and impact-focused venture capital strategies. These vehicles demonstrate how sovereign capital can catalyse market development by providing patient, substantial funding for emerging sectors.

Mubadala participates actively in global sustainability initiatives, joining the Principles for Responsible Investment, supporting renewable energy project development, and engaging in climate-focused investor coalitions. This participation demonstrates commitment while building knowledge networks that strengthen internal capabilities.

The institution's renewable energy portfolio grew substantially through investments in utility-scale solar, offshore wind, and clean technology companies. These investments generate financial returns while supporting UAE's economic diversification and climate objectives, illustrating alignment between commercial success and national sustainability priorities.

Mubadala's sustainability reporting discloses portfolio emissions, investment allocations across sustainable themes, and case studies demonstrating impact. This transparency sets standards for sovereign investors and creates accountability for continued progress.

The institution's evolution shows how large asset owners integrate sustainability without sacrificing return objectives, demonstrating that environmental and financial performance can advance together through strategic frameworks, governance discipline, and systematic implementation[79].

8. Emerging Practices: Technology and Innovation in Institutional Transformation

Financial institutions increasingly leverage technology to accelerate sustainable finance integration. Artificial intelligence analyses vast datasets to identify sustainability risks, assess climate exposure, and generate insights that inform portfolio decisions. Machine learning models predict climate impacts on asset values, improving risk assessment accuracy.

---

[79] *Mubadala Investment Company, Sustainability Report 2023, Mubadala, 2024, https://mubadalaenergy.com/publication/2023-sustainability-report/ , accessed 22 December 2024.*

Blockchain applications support transparency in green finance, tracking use of proceeds, verifying sustainability claims, and enabling automated reporting. These distributed ledger systems reduce verification costs while strengthening trust through immutable records.

Satellite imagery and remote sensing provide independent data on forest cover, agricultural practices, water resources, and infrastructure conditions. This information supplements client disclosures, validates sustainability claims, and enables continuous monitoring that detects deviations from commitments.

Digital platforms connect multiple stakeholders, banks, investors, project developers, and service providers, creating ecosystems that streamline transactions. These platforms match sustainable projects with appropriate capital sources, standardise documentation, and facilitate knowledge sharing.

Climate risk analytics tools model physical hazards and transition pathways at granular levels, asset-by-asset, facility-by-facility. These tools support underwriting decisions, loan covenants, and investment screening by providing location-specific risk assessments.

The adoption of these technologies demonstrates how financial institutions invest in infrastructure that supports long-term sustainable finance objectives while improving operational efficiency and competitive positioning.

Key Takeaways

- Financial intermediaries shape sustainable finance through internal strategies, product innovation, governance evolution, and cross-institutional collaboration.
- Institutional transformation requires board-level commitment, executive accountability, and integration across all business functions rather than isolated sustainability units.
- Product development translates strategy into concrete offerings, green loans, sustainability-linked facilities, thematic funds, and impact investments that serve diverse client needs.
- Governance structures, incentive alignment, and capacity building programmes enable staff to implement sustainability frameworks effectively in daily operations.
- Collaboration across banks, investors, and other intermediaries strengthens market infrastructure through shared standards, coordinated advocacy, and knowledge exchange.
- Practical constraints including data gaps, methodological evolution, regulatory divergence, and talent scarcity require adaptive responses at institutional and systemic levels.
- Case studies from the UAE demonstrate how regional institutions develop comprehensive sustainable finance capabilities through strategic clarity and operational excellence.
- Technology platforms, AI analytics, blockchain applications, and remote sensing accelerate sustainable finance integration while improving decision quality.
- Successful institutional transformation balances commercial objectives with sustainability commitments through structured frameworks that create accountability.

- Systemic financial transformation requires sustained commitment across multiple institutions, markets, and time horizons to achieve meaningful environmental outcomes.

16

Corporates and Project Developers

Corporate sustainability strategies have evolved from voluntary initiatives to strategic imperatives that influence competitiveness, capital access, and long-term resilience. Companies now integrate environmental considerations into capital expenditure decisions, operational planning, and growth strategies because investors, lenders, customers, and regulators increasingly evaluate performance through sustainability lenses.

This transformation requires systematic approaches that align financial planning with transition pathways while maintaining operational excellence and stakeholder confidence.

Project developers occupy a unique position in this landscape. They translate sustainability ambitions into bankable proposals that attract financing, secure partnerships, and deliver measurable outcomes. Whether developing renewable energy installations, green buildings, sustainable infrastructure, or circular economy facilities, developers must demonstrate technical feasibility, financial viability, and environmental credibility simultaneously.

The integration of sustainability into corporate strategy creates tangible value. Research from McKinsey indicates that **companies with strong ESG propositions demonstrate 10-20% lower cost of capital compared to peers, reflecting reduced risk perceptions and improved access to sustainable finance instruments**[80].

This cost advantage translates directly into competitive positioning and expansion capacity.

Yet successful integration extends beyond cost benefits. It encompasses reputation management, regulatory compliance, innovation capacity, operational efficiency, and workforce attraction.

Companies that embed sustainability deeply into strategy position themselves for future markets where clean technologies, circular models, and resource efficiency define competitive advantage.

This chapter explores how corporates and project developers navigate sustainability integration across capital planning, pipeline development, stakeholder engagement, reporting systems, and strategic alignment. It examines practical approaches to building credibility, meeting investor expectations, and structuring projects that achieve both financial and environmental objectives.

Through case studies and structured frameworks, it demonstrates how organizations translate sustainability commitments into operational reality.

---

[80] *McKinsey & Company, Does ESG Really Matter-and why? McKinsey Quarterly, August 2022, https://www.mckinsey.com/capabilities/sustainability/our-insights/does-esg-really-matter-and-why, accessed 23 December 2024.*

OBJECTIVES OF THE CHAPTER

This chapter will help individuals:

- Understand how corporates integrate sustainability considerations into capital expenditure and strategic planning processes.
- Study approaches to building and presenting green project pipelines that attract financing and partnerships.
- Learn how companies prepare for evolving investor and lender expectations around sustainability performance.
- Examine reporting frameworks, verification processes, and credibility mechanisms that strengthen stakeholder confidence.
- Explore methods for aligning financial planning with long-term transition pathways and science-based targets.
- Recognise how strategic sustainability integration creates competitive advantages and reduces capital costs.
- Observe practical examples from corporates and developers demonstrating successful sustainability implementation.
- Build confidence in evaluating corporate sustainability strategies from financial and operational perspectives.
- Understand why systematic approaches to sustainability create value across multiple stakeholder dimensions.
- Appreciate how project-level execution connects to portfolio-wide transformation and sectoral transitions.

1. Integrating Sustainability into Capital Expenditure and Strategy: Building Systematic Approaches

Capital allocation decisions determine whether sustainability commitments translate into operational reality. Companies establish frameworks that evaluate capital expenditure through dual lenses, financial returns and sustainability outcomes. These frameworks ensure major investments advance both profitability and environmental objectives rather than treating them as competing priorities.

Strategic planning processes now incorporate climate scenarios that test business model resilience under different transition pathways. Companies evaluate how policy changes, technology shifts, consumer preferences, and physical climate impacts might affect operations, supply chains, and market demand. This scenario-based planning identifies vulnerabilities early and guides capital allocation toward resilient opportunities.

Many organizations adopt internal carbon pricing mechanisms that incorporate emissions costs into investment decisions before regulatory requirements emerge.

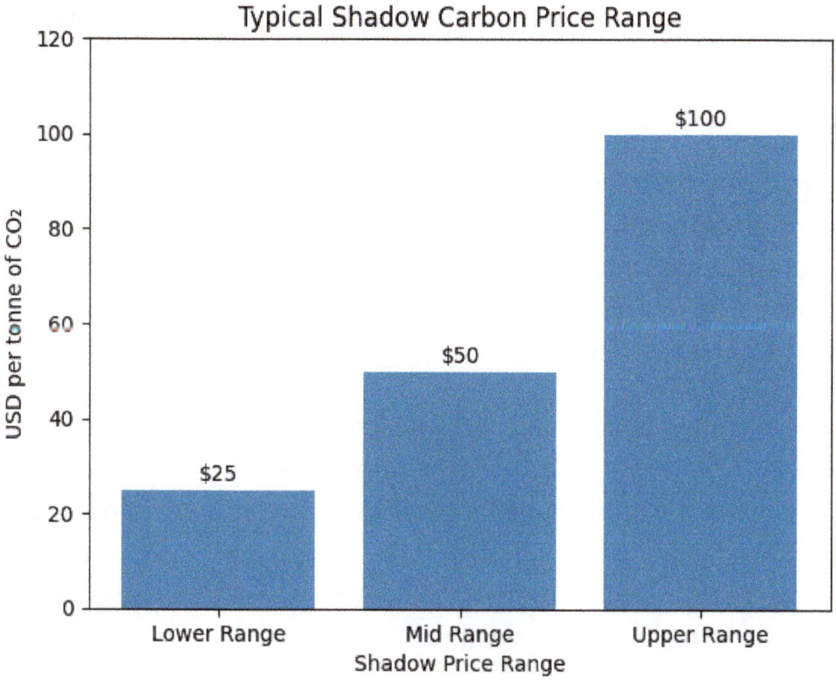

These shadow prices, typically ranging from USD 25 to USD 100 per tonne of CO_2, help companies evaluate long-term competitiveness of capital projects. Equipment with higher efficiency, renewable energy investments, and low-carbon processes gain economic advantage when carbon costs enter calculations.

Capital expenditure categories evolve to include sustainability-specific allocations, renewable energy procurement, energy efficiency retrofits, water conservation systems, waste reduction infrastructure, and circular economy capabilities. These categories receive dedicated budgets and performance tracking separate from traditional expansion or maintenance spending.

Strategic planning timelines extend to match sustainability commitments. Where traditional planning cycles focus on 3-5 years, sustainability strategies often span 10-30 year horizons matching net-zero commitments and asset lifecycles. This temporal expansion requires different analytical approaches, governance structures, and stakeholder communication strategies.

The Science Based Targets initiative provides structure: **over 4,000 companies globally have set science-based emissions reduction targets aligned with limiting global warming to 1.5°C, representing USD 38 trillion in market capitalization**[81]. This widespread adoption demonstrates how structured target-setting frameworks help companies translate climate science into actionable business strategies.

Integration mechanisms include sustainability-linked key performance indicators in executive compensation, board-level sustainability committees with decision-making authority, and cross-functional teams that embed environmental expertise across business units. These governance elements ensure sustainability considerations influence decision-making at all organizational levels.

---

[81] *Science Based Targets initiative (SBTi), Companies Taking Action, SBTi, 2024, https://sciencebasedtargets.org/companies-taking-action, accessed 23 December 2024.*

Investment screening criteria filter capital projects based on emissions intensity, resource efficiency, circular economy alignment, and alignment with sectoral transition pathways. Projects that fail sustainability screens require exceptional justification or redesign before advancing. This systematic filtering shapes capital allocation patterns and encourages innovation in project design.

2. Building and Presenting Green Project Pipelines: Creating Investor Confidence

Project developers succeed by building comprehensive pipelines that demonstrate depth, quality, and alignment with investor priorities. Strong pipelines include diverse project types, staged development timelines, clear eligibility frameworks, and transparent risk assessment. This diversity reduces concentration risk while showing execution capacity across multiple sustainable asset classes.

Pipeline development begins with market assessment, identifying gaps in renewable capacity, efficiency opportunities in building stock, sustainable transport needs, or circular economy infrastructure requirements. This assessment connects market demand with sustainability objectives, ensuring projects serve both commercial and environmental purposes.

Technical feasibility studies establish project viability before seeking financing. These studies examine resource availability, technology suitability, regulatory compliance, grid connectivity, off-take potential, and operational requirements. Thorough technical work reduces execution risk and strengthens lender confidence during due diligence processes. Financial modeling demonstrates project economics under multiple scenarios, base case assumptions, sensitivity analyses around key variables, and stress tests under adverse conditions. Models incorporate construction costs, operating expenses, revenue projections, financing structures, and expected returns. Transparent modeling helps investors understand risk-return profiles and compare opportunities across portfolios.Eligibility alignment ensures projects meet green finance criteria established by taxonomies, bond frameworks, or lending standards. Developers map project characteristics against eligibility requirements early in planning, identifying any gaps that require design adjustments. This proactive alignment streamlines financing processes and reduces transaction costs.

Pipeline presentations emphasize measurable impacts, carbon emissions avoided, renewable energy generated, water conserved, or waste diverted from landfills. Quantified impacts help investors evaluate contribution toward portfolio-level sustainability targets and demonstrate additionality, the incremental environmental benefit created by financing.Phasing strategies allow large pipelines to deploy capital progressively rather than requiring simultaneous financing for all projects. Phased approaches reduce execution risk, allow learning from early projects, and maintain ongoing engagement with financing partners. Clear phase dependencies, milestone definitions, and progression criteria strengthen credibility.

Source: https://www.news.com.au/

A practical example illustrates effective pipeline development: **Masdar, Abu Dhabi's renewable energy company, developed a global project pipeline exceeding 20 GW of clean energy capacity across 40 countries, supported by structured financing arrangements with international development banks and commercial lenders**[82]. This diversified pipeline demonstrates technical capability, geographic reach, and financial strength that attracts substantial capital commitments.

Developers maintain pipeline databases that track project status, financing requirements, development timelines, and stakeholder engagement. These systems provide real-time visibility for internal teams and support transparent communication with investors, lenders, and partners. Digital platforms increasingly automate pipeline management, improving efficiency and accuracy.

Pipeline Element	Purpose	Key Content	Stakeholder Benefit
Project Database	Comprehensive tracking	Status, timelines, requirements	Transparency, planning
Technical Studies	Feasibility validation	Resource data, technology specs	Risk reduction
Financial Models	Economic viability	Costs, revenues, returns	Investment decision support
Impact Metrics	Environmental contribution	Emissions avoided, energy produced	Portfolio alignment

[82] *Masdar, About Masdar, Masdar Clean Energy, 2024, https://www.masdar.ae/en/about-us, accessed 23 December 2024.*

Eligibility Mapping	Finance qualification	Taxonomy alignment, criteria match	Streamlined transactions

This table clarifies how different pipeline elements serve distinct purposes while collectively building investor confidence through systematic preparation and transparent communication.

3. Preparing for Investor and Lender Expectations: Meeting Evolving Standards

Investor and lender expectations around sustainability have intensified significantly. Financial institutions now conduct environmental due diligence that examines emissions profiles, resource management practices, climate risk exposure, and transition planning quality. Companies must anticipate these reviews and prepare documentation that demonstrates systematic sustainability management.

Environmental, social, and governance data requirements have expanded dramatically. Investors expect comprehensive Scope 1, 2, and 3 emissions data, water usage metrics, waste generation figures, biodiversity impact assessments, and social performance indicators. Companies invest in measurement systems, third-party verification, and digital platforms that collect, validate, and report this information accurately.

Transition plans receive particularly close scrutiny. Investors evaluate whether targets align with science-based pathways, whether interim milestones provide measurable progress points, whether capital expenditure plans support stated objectives, and whether governance structures ensure accountability. Weak transition plans create financing barriers while strong plans unlock preferential terms.

Engagement readiness determines relationship quality with investors and lenders. Companies establish dedicated investor relations capabilities focused on sustainability topics, prepare executives to discuss climate strategy in depth, and maintain regular communication about progress. Proactive engagement builds trust and creates opportunities to shape expectations through dialogue rather than simply responding to demands.

Sustainability-linked financing structures require specific preparation. Companies identify material key performance indicators, establish credible baselines supported by historical data, set ambitious yet achievable targets, and build monitoring systems that track progress transparently. These preparations enable companies to access sustainability-linked loans and bonds that reward performance improvements through pricing benefits.

The International Finance Corporation notes that **investors managing over USD 130 trillion in assets have committed to measuring and disclosing portfolio emissions through the TCFD framework, creating consistent expectations across global markets**[83]. This convergence means companies can prepare for relatively standardized disclosure requirements rather than navigating completely divergent expectations across investor types.

Credit rating agencies increasingly incorporate ESG factors into assessments, influencing borrowing costs and market access. Companies prepare by understanding rating methodologies, addressing material ESG issues proactively, and communicating sustainability strategies clearly to rating analysts. Strong ESG profiles can enhance credit ratings by 1-2 notches, translating into significant cost savings on large financing programs.

---

[83] *International Finance Corporation (IFC), Task Force on Climate-related Financial Disclosures: Investor Use of TCFD Disclosures, IFC, 2023, https://www.ifc.org/sustainability, accessed 23 December 2024.*

Sector-specific expectations require tailored preparation. Real estate developers face questions about building certifications and energy performance. Manufacturing companies address production process emissions and circular economy integration. Energy companies discuss transition strategies and renewable portfolio development. Understanding sector-specific priorities allows companies to focus preparation efforts effectively.

4. Reporting, Verification and Credibility: Building Stakeholder Trust

Sustainability reporting has evolved from voluntary disclosure to comprehensive frameworks that inform investment decisions, regulatory compliance, and stakeholder engagement. Companies adopt international standards, GRI, SASB, TCFD, ISSB, that provide structured guidance on disclosure content, materiality assessment, and presentation formats. These frameworks create comparability across companies and sectors while ensuring relevant information reaches stakeholders.

Materiality assessments identify which sustainability topics most significantly affect business performance and stakeholder interests. Companies engage with investors, customers, employees, communities, and regulators to understand priorities. This engagement process reveals where disclosure efforts deliver most value and helps companies focus reporting on material issues rather than attempting comprehensive coverage of every possible sustainability metric.

Data quality determines reporting credibility. Companies invest in measurement systems, establish data governance processes, implement controls that ensure accuracy, and maintain documentation that supports reported figures. Regular internal audits test data integrity while identifying improvement opportunities in collection and validation processes.

External verification strengthens credibility by providing independent assessment of reported information. Third-party assurers examine data accuracy, review calculation methodologies, assess disclosure completeness, and validate alignment with reporting standards. Assurance statements accompany sustainability reports, giving stakeholders confidence in information reliability.

Impact reporting translates activities into measurable environmental and social outcomes. Rather than simply stating that renewable energy was installed, impact reports quantify emissions avoided, compare performance against baselines, and demonstrate progress toward targets. This outcome focus helps stakeholders understand real-world effects of corporate actions.

The UAE demonstrates regional leadership: **the Abu Dhabi Securities Exchange mandated ESG disclosure for all listed companies starting in 2019, requiring structured reporting across environmental, social, and governance dimensions**[84]. This regulatory framework accelerated corporate reporting maturity and created consistent information availability that supports investor decision-making across the market.

Digital reporting platforms improve accessibility and usability. Interactive dashboards allow stakeholders to explore data at granular levels, compare performance across time periods, and download information in usable formats. These platforms often integrate with financial reporting systems, ensuring consistency between sustainability and financial disclosures.

Forward-looking disclosure helps stakeholders understand future direction. Companies describe strategic plans, capital allocation intentions, technology deployment roadmaps, and expected performance trajectories. This forward guidance helps investors evaluate whether

---

[84] *Abu Dhabi Securities Exchange (ADX), ESG Disclosure Guidelines, ADX, 2019, https://www.adx.ae/ , accessed 23 December 2024.*

companies are positioning for successful transitions rather than simply reporting historical performance.

Transparency around challenges and setbacks builds trust more effectively than exclusively positive narratives. Companies that acknowledge where performance fell short, explain contributing factors, and describe corrective actions demonstrate management maturity and commitment to continuous improvement. This honesty strengthens credibility with sophisticated investors who recognize that sustainability transformation involves learning and adaptation.

5. Aligning Financial Planning with Transition Pathways: Creating Strategic Coherence

Financial planning alignment ensures that annual budgets, multi-year capital programs, and long-term strategies work coherently toward transition objectives. Companies establish clear linkages between sustainability targets and resource allocation decisions, making abstract commitments concrete through systematic funding.

Scenario-based financial planning tests business model resilience under different transition speeds and policy environments. Companies model financial performance assuming rapid decarbonization, delayed action, disorderly transition, or orderly pathway scenarios. This analysis reveals which business lines require strategic repositioning, where capital reallocation creates value, and what financial resources support successful adaptation.

Capital reallocation strategies gradually shift spending from carbon-intensive activities toward sustainable alternatives. This reallocation doesn't happen overnight but follows phased approaches that maintain operational stability while progressively transforming asset portfolios. Companies set interim allocation targets, for example, 30% of capital expenditure in sustainable projects by 2025, increasing to 60% by 2030.

Cash flow planning incorporates sustainability-linked revenues and cost structures. Companies forecast revenue growth from sustainable products, premium pricing opportunities, and new market access. They also model changing cost structures, carbon pricing impacts, efficiency savings, renewable energy procurement costs, and potential subsidies or incentives.

Financing strategy diversification includes accessing multiple sustainable finance instruments, green bonds for project finance, sustainability-linked loans for general corporate purposes, transition bonds for transformation programs, and impact investment for innovation initiatives. This diversification reduces dependency on single financing sources while building relationships across investor types.

Partnership structures support financial planning by sharing risks and capital requirements. Joint ventures with technology providers, co-investment arrangements with financial institutions, and strategic alliances with supply chain partners distribute financial burden while accelerating implementation timelines.

A compelling example demonstrates strategic alignment: **ACWA Power, a Saudi Arabian developer, structured its business model around renewable energy and water desalination, securing over USD 70 billion in project finance across its portfolio through strategic alignment of project selection, financial structuring, and partnership development**[85].

This model shows how developers build substantial businesses by systematically aligning financial planning with sustainable infrastructure development.

---

[85] *ACWA Power, About Us, ACWA Power, 2024, https://www.aldar.com/en/explore-aldar/sustainability/netzero , accessed 23 December 2024.*

Source: https://eurasiamagazine.com

Risk management integration ensures financial planning accounts for climate-related risks, physical hazards affecting assets, transition risks from policy changes, liability risks from stakeholder actions, and reputational risks from sustainability performance. Insurance strategies, hedging mechanisms, and reserve policies address these risks systematically.

Performance monitoring systems track financial and sustainability metrics in parallel, allowing companies to understand relationships between environmental performance and financial outcomes.

These integrated dashboards reveal where sustainability investments deliver financial returns, which interventions require adjustment, and how overall strategy execution progresses.

Case Study: Aldar Properties' Sustainable Development Framework

Aldar Properties, Abu Dhabi's leading real estate developer, demonstrates comprehensive sustainability integration across its development portfolio. The company established ambitious targets including achieving net-zero carbon emissions by 2050, implementing Estidama sustainability standards across all new projects, and securing green building certifications for its entire portfolio.

Aldar's approach integrates sustainability into capital expenditure decisions through mandatory sustainability assessments for all major investments, incorporation of lifecycle cost analysis that includes energy and water consumption, and preference for materials and technologies with lower environmental impacts. This systematic integration ensures sustainability influences project economics from initial concept stages.

The company developed a substantial green project pipeline including energy-efficient residential communities, sustainable mixed-use developments, and retrofit programs for existing assets. Aldar secured green financing through multiple instruments, issuing a USD 500 million green bond in 2023, establishing sustainability-linked loan facilities, and attracting ESG-focused investors to specific projects.

Sustainability reporting evolved to include comprehensive disclosures aligned with international frameworks, third-party verification of key metrics, and transparent progress tracking against targets.

The company publishes annual sustainability reports that detail environmental performance, social initiatives, and governance structures, building stakeholder confidence through transparency.

Aldar's strategic planning explicitly connects financial objectives with sustainability outcomes. Development timelines incorporate sustainability milestones, capital budgets allocate specific resources to green building features, and executive compensation links to ESG performance indicators. This alignment ensures sustainability receives consistent priority in resource allocation decisions.

The company's efforts received recognition through strong ESG ratings from international agencies, inclusion in sustainable investment indices, and awards for green building leadership.

More importantly, the strategy delivered tangible benefits, reduced operating costs in efficient buildings, premium pricing for certified developments, and enhanced reputation that strengthens market positioning.

This case illustrates how regional real estate developers systematically integrate sustainability across strategy, operations, and financial planning, demonstrating that comprehensive approaches create competitive advantages while advancing environmental objectives[86].

7. Case Study: Taqa's Energy Transition Strategy

Abu Dhabi National Energy Company (Taqa) exemplifies how established energy companies execute strategic transitions toward clean energy while maintaining financial strength. The company established clear transition targets including achieving net-zero emissions by 2050, growing renewable energy capacity to 23 GW by 2030, and increasing clean energy's share of generation portfolio to 30% by 2030.

Taqa's capital allocation strategy shifted substantially toward renewable energy and enabling infrastructure, investing over USD 5 billion in clean energy projects, expanding into offshore wind development, and building transmission capabilities that support renewable integration. This capital reallocation demonstrates commitment backed by concrete financial resources.

---

[86] *Aldar Properties, Sustainability Report 2023, Aldar Properties PJSC, 2024, https://www.aldar.com/en/sustainability, accessed 23 December 2024.*

Source: https://www.energyintel.com/

The company developed comprehensive project pipelines across solar, wind, and hydroelectric generation. These pipelines include utility-scale installations, distributed generation systems, and innovative hybrid projects that combine multiple technologies. Strong pipelines positioned Taqa as a preferred partner for governments and international developers seeking local expertise and financial strength.

Financial planning aligned with transition timelines through phased capacity additions, diversified financing structures including green bonds and sustainability-linked facilities, and strategic partnerships that share risks while accelerating development. The company's strong balance sheet enabled patient capital deployment that matches long-term nature of energy infrastructure.

Sustainability reporting transparency strengthened stakeholder confidence. Taqa publishes detailed emissions data, tracks progress against targets with clear metrics, and discusses challenges openly while describing mitigation strategies. This transparency supports investor engagement and demonstrates management accountability.

The transition strategy delivered financial benefits alongside environmental progress, improved ESG ratings enhanced capital access, renewable projects generated stable long-term cash flows, and strategic positioning strengthened competitiveness in evolving energy markets.

The company's experience demonstrates that energy transitions can advance through systematic strategies that balance operational continuity with transformational change.This case shows how established energy companies in the region execute strategic transitions through clear targets, substantial capital allocation, pipeline development, and transparent reporting, creating models for sectoral transformation that maintains financial strength while advancing sustainability objectives[87].

---

[87] *Taqa, Sustainability Report 2023, Abu Dhabi National Energy Company PJSC, 2024, https://www.taqa.com/sustainability/, accessed 23 December 2024.*

Key Takeaways

- Corporate sustainability integration requires systematic approaches that embed environmental considerations into capital expenditure, strategic planning, and operational decisions.
- Strong green project pipelines demonstrate depth, diversity, and clear alignment with investor priorities through comprehensive technical and financial preparation.
- Evolving investor and lender expectations demand robust ESG data, credible transition plans, and proactive engagement that builds relationship quality.
- Sustainability reporting frameworks, external verification, and transparent disclosure strengthen stakeholder confidence and support capital access.
- Financial planning alignment with transition pathways creates strategic coherence through scenario analysis, capital reallocation, and integrated performance monitoring.
- Companies with strong ESG propositions demonstrate 10-20% lower cost of capital, translating sustainability into tangible competitive advantage.
- Regional case studies from the UAE demonstrate comprehensive sustainability integration across real estate development and energy transition.
- Successful approaches combine clear target-setting, substantial capital commitment, pipeline development, transparent reporting, and governance structures that ensure accountability.
- Project developers build investor confidence through technical feasibility validation, financial modeling transparency, impact quantification, and eligibility alignment.

- Strategic sustainability integration creates value across multiple dimensions, capital costs, operational efficiency, reputation, regulatory compliance, and workforce attraction.

17

Governments, Cities and Public Agencies

Governments shape the velocity and direction of sustainable finance through their unique capacity to set priorities, mobilize capital, coordinate stakeholders, and create enabling conditions that private markets build upon.

As sovereign borrowers, budget authorities, guarantee providers, and policy architects, public entities hold instruments of transformation that extend far beyond direct expenditure. Their decisions influence how trillions of dollars flow across economies, how cities develop infrastructure, and how national transitions unfold across decades.

The evolution of sovereign green finance represents one of the most significant developments in modern capital markets. When national governments issue green bonds, establish sustainability-linked frameworks, or integrate climate considerations into fiscal planning, they send powerful signals that reshape investor behavior, corporate strategy, and subnational priorities. These actions demonstrate commitment that extends beyond political cycles, creating confidence that encourages long-term investment in sustainable infrastructure, clean technologies, and resilient systems.

Cities and subnational governments occupy equally critical positions as implementers of climate action. Urban centers account for the majority of global emissions while holding responsibility for transport systems, buildings, waste management, and water infrastructure, the physical assets that determine environmental outcomes.

Municipal finance instruments, creditworthiness enhancement, and capacity building enable cities to access capital markets directly, transforming them from passive recipients of transfers into active issuers shaping their own sustainable development pathways.

Sovereign and subnational green bond issuance exceeded USD 400 billion cumulatively by 2023, demonstrating how public sector leadership catalyzes market development and establishes standards that private issuers subsequently adopt[88]. This scale reflects growing recognition among governments that capital markets offer complementary resources to traditional taxation and borrowing, provided public entities demonstrate the transparency, governance, and project preparation that investors require.

The coordination challenge extends across multiple dimensions, horizontally between ministries with different mandates, vertically between national and local authorities, and systemically between public entities and private partners. Green budgeting frameworks, inter-ministerial coordination mechanisms, and multilevel governance structures address these complexities, creating coherence that strengthens implementation effectiveness. When coordination succeeds,

---

[88] *Climate Bonds Initiative, Sustainable Debt Global State of the Market 2023, Climate Bonds Initiative, 2024, https://www.climatebonds.net/data-insights/publications , accessed 21 December 2024.*

public resources catalyze private capital, policies align across sectors, and transitions accelerate through reinforcing actions rather than fragmented initiatives.

This chapter explores how governments, cities, and public agencies deploy their distinctive capabilities to advance sustainable finance. It examines sovereign green borrowing structures, fiscal policy integration, public-private partnership models, guarantee mechanisms, and coordination frameworks that enable effective implementation across complex institutional landscapes.

OBJECTIVES OF THE CHAPTER

This chapter will help individuals:

- Understand how sovereign green bonds and sustainability-linked instruments strengthen national climate commitments while accessing capital markets.
- Study how green budgeting integrates environmental priorities into fiscal policy and expenditure decisions.
- Explore public-private partnership models and guarantee structures that de-risk sustainable infrastructure investments.
- Learn how coordination across ministries and government levels improves policy coherence and implementation effectiveness.
- Examine practical examples of sovereign issuances, municipal finance innovations, and multilevel governance from the UAE, GCC, and global contexts.
- Recognize how public sector leadership establishes market standards and creates conditions for private capital mobilization.

- Build confidence in evaluating government sustainability strategies, fiscal frameworks, and institutional coordination mechanisms.

- Appreciate why public entities serve as both direct implementers and systemic enablers of sustainable finance.

- Understand how subnational governments access capital markets and strengthen creditworthiness through transparent governance.

- Identify opportunities where public finance catalyzes broader market transformation beyond direct public expenditure.

Sovereign and Sub-Sovereign Green Borrowing: Public Sector Market Leadership

Sovereign green bonds represent more than financing instruments, they embody national commitments to sustainability translated into actionable investment frameworks.

When governments enter capital markets with labeled debt, they submit to disclosure standards, external verification, and impact reporting that creates accountability mechanisms extending beyond domestic political processes. This transparency strengthens credibility while demonstrating concrete linkages between borrowed capital and environmental outcomes.

Early sovereign issuances established templates that subsequent markets built upon. Poland's pioneering 2016 sovereign green bond demonstrated that national governments could access debt markets under green frameworks without interest rate penalties, dispelling concerns that sustainability labeling might increase borrowing costs.

France's landmark EUR 7 billion issuance in 2017 showed that large, liquid sovereigns could scale green bonds to meaningful size while maintaining robust investor demand. These precedents encouraged broader sovereign participation that transformed green bonds from specialized instruments into mainstream sovereign debt management tools.

Sovereign green bond frameworks typically align with national climate strategies, creating explicit connections between borrowed funds and policy priorities. Eligible categories often include renewable energy infrastructure, clean transportation systems, energy efficiency programs, sustainable water management, climate adaptation investments, and biodiversity conservation.

This alignment ensures that debt issuance supports rather than substitutes for existing budget commitments, addressing investor concerns about additionality while strengthening overall climate finance architecture.

The UAE issued its inaugural sovereign green bond in September 2022, raising USD 2 billion with strong international investor participation that demonstrated confidence in the nation's sustainability strategy and fiscal management[89]. The framework covers renewable energy, clean transportation, energy efficiency, sustainable water management, and green buildings, categories aligned with national development priorities. The successful issuance positioned the UAE as a regional green finance leader while establishing a benchmark for other GCC sovereigns.

Sub-sovereign entities, states, provinces, municipalities, increasingly access green bond markets independently, demonstrating financial sophistication and governance capacity that attracts institutional investors. Municipal green bonds finance local infrastructure like public

---

[89] *Ministry of Finance UAE, UAE Federal Government Issues Inaugural Green Bond, Ministry of Finance UAE, September 2022,* https://masdar.ae/-/media/corporate-revamp/downloads/investors/masdar_green-finance-report_2023-2024_v3f_.pdf *, accessed 21 December 2024.*

transport upgrades, district heating systems, waste-to-energy facilities, and building retrofits. These instruments allow cities to address specific urban challenges while building direct relationships with capital markets rather than depending solely on national transfers or traditional bank lending.

Creditworthiness remains central to subnational market access. Cities strengthen credit profiles through transparent accounting, stable revenue bases, professional financial management, and predictable regulatory environments. Credit enhancement mechanisms, national guarantees, pooled financing vehicles, reserve funds, help municipalities with developing credit histories access markets at reasonable costs. Rating agencies evaluate subnational entities using criteria that increasingly incorporate climate risk management and sustainability strategy alignment.

The table below illustrates sovereign and subnational green bond characteristics across different contexts:

Issuer Type	Typical Size	Key Eligible Categories	Investor Base	Credit Enhancement
Developed Sovereign	USD 2-10 billion	Renewable energy, transport, buildings, adaptation	International institutional, central banks	Sovereign credit rating
Emerging Sovereign	USD 500 million - 2 billion	Energy, transport, water, agriculture	Regional + international	Sometimes guaranteed by MDBs

Large Municipality	USD 200-800 million	Urban transport, buildings, waste, water	Domestic + international	Municipal credit, sometimes sovereign guarantee
Smaller Municipality	USD 50-200 million	Local infrastructure, efficiency, resilience	Primarily domestic	Pooled structures, guarantees

This differentiation helps readers understand how issuer capacity, market development, and institutional context shape sovereign and subnational green finance approaches.

Sovereign sustainability-linked bonds represent an innovation extending beyond use-of-proceeds models. Chile issued the world's first sustainability-linked sovereign bond in 2022, tying coupon rates to achieving renewable energy and greenhouse gas reduction targets. Uruguay followed with an instrument linking payments to forest cover, renewable energy share, and emissions reductions. These structures demonstrate national commitment to measurable outcomes rather than merely financing eligible projects, creating accountability mechanisms that strengthen policy implementation.

Green sukuk, Islamic finance instruments compliant with Sharia principles, expand sovereign green finance reach in Muslim-majority nations. Indonesia pioneered sovereign green sukuk issuance, channeling funds toward renewable energy and sustainable infrastructure while adhering to Islamic finance principles.

The GCC region shows growing interest in green sukuk structures that align with both sustainability objectives and religious requirements, demonstrating how green finance adapts to diverse cultural and financial contexts.

Public development banks and national green banks complement sovereign borrowing through specialized lending that targets market gaps. These institutions provide concessional finance, technical assistance, and risk mitigation for projects too early-stage or complex for commercial lenders.

Germany's KfW, France's Caisse des Dépôts, and Brazil's BNDES exemplify development banks advancing sustainability through specialized programs that leverage sovereign backing to mobilize broader capital.

Budgeting, Fiscal Policy and Green Priorities: Integrating Sustainability into Public Finance

Green budgeting represents systematic integration of environmental considerations throughout fiscal planning, expenditure allocation, and budget execution. Rather than treating environmental spending as a separate category, green budgeting examines climate and environmental implications across all budget lines, energy subsidies, transport investment, agricultural support, housing programs, identifying opportunities to align expenditure with sustainability goals while eliminating subsidies that undermine environmental objectives.

France pioneered comprehensive green budgeting at national level, publishing annual assessments of how budget expenditures impact climate goals. The framework evaluates each spending program against climate objectives, categorizing them as favorable, unfavorable, or neutral.

This transparency enables parliamentary oversight and public scrutiny while identifying areas where expenditure conflicts with climate commitments. Other OECD members increasingly adopt similar approaches, recognizing that budget documents provide powerful tools for policy coherence.

Tax policy serves as another lever for sustainability integration. Carbon pricing, whether through explicit taxes or emissions trading systems, creates financial signals that reshape economic decisions across households, businesses, and industries.

Environmental tax reform shifts tax burdens from income and labor toward resource consumption and pollution, creating incentives for efficiency while maintaining revenue neutrality. Green tax incentives, accelerated depreciation for clean technologies, VAT reductions on efficient appliances, property tax breaks for green buildings, encourage private investment aligned with public priorities.

The International Monetary Fund estimates that eliminating fossil fuel subsidies globally could reduce CO2 emissions by 28% while freeing fiscal resources exceeding USD 300 billion annually for reallocation toward sustainable development priorities[90]. This analysis demonstrates how budget reorientation, not merely increased spending, can advance climate goals while strengthening fiscal sustainability.

Fiscal rules increasingly incorporate climate considerations alongside traditional macroeconomic objectives. The European Union's reformed fiscal framework allows greater flexibility for green investments. Some proposals suggest excluding certain climate infrastructure spending from deficit calculations, recognizing that such investments generate long-term economic and environmental returns that justify temporary deficit increases.

---

[90]*International Monetary Fund, Still Not Getting Energy Prices Right: A Global and Country Update of Fossil Fuel Subsidies, IMF Working Paper, September 2021, https://www.imf.org/en/Publications/WP/Issues/2021/09/23/Still-Not-Getting-Energy-Prices-Right-A-Global-and-Country-Update-of-Fossil-Fuel-Subsidies-466004, accessed 21 December 2024.*

These discussions reflect evolving understanding that fiscal sustainability depends partly on preventing climate damages that would impose massive future costs.

Public procurement represents substantial purchasing power that governments leverage to stimulate sustainable markets. When public entities commit to buying electric vehicles, renewable energy, low-carbon cement, or sustainable food, they create guaranteed demand that encourages private sector production scaling.

Green procurement standards, lifecycle carbon assessment, circular economy criteria, social standards, embed sustainability requirements into tendering processes that shape market development.

The UAE demonstrates comprehensive fiscal integration of sustainability priorities through multiple channels. National budgets allocate substantial resources toward renewable energy, water efficiency, sustainable transport, and climate adaptation. Tax structures incentivize clean technology adoption.

Public procurement increasingly favors sustainable products and services. Strategic reserves invest in sustainable assets. This multifaceted approach shows how fiscal policy, budget allocation, procurement power, and investment strategy reinforce each other in advancing national sustainability objectives.

Climate-responsive budgeting extends analysis to examine how climate impacts affect fiscal positions. Extreme weather events impose emergency response costs, damage public infrastructure, reduce tax revenues, and increase social protection needs.

Proactive investment in resilience, flood defenses, drought-resistant agriculture, heat-resilient infrastructure, reduces future fiscal exposure while protecting communities. This forward-looking fiscal approach treats climate adaptation as prudent risk management rather than discretionary spending.

Intergovernmental fiscal transfers increasingly incorporate climate and environmental criteria. National governments can incentivize subnational climate action through transfer formulas rewarding forest conservation, renewable energy adoption, or emissions reduction. Brazil's ICMS Ecológico allocates state tax revenues partly based on protected area establishment. These fiscal mechanisms align incentives across government levels, encouraging local action that contributes to national climate objectives.

Public-Private Models and Guarantees: De-Risking Sustainable Infrastructure Investment

Public-private partnerships mobilize private capital and expertise for public infrastructure by sharing risks, responsibilities, and returns between government and private partners. PPP structures suit sustainable infrastructure particularly well because they align long-term asset lifespans with patient private capital while transferring operational efficiencies to specialized private operators. Renewable energy, urban transport, water systems, and waste management, sectors central to climate transitions, have extensive PPP experience.

Guarantee mechanisms represent particularly powerful tools for de-risking private investment in sustainable sectors. Sovereign guarantees backstop revenue or performance risks that private investors cannot fully manage, enabling projects to proceed that otherwise would not attract commercial finance.

Development finance institutions provide partial credit guarantees that cover specific risk layers, construction completion, demand shortfalls, currency convertibility, allowing commercial lenders to participate in projects they would otherwise decline.

First-loss capital structures place public or concessional funds in subordinated positions, absorbing initial losses and thereby protecting senior commercial investors.

This risk layering allows projects with acceptable overall risk but uncertain early performance to access mainstream finance. Blended finance vehicles combine these mechanisms, first-loss tranches, guarantees, technical assistance grants, creating comprehensive support that mobilizes commercial capital at scale for sustainable infrastructure.

The World Bank Group's Multilateral Investment Guarantee Agency (MIGA) provided USD 5.4 billion in political risk insurance and credit enhancement guarantees in fiscal 2023, mobilizing approximately USD 3 of private investment for every USD 1 of

MIGA exposure[91]. This multiplier effect demonstrates how strategic public risk-sharing catalyzes substantially larger private capital flows than would emerge from direct public spending alone.

Availability payment models separate revenue risk from demand variability, making sustainable infrastructure more attractive to private investors. Rather than collecting user fees subject to uncertain ridership or consumption, private partners receive payments based on asset availability and performance standards.

Governments assume demand risk while benefiting from private sector efficiency in construction and operation. This model proved successful for renewable energy, where power purchase agreements guarantee off-take, and can extend to other infrastructure types.

Public sector comparator analysis helps governments evaluate whether PPP structures offer value compared to direct public provision. These assessments examine whole-life costs, risk allocation efficiency, service quality outcomes, and fiscal implications. Transparent methodology and independent review prevent PPPs from being selected merely to circumvent budget constraints, ensuring they genuinely deliver better value through appropriate risk transfer and private sector capabilities.

The UAE employs PPP structures extensively in sustainable infrastructure development, combining clear regulatory frameworks, strong public institutions, and active private sector participation. Dubai's solar park expansions through independent power producer models attracted international developers and low-cost capital while transferring technical and operational risks to experienced private partners.

---

[91] *Multilateral Investment Guarantee Agency (MIGA), MIGA Annual Report 2023, World Bank Group, 2023, https://www.miga.org/annual-report, accessed 21 December 2024.*

Abu Dhabi's waste-to-energy facilities use PPP structures that ensure private sector efficiency while meeting public service requirements. These implementations demonstrate how well-designed PPPs accelerate infrastructure deployment while managing public fiscal exposure.

Challenges in PPP implementation require careful management. Contract complexity demands sophisticated legal and technical capabilities that some jurisdictions lack. Renegotiation risks emerge when circumstances change during long contract periods.

Political economy considerations arise when private profits from public services generate controversy. Capacity building, training public officials, developing standardized contracts, establishing transparent processes, addresses these challenges and builds institutional capabilities for successful PPP programs.

Green guarantee facilities specifically target sustainable infrastructure by offering terms unavailable in commercial markets. Partial risk guarantees cover specific project risks.

Portfolio guarantees enable lending programs rather than individual transactions. Revenue guarantees mitigate demand uncertainty during early project years. These specialized instruments recognize that sustainable infrastructure often faces distinct risk profiles requiring tailored support.

Coordinating Across Ministries and Levels of Government: Building Policy Coherence

Sustainability transitions require coordination across government entities with different mandates, timelines, and priorities. Energy ministries focus on grid reliability and fuel security. Finance ministries prioritize fiscal sustainability and economic growth. Environment ministries emphasize ecosystem protection. Transport ministries manage infrastructure networks.

Agriculture ministries support rural livelihoods. Without coordination mechanisms, these entities may pursue conflicting objectives that undermine overall transition effectiveness.

Inter-ministerial coordination bodies create forums for policy alignment and conflict resolution. Climate cabinets or green growth committees bring together ministers responsible for climate-relevant sectors, encouraging integrated strategies that consider cross-sectoral implications. These bodies develop whole-of-government approaches where energy policy aligns with industrial strategy, transport planning considers emissions targets, and fiscal policy supports rather than contradicts climate objectives.

National climate strategies provide overarching frameworks that guide sectoral planning. When properly designed, these strategies establish clear targets, allocate responsibilities across government entities, define timelines, and create monitoring mechanisms. They transform abstract climate commitments into concrete action plans with assigned accountability. Regular review processes ensure strategies adapt as circumstances change, technologies evolve, or new challenges emerge.

The UAE established the Higher Committee for Green Development and Climate Change in 2021, chaired by the Prime Minister, to coordinate national climate action across ministries, align with international commitments, and oversee implementation of the Net Zero by 2050 Strategic Initiative[92].

This high-level coordination mechanism demonstrates institutional commitment to policy coherence and ensures climate considerations integrate into decisions across all government sectors.

---

[92] *UAE Government Portal, Higher Committee for Green Development and Climate Change, Government of UAE, https://u.ae/en/about-the-uae/strategies-initiatives-and-awards/federal-governments-strategies-and-plans/higher-committee-for-green-development-and-climate-change, accessed 21 December 2024.*

Vertical coordination between national and subnational governments proves equally important. National governments set overall targets and regulatory frameworks while local governments implement infrastructure projects, land-use planning, and service delivery.

Effective coordination requires clear allocation of responsibilities, adequate resource transfers, capacity building support, and accountability mechanisms that neither impose inflexible mandates nor allow complete local discretion that fragments national efforts.

Fiscal federalism arrangements determine resource flows and decision-making authority between government levels. Intergovernmental transfers can incentivize local climate action through performance-based allocation formulas.

Local revenue-raising authorities, environmental taxes, congestion charges, development fees, enable cities to finance sustainability investments without complete dependence on national transfers.

Clear frameworks prevent unfunded mandates where national regulations impose requirements without providing resources for implementation.

Regional coordination addresses sustainability challenges transcending political boundaries. River basin management requires cooperation across upstream and downstream jurisdictions.

Air quality improvement needs coordinated action across interconnected urban areas. Grid integration of renewable energy depends on regional cooperation for transmission infrastructure.

Cross-border agreements, joint authorities, and coordinated planning processes enable collective action at appropriate geographic scales.

The table below illustrates coordination mechanisms and their applications:

Coordination Type	Mechanism	Purpose	Example
Horizontal (National)	Inter-ministerial committee	Policy alignment across sectors	UAE Higher Committee for Green Development
Vertical (National-Local)	Performance-based transfers	Incentivize local climate action	Brazil's ICMS Ecológico
Regional (Subnational)	Joint authorities	Manage shared resources	European river basin districts
International (Cross-border)	Climate coalitions	Knowledge sharing, joint advocacy	C40 Cities Climate Leadership Group

This framework helps readers understand how different coordination challenges require distinct institutional mechanisms and governance structures.

Digital governance platforms enhance coordination by providing shared data, transparent tracking, and collaborative decision-making tools. When ministries access common information about emissions sources, project pipelines, budget allocations, and policy impacts, they make better-informed decisions that consider trade-offs explicitly rather than creating accidental conflicts. Open data platforms enable public scrutiny and stakeholder engagement that strengthen accountability.

Institutional capacity building supports effective coordination by developing skills, processes, and culture required for collaborative governance. Training programs educate public officials across technical aspects of climate action, financial mechanisms, project preparation, and stakeholder engagement. Exchange programs share lessons between jurisdictions. Technical assistance supports development of strategies, frameworks, and monitoring systems. These investments in institutional capabilities often determine implementation success more than direct project funding.

Saudi Arabia's Vision 2030 exemplifies comprehensive national coordination for sustainable development. The strategy aligns efforts across ministries, regions, and sectors toward common objectives including renewable energy expansion, economic diversification, and environmental conservation.

Clear governance structures assign responsibilities while allowing sectoral flexibility in implementation approaches. Regular monitoring tracks progress and identifies obstacles requiring policy adjustments or additional resources.

Practical Examples: Public Sector Leadership in Action

Chile's Sustainability-Linked Sovereign Bond Framework

Chile pioneered sustainability-linked sovereign bonds with a March 2022 issuance integrating key performance indicators into bond structure. The framework links coupon adjustments to achieving renewable energy and greenhouse gas reduction targets. Independent verification ensures credibility.

The innovation demonstrates how national commitments translate into financial accountability mechanisms that extend beyond political cycles. Success has encouraged other sovereigns, Uruguay, Austria, to explore similar structures that reward measurable progress rather than merely financing eligible projects.

The Chilean framework provides valuable lessons about KPI selection, baseline establishment, target ambition, and verification processes. Indicators chosen reflect both materiality to national climate strategy and data availability for reliable measurement.

Targets balance ambition with achievability, avoiding either greenwashing through easy goals or unrealistic commitments that undermine credibility. These design considerations apply broadly to sustainability-linked instruments across public and private issuers[93].

---

[93] *Ministry of Finance Chile, Sustainable Finance Framework, Government of Chile, 2022, https://greenfinancelac.org/resources/news/chile-presents-an-update-to-the-sustainability-linked-bond-framework/*

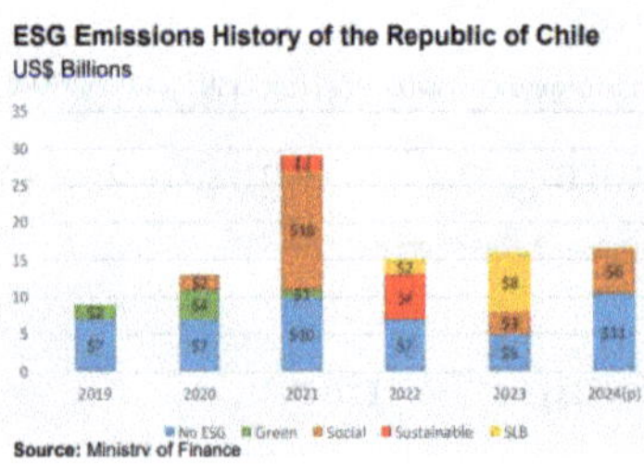

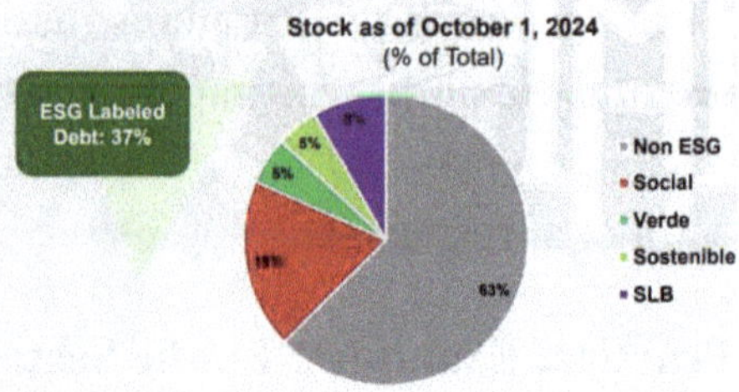

France's Green Budgeting Initiative

France's pioneering green budget assessment evaluates environmental impacts across all government expenditure. Annual reports classify spending as favorable, unfavorable, or neutral toward climate objectives.

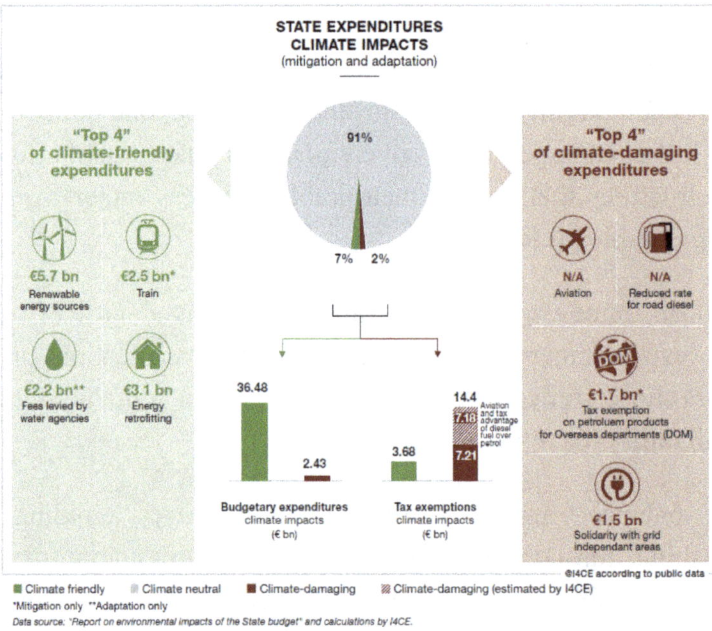

This transparency enables systematic identification of inconsistencies, agricultural subsidies undermining biodiversity goals, tax provisions favoring fossil fuels, and creates accountability for reform. The methodology has been refined through successive budget cycles and shared internationally, influencing green budgeting adoption across European Union members and beyond.

The French approach demonstrates that green budgeting requires neither perfect data nor complete methodology before beginning. Starting with available information and reasonable assumptions creates baseline assessments that improve iteratively. Political commitment matters more than technical perfection initially. Once frameworks establish themselves, data quality improves, methodologies refine, and institutional cultures shift toward routine consideration of environmental implications across fiscal decisions[94].

UAE Federal and Emirate-Level Coordination

The UAE's federal structure coordinates climate action across emirates while allowing local flexibility suited to distinct economic profiles and geographic conditions.

The federal Higher Committee for Green Development provides overall direction and coordinates international commitments. Individual emirates, Dubai, Abu Dhabi, Sharjah, implement strategies aligned with federal goals but tailored to local circumstances. Dubai emphasizes smart city technologies and clean energy.

Abu Dhabi focuses on large-scale renewables and carbon management. Sharjah advances circular economy and conservation.

Regular coordination meetings ensure alignment while knowledge-sharing platforms distribute lessons across emirates. Federal-level green bond frameworks establish standards that individual emirates can adopt, creating consistency while avoiding rigid uniformity.

---

[94] *French Ministry of Economy, Finance and Industrial and Digital Sovereignty, Green Budgeting, Government of France, https://www.tresor.economie.gouv.fr/Articles/tags/Green-budgeting, accessed 21 December 2024.*

This flexible coordination balances unity of purpose with diversity of implementation approaches suited to UAE's governance structure. The model offers insights for other federations navigating multilevel climate governance[95].

[95] *Ministry of Climate Change and Environment UAE, Federal Decree-Law No. (11) of 2024 on the Reduction of Climate Change Effects,* https://uaelegislation.gov.ae/en/legislations/2558., *accessed 21 December 2024.*

Key Takeaways

- Sovereign green bonds demonstrate national climate commitments through capital market instruments subject to disclosure, verification, and impact reporting standards.
- Sub-sovereign entities increasingly access green bond markets independently, demonstrating governance capacity and financial sophistication that attracts institutional investors.
- Green budgeting integrates environmental considerations throughout fiscal planning, expenditure allocation, and policy implementation rather than treating sustainability as separate category.
- Tax policy, procurement standards, and fiscal transfers provide powerful levers for aligning economic incentives with sustainability objectives across households, businesses, and subnational governments.
- Public-private partnerships mobilize private capital and expertise while sharing risks through well-designed contracts, guarantee mechanisms, and blended finance structures.
- Guarantee instruments and first-loss capital structures de-risk sustainable infrastructure investments, creating multiplier effects where modest public resources catalyze substantially larger private flows.
- Inter-ministerial coordination mechanisms and climate cabinets ensure policy coherence across sectors with different mandates but interconnected impacts on transition effectiveness.
- Vertical coordination between national and subnational governments requires clear responsibility allocation, adequate resource transfers, and accountability mechanisms that balance direction with flexibility.

- The UAE demonstrates comprehensive public sector leadership through sovereign green issuance, federal-emirate coordination, strategic budget allocation, and PPP deployment across sustainable infrastructure.
- Institutional capacity building, training, technical assistance, knowledge sharing, often determines implementation success more than direct project funding levels.

18

Academia, Research and Civil Society

Academia and civil society occupy essential positions in the sustainability ecosystem, they generate knowledge, challenge assumptions, build capacity, ensure accountability, and shape public discourse that determines whether green finance achieves transformative impact or remains confined to specialized circles.

Universities develop research methodologies, train future practitioners, and create intellectual frameworks that guide policy and practice. Civil society organizations monitor implementation, advocate for inclusion, and ensure that sustainability transitions serve public interest rather than narrow stakeholder groups.

The relationship between research institutions, civil society, and green finance practitioners has evolved from occasional consultation toward systematic collaboration. Universities increasingly engage with financial institutions, governments, and corporations as research partners rather than distant observers.

Civil society organizations participate in standard-setting processes, contribute to verification frameworks, and provide ground-level insights that improve project design. This collaborative ecosystem strengthens green finance through diverse perspectives, rigorous analysis, and public legitimacy.

Research institutions generate evidence that underpins effective sustainability action. They develop climate models that inform policy targets, create impact measurement methodologies that enable credible reporting, and analyze case studies that identify success factors and implementation barriers.

Yet significant data gaps persist, particularly around social impacts, nature-related risks, and emerging market contexts, that limit understanding and create space for greenwashing. Addressing these gaps requires sustained research investment, interdisciplinary collaboration, and partnerships between academic institutions and practitioners.

Global spending on climate research reached approximately USD 15 billion annually by 2023, yet developing countries receive less than 10% of climate research funding despite facing the most severe impacts and implementation challenges[96].

This disparity highlights how research agendas must expand geographically and thematically to support equitable transitions. Universities in emerging markets increasingly build research capabilities that address locally relevant questions while contributing to global knowledge.

Teaching green finance requires integration across traditional disciplinary boundaries. Finance students need environmental science literacy.

---

[96] *UNESCO, Global Investment in Climate Change Research, UNESCO Institute for Statistics, 2023, http://data.uis.unesco.org, accessed 22 December 2024.*

Engineers require understanding of capital markets. Policy students must grasp both technical feasibility and financial viability. These interdisciplinary imperative challenges conventional academic structures organized around distinct departments and specializations. Innovative programs blend perspectives, create team-teaching models, and emphasize problem-based learning that mirrors real-world complexity.

Civil society's role extends beyond advocacy to include transparency monitoring, accountability mechanisms, and bridge-building between technical experts and affected communities.

Organizations track corporate commitments against actual performance, expose greenwashing, and ensure that transition planning includes voices of workers, indigenous peoples, and vulnerable populations. This accountability function strengthens rather than obstructs green finance by building trust and directing capital toward genuinely impactful initiatives.

OBJECTIVES OF THE CHAPTER

This chapter will help individuals:

- Understand research priorities and data gaps that constrain green finance effectiveness and how academic institutions address them.
- Study innovative approaches to teaching sustainability finance across disciplines and building practitioner capacity.
- Explore civil society's role in ensuring transparency, accountability, and inclusion throughout sustainability transitions.
- Learn how universities engage communities through research partnerships, extension services, and public education.

- Examine examples from global contexts demonstrating academic-practitioner collaboration and civil society contributions.
- Recognize how research institutions, civil society, and financial sectors create mutually reinforcing ecosystems.
- Build confidence in evaluating research quality, educational program design, and civil society engagement strategies.
- Appreciate why informed public discourse determines political feasibility and social legitimacy of sustainability transitions.
- Understand how knowledge generation, capacity building, and accountability mechanisms strengthen green finance architecture.
- Identify opportunities for academic-practitioner partnerships and civil society collaboration in sustainability initiatives.

Research Agendas and Data Gaps: Building the Evidence Base

Research priorities in green finance span technical, social, and institutional dimensions. Climate modeling advances enable more precise scenario analysis and risk assessment. Nature-related financial disclosure methodologies develop frameworks for valuing ecosystem services and biodiversity impacts.

Social impact measurement evolves beyond anecdotal evidence toward rigorous metrics. Transition finance research examines how carbon-intensive sectors can achieve credible decarbonization pathways. Each area requires sustained investigation that combines theoretical development with empirical validation.

Data availability constrains research progress and practical implementation. While climate data has improved dramatically through satellite monitoring and global cooperation, social impact data remains fragmented and inconsistent. Nature-related information exists in ecological databases disconnected from financial systems. Small and medium enterprise sustainability performance lacks systematic measurement. Emerging market data often suffers from limited coverage, inconsistent standards, and access restrictions.

Academic institutions address data gaps through multiple approaches. Research consortia pool resources to create shared databases accessible to researchers globally.

University partnerships with corporations and governments facilitate data access while maintaining research independence. Open-access publications ensure findings reach practitioners in developing countries who cannot afford subscription fees.

Data science programs train students in techniques for extracting insights from imperfect, incomplete datasets, a critical skill for real-world application.

The Network for Greening the Financial System, comprising 135 central banks and supervisors, identified data quality and availability as top challenges facing climate risk assessment, with institutions calling for standardized, granular, and forward-looking data that current systems often cannot provide[97]. This recognition from financial authorities validates research community concerns and creates demand for academic contributions toward data solutions.

Methodological innovation advances research capabilities across multiple dimensions. Machine learning analyzes satellite imagery to monitor deforestation, land use changes, and agricultural practices at

---

[97] *Network for Greening the Financial System (NGFS), Progress Report on Bridging Data Gaps, NGFS, 2023, https://www.ngfs.net/en/progress-report-bridging-data-gaps, accessed 22 December 2024.*

scale impossible through ground surveys. Natural language processing evaluates corporate sustainability disclosures for specificity, consistency, and credibility.

Blockchain technologies enable transparent supply chain tracking that researchers can verify independently. Agent-based modeling simulates how policy changes ripple through complex economic systems, revealing unintended consequences before implementation. These computational tools transform researchers' ability to answer questions previously considered intractable due to scale, complexity, or data limitations.

Interdisciplinary collaboration addresses sustainability challenges that transcend traditional academic boundaries. Climate finance research requires expertise in atmospheric science, economics, engineering, and social sciences simultaneously.

Effective research teams combine specialists who understand both technical dimensions, how carbon sequestration actually works, and financial dimensions, how carbon markets function. Universities create formal interdisciplinary centers, joint appointments, and collaborative research grants that overcome departmental silos that historically fragmented knowledge production.

Regional research hubs build specialized expertise addressing geographic priorities. European institutions lead in circular economy finance and green taxonomy development. Asian universities advance renewable energy integration and industrial transition pathways. Latin American researchers pioneer nature-based solution finance and biodiversity credit markets.

African institutions develop off-grid energy finance and climate adaptation models. Middle Eastern centers focus on water-energy nexus, extreme heat resilience, and arid climate sustainability. This geographic diversity ensures research agendas reflect varied contexts rather than presuming universal solutions.

Action research methodologies engage practitioners as research partners rather than passive subjects. University teams collaborate with financial institutions to develop and test new green finance products. Academic researchers work alongside government agencies to evaluate policy effectiveness.

This embedded approach ensures research addresses real implementation barriers rather than theoretical abstractions while providing practitioners with rigorous evaluation of their innovations. The methodology recognizes that knowledge emerges from practice as much as from controlled studies, particularly in rapidly evolving fields where established theory lags behind market development.

Teaching Green Finance Across Disciplines: Building Capacity for Transition

Educational programs in sustainable finance must serve diverse audiences, finance professionals requiring environmental literacy, engineers needing capital markets understanding, public sector officials managing policy implementation, and community leaders advocating for equitable transitions. This diversity demands flexible curricula, varied pedagogical approaches, and recognition that no single course format serves all learning needs effectively.

Master's programs in sustainable finance integrate core finance competencies, corporate finance, asset management, risk analysis, with sustainability content on climate science, environmental policy, and impact measurement.

The integration approach ensures graduates combine financial rigor with environmental understanding rather than treating sustainability as optional addition to traditional finance. Programs increasingly require experiential components, internships, consulting projects, case competitions, that develop practical skills alongside theoretical knowledge.

Leading programs include Imperial College London's MSc in Climate Change, Management and Finance, Columbia University's MBA concentration in Social Enterprise, and National University of Singapore's MSc in Environmental Management.

Certificate programs serve working professionals unable to pursue full-time study. Intensive short courses, executive education, and online modules allow bankers, investors, corporate managers, and government officials to develop green finance capabilities without career interruption. Flexible formats accommodate learners across time zones and contexts. Micro-credentials validate specific competencies, carbon accounting, sustainable portfolio management, climate risk assessment, that professionals add to existing qualifications.

The Cambridge Institute for Sustainability Leadership and Oxford Sustainable Finance Programme exemplify executive education meeting practitioner needs for advanced, immediately applicable knowledge.

Universities globally launched over 400 degree programs focused on sustainability finance, business, and management between 2020 and 2023, reflecting surging student demand and employer requirements

for sustainability competencies[98]. This proliferation creates both opportunity and quality assurance challenges. Accreditation standards, faculty qualifications, and employer feedback help distinguish substantive programs from superficial offerings that add sustainability labels without genuine curricular transformation.

Interdisciplinary teaching challenges traditional academic structures where faculty expertise and course offerings concentrate within departments. Team-teaching brings together finance professors, environmental scientists, and social scientists to co-design and co-deliver courses that authentically integrate perspectives.

Guest practitioners share implementation experiences and real-world challenges that ground theoretical frameworks. Problem-based learning organizes courses around actual sustainability projects requiring students to integrate knowledge from multiple disciplines, a structure mirroring professional practice more closely than traditional lecture formats.

Case method teaching proves particularly effective for sustainability finance education.

Cases present complex decisions, should a bank finance this coal transition project, how should an investor evaluate nature-positive bonds, what frameworks should regulators adopt, that require students to wrestle with trade-offs, incomplete information, and stakeholder conflicts. Well-designed cases based on actual situations develop judgment alongside technical knowledge.

Harvard Business School, INSEAD, and other institutions build case libraries documenting sustainability finance decisions across geographies and sectors.

---

[98] *QS World University Rankings, Sustainability in Higher Education Report 2023, QS Quacquarelli Symonds, 2023, https://www.qs.com/portfolio-items/qs-sustainability-rankings/, accessed 22 December 2024.*

Online learning platforms democratize access to sustainability education. Coursera, edX, and FutureLearn host courses from leading universities reaching millions globally. These massive open online courses introduce foundational concepts to learners who might never attend traditional universities.

While completion rates vary, successful participants gain knowledge previously accessible only through expensive degree programs. The open-access model particularly benefits learners in developing countries where university capacity for specialized sustainability programs remains limited.

Simulation exercises immerse students in realistic decision-making environments. Climate negotiation simulations prepare students for international policy processes. Investment portfolio simulations require balancing financial returns with impact objectives under realistic constraints.

Supply chain simulations reveal trade-offs between cost, sustainability, and resilience. These experiential methods develop skills that traditional exams cannot assess, negotiation, judgment under uncertainty, stakeholder management, that prove essential in professional roles.

Faculty development ensures teaching quality matches program ambitions. Professional development workshops help finance faculty integrate sustainability content authentically rather than superficially. Environmental science faculty gain understanding of financial markets and investment processes that inform how they present concepts to business students.

Teaching materials, case libraries, and curriculum resources shared across institutions reduce development burden while disseminating best practices. Sabbatical programs place faculty in financial institutions or government agencies, building practical knowledge that enriches classroom teaching upon return.

Civil Society as Transparency and Accountability Partner: Strengthening Implementation

Civil society organizations fulfill essential accountability functions that strengthen green finance credibility and effectiveness. Environmental groups monitor corporate environmental performance, exposing gaps between commitments and actual results. Development organizations ensure transition policies include rather than marginalize vulnerable populations.

Research organizations evaluate policy effectiveness and propose improvements. Advocacy coalitions build political support for ambitious climate action. Together, these organizations create accountability ecosystems that complement rather than substitute for government oversight and market discipline.

Transparency monitoring represents civil society's most visible accountability contribution. Organizations track corporate climate commitments against disclosed emissions, investment patterns, and lobbying activities. ShareAction evaluates asset manager climate strategies and votes on climate-related shareholder resolutions across Europe.

Climate Action 100+ coordinates investor engagement with major emitters globally. Carbon Tracker analyzes fossil fuel company business models against climate scenarios. This scrutiny creates reputational incentives for alignment between stated commitments and actual practices. Public reporting makes information accessible to investors, consumers, and voters who can reinforce accountability through their own decisions.

Standard-setting processes increasingly include civil society representatives ensuring that frameworks serve broad public interest rather than narrow stakeholder preferences. Environmental NGOs participate in developing green taxonomies, ensuring technical criteria reflect scientific consensus rather than politically convenient thresholds. Social organizations contribute to just transition frameworks, bringing worker and community perspectives that might otherwise receive insufficient attention. Indigenous representatives shape nature-based solution standards, ensuring traditional knowledge and rights receive appropriate recognition in frameworks governing forest finance and conservation credits.

The Principles for Responsible Investment, with over 5,000 signatory institutions representing USD 128 trillion in assets, incorporates civil society perspectives through advisory committees and working groups that include NGO representatives alongside investors, demonstrating how standard-setting benefits from diverse stakeholder engagement[99]. This inclusive approach strengthens legitimacy while surfacing issues, forced labor in supply chains, community displacement from conservation, energy poverty in transitions, that technical experts might overlook without civil society input.

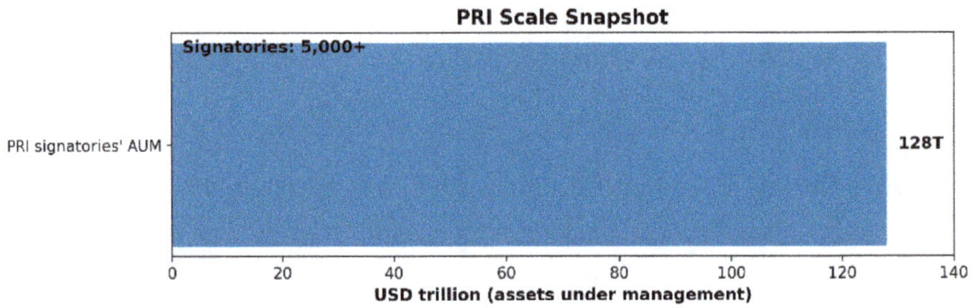

Civil society organizations serve as intermediaries connecting technical experts with affected communities. They translate complex policy proposals into accessible language that community members can evaluate.

[99] *Principles for Responsible Investment (PRI), Annual Report 2023, PRI Association, 2023, https://www.unpri.org/annual-report-2023, accessed 22 December 2024.*

Organizations gather community input on project design, ensuring local knowledge informs planning. They advocate for populations lacking direct voice in decision-making forums, informal workers, indigenous peoples, small farmers, whose participation determines whether transitions prove equitable. This bridge function ensures that green finance addresses ground-level realities rather than abstract models disconnected from implementation contexts.

Legal accountability mechanisms enforced by civil society organizations include climate litigation, disclosure challenges, and human rights complaints. ClientEarth uses legal action to compel stronger government climate policies across Europe.

Urgenda successfully sued the Dutch government for inadequate climate action, setting precedent for rights-based climate litigation. Earthrights International challenges corporate projects lacking adequate community consultation.

Strategic litigation creates precedents that shape behavior beyond individual cases while demonstrating that environmental and social commitments carry legal weight enforceable through courts.

Collaborative partnerships between civil society and financial institutions generate mutual learning that improves practice. WWF partnered with financial institutions to develop Principles for Sustainable Insurance.

The Nature Conservancy works with banks on conservation finance mechanisms. Oxfam engages investors on living wage standards in supply chains. These partnerships work best when structured as genuine collaboration rather than co-option, with civil society maintaining independence while engaging constructively on shared objectives.

Source: https://rw.wikipedia.org/wiki/Dosiye:Oxfam,_King_Street,_Hammersmith.jpg

Grassroots organizing complements technical advocacy by building political constituencies supporting ambitious climate action. 350.org mobilizes youth and community groups demanding fossil fuel divestment. Extinction Rebellion uses direct action to raise climate urgency.

The Sunrise Movement advocates for Green New Deal policies connecting climate and economic justice.

These movements create political space for policymakers to adopt policies that technical analysis supports but political calculation might otherwise delay. Mass mobilization demonstrates public demand that elected officials and corporate leaders cannot ignore.

Building an Informed Public Conversation: Democratizing Sustainability Knowledge

Public understanding of climate change, sustainability transitions, and green finance determines political feasibility and social legitimacy of ambitious action. Complex technical issues, carbon markets, sustainable taxonomies, just transition mechanisms, require translation into accessible language that enables informed citizen participation in democratic processes.

Academic institutions and civil society organizations share responsibility for public education that goes beyond advocacy to build genuine understanding of choices, trade-offs, and pathways forward.

Public lectures, community forums, and open courses make research findings accessible to general audiences beyond university walls. Institutions host events where faculty explain climate science without jargon, economists discuss carbon pricing trade-offs, and finance professors clarify green bond mechanics.

These educational initiatives serve civic functions beyond traditional teaching, creating informed citizenry capable of evaluating policy proposals and holding leaders accountable. Recording and distributing these presentations extends reach beyond those physically present.

Media engagement amplifies research reach when academics translate findings for journalists, write opinion pieces for general publications, and provide expert commentary on sustainability developments.

\Effective science communication requires different skills than academic writing, brevity, clarity, practical relevance, that academics must develop to contribute meaningfully to public discourse beyond specialized journals.

Communication training helps researchers present complex ideas without oversimplification that distorts while avoiding jargon that alienates general audiences unfamiliar with technical terminology.

A 2023 survey across 23 countries found that 69% of respondents expressed concern about climate change, yet only 37% felt they understood what actions would effectively address it, revealing a critical gap between awareness and actionable knowledge that education and communication must address[100].

This finding underscores the responsibility of experts to make knowledge accessible and practical for public engagement rather than remaining confined to academic or professional circles.

Digital platforms expand public education reach dramatically beyond geographic constraints. Massive open online courses make university content accessible globally at minimal cost.

Podcasts like "Drilled," "How to Save a Planet," and "Warm Regards" discuss sustainability topics in conversational formats accessible during commutes or exercise.

Social media enables researchers to share findings directly with interested audiences, bypassing traditional gatekeepers.

Webinars connect experts with professionals seeking continuing education across time zones. These digital channels democratize access to knowledge previously confined to university campuses, expensive conferences, or subscription publications.

[100] *Pew Research Center, International Attitudes Toward Climate Change, Pew Research Center, 2023, https://www.pewresearch.org/global/, accessed 22 December 2024.*

Source: *https://www.france-voyage.com/tourism/photos-city-science-industry-618.htm*

Visualization techniques make abstract concepts concrete and data comprehensible to audiences processing information graphically. Interactive maps show climate vulnerability overlaid with renewable energy potential and population density. Carbon footprint calculators personalize climate impact, making abstract emissions tangible through everyday activities.

Budget visualizations illustrate green spending as proportion of total government expenditure with comparison to subsidies undermining climate goals. Infographics distill complex reports into shareable formats circulatable through social networks. Climate Central, Carbon Brief, and Our World in Data exemplify organizations making data accessible through sophisticated visualization.

Cultural approaches to climate communication recognize that different communities respond to distinct framing, messengers, and narratives.

Faith-based organizations emphasize stewardship values and moral obligations to creation. Business networks highlight economic opportunities, competitive advantages, and market leadership. Youth movements center intergenerational justice and betrayal by previous generations.

Community organizations focus on local health improvements, job quality, and neighborhood prosperity. Effective public engagement meets audiences where they are rather than imposing uniform messaging that resonates with educated urban professionals but fails elsewhere.

Museums and science centers provide informal learning environments reaching audiences who might not attend university lectures or read academic publications. Climate exhibitions explain science through interactive displays. Planetarium shows visualize future climate scenarios.

Maker spaces enable hands-on experimentation with renewable energy technologies. These institutions reach families, school groups, and tourists, expanding climate literacy beyond those actively seeking information through traditional educational channels.

University and Community Engagement Initiatives: Connecting Knowledge with Action

Universities advance sustainability beyond research and teaching through community engagement that applies knowledge to local challenges, builds partnerships with diverse stakeholders, and demonstrates institutional commitment to societal wellbeing. Campus sustainability initiatives model practices that communities can adapt to their contexts.

Extension services share expertise with businesses and governments lacking internal capacity. Student engagement programs channel youthful energy toward practical projects producing tangible results while developing professional capabilities.

Campus operations as living laboratories allow universities to test sustainability innovations before broader deployment reduces risk for early adopters. Green building retrofits demonstrate efficiency technologies while generating performance data validating savings claims.

Renewable energy installations provide training opportunities for students while producing electricity. Waste reduction programs pilot circular economy approaches at manageable scale. Transportation demand management experiments with behavior change strategies before cities attempt system-wide implementation.

These implementations generate learning that informs regional adoption while reducing university environmental footprints, creating alignment between institutional values and operational practice.

Universities representing over 50 million students across 70 countries committed to carbon neutrality by 2030 or 2050 through initiatives like the UN Race to Zero campaign, making higher education a significant force in climate action while creating models for other institutions to follow[101].

These commitments translate into tangible investments in renewable energy, efficiency upgrades, and operational transformation that students experience directly. Arizona State University, University of British Columbia, and ETH Zurich exemplify institutions achieving substantial emissions reductions while maintaining research excellence and student services.

---

[101] *UN Climate Change, Race to Zero Campaign, United Nations Framework Convention on Climate Change,* https://unfccc.int/climate-action/engagement/marrakech-partnership-for-global-climate-action/actors/meet-the-champions/work-of-the-climate-high-level-champions *accessed 22 December 2024.*

Extension services connect university expertise with community needs through technical assistance, training programs, and collaborative problem-solving addressing locally relevant challenges. Agricultural extension helps farmers adopt climate-smart practices appropriate for regional conditions.

Business extension advises small enterprises on sustainability integration within budget constraints. Municipal extension supports local governments with sustainability planning, grant applications, and project preparation. These services ensure research benefits reach populations beyond university walls while grounding academic work in practical realities that inform future research agendas.

Student engagement initiatives channel learning toward community impact that develops professional capabilities alongside civic commitment. Service-learning courses combine academic study with community projects addressing sustainability challenges, students might conduct energy audits for nonprofits, develop business plans for social enterprises, or assist municipalities with climate action planning. Student consulting programs offer pro bono sustainability advice to organizations lacking resources for professional consultants. Research assistantships involve students in faculty projects while building technical skills, professional networks, and experience with rigorous methodology.

University-community partnerships address sustainability challenges requiring sustained collaboration over years rather than one-time interventions. A university might partner with municipalities on climate adaptation planning, providing technical analysis, student research support, and access to climate modeling tools.

Partnerships with corporations might pilot green finance products, combining academic rigor with industry implementation capacity and market knowledge. Relationships with civil society organizations might co-design research agendas ensuring academic work addresses practitioner priorities rather than merely pursuing questions interesting to rcscarchcrs.

Technology transfer offices facilitate commercialization of university research, creating pathways from laboratory discoveries to market deployment at scale. These offices help faculty navigate patents, licensing, and startup formation, processes unfamiliar to most academics. Incubators provide physical space, mentorship, and seed funding for university spin-offs developing clean technologies.

When successful, these ventures create employment, demonstrate innovation pathways, and generate revenue supporting further research, creating virtuous cycles linking discovery, education, and economic development.

Community science projects engage non-academics in research, democratizing knowledge production while expanding data collection capacity. Volunteers monitor water quality in local streams, providing data supplementing professional monitoring. Citizens document species observations through platforms like iNaturalist, contributing to biodiversity research. Community members map neighborhood heat islands, revealing patterns that official weather stations miss. These collaborations build public understanding of scientific methods while generating data researchers cannot collect alone, creating authentic partnerships rather than token participation.

Key Takeaways

- Research institutions generate evidence, methodologies, and frameworks underpinning effective green finance while addressing critical data gaps through methodological innovation and global collaboration.
- Teaching sustainable finance requires interdisciplinary integration, experiential learning, and flexible formats serving diverse audiences from undergraduate students to senior executives across sectors.
- Civil society organizations strengthen green finance through transparency monitoring, standard-setting participation, legal accountability mechanisms, and ensuring inclusion of marginalized voices.
- Public education initiatives translate complex sustainability concepts into accessible knowledge enabling informed citizen participation in democratic processes shaping climate policy.
- University community engagement applies academic expertise to local challenges while creating living laboratories testing innovations before broader deployment reduces risk.
- Geographic diversity in research priorities ensures knowledge production reflects varied contexts, European circular economy expertise, Asian industrial transition experience, African off-grid energy innovation, Latin American nature-based solutions, Middle Eastern water-energy nexus focus.
- Academic-practitioner partnerships generate mutual learning improving both research relevance and implementation effectiveness through embedded researchers and action research methodologies.

19

Tools and Skills for Future Professionals

The transformation toward sustainable finance creates demand for professionals who combine financial acumen with environmental literacy, technical precision with interdisciplinary thinking, and analytical rigor with practical implementation capabilities.

This convergence reshapes professional development across sectors, creating pathways where diverse backgrounds, finance, engineering, policy, data science, environmental studies, contribute meaningfully to climate-aligned capital flows and sustainability transitions.

Professional readiness in green finance extends beyond mastering isolated competencies. It requires building integrated skill sets where financial analysis informs environmental decisions, sustainability frameworks guide investment choices, and data literacy enables credible impact measurement.

The field rewards professionals who move fluidly between quantitative analysis and qualitative judgment, between specialized technical depth and cross-functional collaboration, between theoretical frameworks and practical application.

Global labor markets reflect this evolution. **The LinkedIn Global Green Skills Report 2023 indicates that green skills appeared in 13.3% of job postings across major economies, up from 9.6% in 2015, with demand growing fastest in financial services, professional services, and corporate functions**[102]. This acceleration signals how sustainability competencies transition from specialized niches into mainstream professional requirements across industries and geographies.

The tools and skills explored in this chapter form foundational elements for professionals entering or advancing within sustainable finance. Financial literacy enables non-finance professionals to communicate value propositions effectively. Sustainability frameworks help finance

---

[102] *LinkedIn Economic Graph, Global Green Skills Report 2023, LinkedIn Corporation, 2023, https://economicgraph.linkedin.com/research/global-green-skills-report, accessed 23 December 2024.*

professionals integrate environmental and social considerations systematically.

Data capabilities transform raw information into actionable insights. Interdisciplinary collaboration amplifies individual expertise through collective intelligence. Project-based learning accelerates development through authentic challenges requiring applied knowledge.

Understanding these capabilities as interconnected rather than isolated strengthens professional effectiveness. Financial literacy without sustainability knowledge produces analysis blind to long-term risks. Sustainability expertise without financial fluency struggles to influence capital allocation decisions. Technical skills without collaboration capabilities limit implementation impact. Each dimension reinforces others, creating professional versatility that organizations increasingly value and seek.

OBJECTIVES OF THE CHAPTER

This chapter will help individuals:

- Build essential financial literacy enabling non-finance professionals to communicate sustainability value in business terms.
- Master sustainability frameworks that integrate environmental and social considerations into financial analysis.
- Develop data analysis capabilities for measuring, monitoring, and verifying sustainability impacts credibly.
- Strengthen interdisciplinary collaboration skills essential for addressing complex sustainability challenges.

- Apply project-based learning approaches that accelerate professional development through hands-on experience.
- Understand how different skill dimensions interconnect to create comprehensive professional capabilities.
- Identify specific competencies most relevant to target roles and career trajectories in green finance.
- Recognize learning pathways suited to different professional contexts and development stages.
- Build confidence in translating technical knowledge into practical application across diverse settings.
- Appreciate how continuous capability building positions professionals for emerging opportunities in evolving markets.

Essential Financial Literacy for Non-Finance Readers: Speaking the Language of Value

Financial literacy enables professionals from environmental science, engineering, policy, and social sectors to translate sustainability initiatives into business value propositions. When professionals understand how organizations measure success and allocate resources, they position environmental improvements as strategic opportunities rather than compliance obligations or cost centers.

Core financial concepts provide universal frameworks for decision-making across sectors. Return on investment quantifies value created relative to capital deployed. Payback period indicates how quickly initial investments generate returns.

Net present value accounts for time value of money when evaluating long-term projects. Internal rate of return enables comparison across investment opportunities with different scales and timeframes. These metrics form the analytical language executives use daily when prioritizing initiatives and allocating budgets.

Understanding financial statements reveals organizational priorities and constraints. Balance sheets show capital allocation across assets and financing sources. Income statements track revenue generation and cost structures. Cash flow statements reveal liquidity patterns and investment cycles.

Reading these documents helps professionals identify where sustainability improvements strengthen financial performance, reducing operating costs, mitigating risks, unlocking revenue opportunities, or enhancing asset values.

The Global Reporting Initiative's 2023 analysis found that 78% of large corporations worldwide now publish sustainability reports, yet only 43% effectively integrate financial and sustainability data in ways that inform capital allocation decisions[103]. This gap highlights opportunities for professionals who bridge financial and sustainability domains, translating environmental performance into financially material insights that influence strategic decisions.

Capital budgeting frameworks structure how organizations evaluate potential investments. Presenting sustainability projects using established evaluation criteria, payback analysis, NPV calculations, risk-adjusted returns, demonstrates financial sophistication while making proposals comparable to conventional alternatives.

When renewable energy installations show competitive returns, efficiency upgrades deliver measurable savings, or circular economy

---

[103] *Global Reporting Initiative, The State of Sustainability Reporting 2023, GRI, 2023, https://www.globalreporting.org/news/news-center/gri-report-shows-exponential-rise-in-sustainability-reporting/, accessed 23 December 2024.*

models reduce input costs, financial analysis makes value visible to decision-makers.

Risk assessment represents another dimension where financial literacy strengthens sustainability work. Understanding how organizations evaluate and price risks, credit risk, operational risk, market risk, enables professionals to frame climate risks, nature-related dependencies, and social factors using familiar analytical structures. When physical climate risks translate into asset impairment calculations or transition risks appear in scenario-based valuations, sustainability considerations integrate naturally into risk management frameworks.

The table below illustrates core financial concepts and their sustainability applications:

Financial Concept	Definition	Sustainability Application	Example
Return on Investment (ROI)	Net return divided by investment cost	Quantifying financial value from efficiency upgrades	Solar installation generating 18% ROI through energy savings
Payback Period	Time required to recover initial investment	Demonstrating quick wins for resource efficiency	LED retrofit paying back investment in 2.3 years
Net Present Value (NPV)	Present value of future cash flows minus initial cost	Evaluating long-term green infrastructure	Waste-to-energy facility with positive NPV over 20-year horizon

Internal Rate of Return (IRR)	Discount rate making NPV equal to zero	Comparing renewable energy alternatives	Wind project achieving 12% IRR vs. 8% threshold

This framework helps non-finance professionals structure sustainability proposals using analytical approaches familiar to finance decision-makers.

Professional development in financial literacy follows multiple pathways. Formal coursework through business schools or executive education provides structured learning. Industry certifications validate competencies. Online platforms offer flexible, self-paced modules.

Mentorship relationships with finance colleagues enable contextual learning within specific organizational settings. Reading financial publications builds vocabulary and familiarity with current discussions. Practical application through actual project analysis accelerates understanding more effectively than passive study alone.

Sustainability Tools for Finance Professionals: Integrating Environmental and Social Factors

Finance professionals entering sustainability discover structured frameworks that bring analytical rigor to environmental and social performance measurement. These tools enable systematic integration of sustainability factors into traditional financial analysis, investment decisions, and risk management processes.

The Task Force on Climate-related Financial Disclosures provides globally recognized frameworks for assessing climate risks and opportunities. TCFD organizes disclosure around four pillars, governance, strategy, risk management, metrics and targets, helping finance professionals integrate climate considerations systematically rather than treating them as separate reporting exercises.

The framework's scenario analysis component encourages forward-looking assessment across different climate pathways, complementing historical financial analysis with prospective risk evaluation.

The Sustainability Accounting Standards Board offers industry-specific guidance on financially material sustainability topics. SASB identifies environmental, social, and governance issues most likely to affect financial performance within each sector, helping analysts prioritize attention on factors with genuine business implications.

This materiality focus aligns naturally with financial analysis principles, making SASB particularly accessible for finance professionals seeking structured entry into sustainability integration.

SASB standards now cover 77 industries across 11 sectors, with research demonstrating that companies performing well on SASB-identified material factors show 2.7 percentage points higher return

on equity compared to industry peers over five-year periods[104]. This performance correlation strengthens the business case for systematic sustainability integration within investment analysis and corporate strategy.

The Science Based Targets initiative provides methodologies for setting corporate emissions reduction goals aligned with climate science. Finance professionals evaluate SBTi-verified targets when assessing corporate transition credibility, using these commitments as indicators of strategic alignment with global climate pathways. Understanding SBTi frameworks helps analysts distinguish ambitious, science-aligned targets from less credible commitments.

Impact measurement frameworks guide assessment of social and environmental outcomes alongside financial returns.

The Impact Management Project's five dimensions, what outcomes, who experiences them, how much change occurs, contribution beyond counterfactual, and risk of outcomes differing from expectations, structure comprehensive impact analysis.

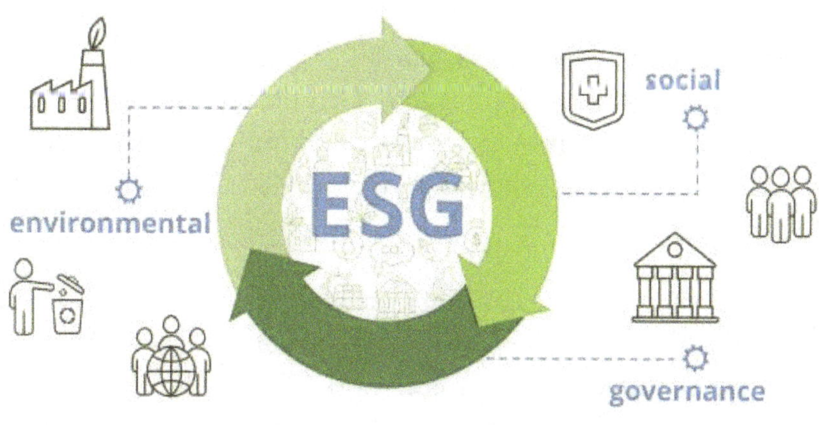

[104] *SASB, Research on the Sustainability Accounting Standards Board, SASB Foundation, 2022, https://www.sasb.org/research/, accessed 23 December 2024.*

The IRIS+ system from GIIN offers standardized metrics enabling comparison across investments and portfolios.

Portfolio construction tools help investors integrate sustainability systematically. ESG rating methodologies from providers like MSCI, Sustainalytics, and ISS ESG inform security selection and risk assessment. Portfolio carbon footprinting techniques measure emissions exposure across holdings.

Climate value-at-risk models estimate potential losses under different climate scenarios. These quantitative tools complement qualitative sustainability assessment with measurable metrics suitable for portfolio management disciplines.

Blended finance structures represent another toolkit finance professionals master when working across public, private, and philanthropic capital. Understanding how concessional capital, guarantees, first-loss tranches, and performance-based payments de-risk sustainable infrastructure enables structuring transactions that mobilize commercial capital for projects serving development and environmental objectives alongside financial returns.

Professional development in sustainability tools often combines formal training with practical application. Certification programs provide structured learning pathways. Industry working groups share emerging practices. Conferences showcase tool application across different contexts.

Internal pilots within organizations enable experimentation before full deployment. Collaboration with sustainability specialists builds understanding through joint project work. This multifaceted approach develops genuine fluency rather than superficial familiarity with frameworks.

Working with Data, Scenarios and Impact Metrics: Building Analytical Foundations

Data capabilities distinguish exceptional professionals in sustainable finance as organizations face increasing expectations for quantifying sustainability performance. Professionals skilled in gathering, validating, analyzing, and communicating complex data become invaluable as markets demand credible measurement backing sustainability claims.

Data quality assessment represents a foundational skill. Unlike financial data governed by standardized accounting principles, sustainability data originates from diverse sources using varied methodologies and reporting boundaries.

Developing judgment about data reliability, completeness, and comparability ensures analyses rest on solid foundations. This includes understanding differences between modeled estimates and measured data, recognizing reporting boundary variations, and identifying potential gaps or inconsistencies requiring deeper investigation.

Scenario analysis tools enable exploration of uncertainty across climate pathways, policy trajectories, technology developments, and market shifts. Rather than predicting single outcomes, scenario thinking examines multiple plausible futures to test strategic resilience.

The Network for Greening the Financial System provides standardized climate scenarios, orderly transition, delayed transition, current policies, that financial institutions use for risk assessment. Mastering scenario frameworks helps professionals evaluate how different futures might affect business models, asset valuations, and investment strategies.

The NGFS climate scenarios, released in 2020 and updated regularly, are now used by over 300 financial institutions globally for climate risk assessment, representing combined assets exceeding USD 130 trillion and establishing scenario analysis as standard practice in

financial risk management[105]. This widespread adoption demonstrates how forward-looking analytical approaches complement traditional backward-looking financial analysis.

Impact measurement frameworks quantify environmental and social outcomes from investments and projects. This includes carbon accounting methodologies tracking emissions across scopes and value chains, biodiversity metrics assessing ecosystem health and species impacts, water footprint calculations measuring consumption and pollution, social indicators evaluating employment quality and community wellbeing, and financial inclusion metrics assessing access and affordability.

Each domain requires understanding both measurement methodologies and interpretation nuances.

Data visualization transforms complex information into accessible insights for diverse audiences. Learning visualization principles and tools, whether Excel, Tableau, Power BI, or programming languages like Python and R, amplifies communication effectiveness.

Effective visualizations highlight patterns, enable comparisons, show trends over time, and make technical findings accessible to non-technical stakeholders. This translation capability proves essential when presenting sustainability analysis to boards, investors, or public audiences.

Statistical literacy supports rigorous analysis. Understanding correlation versus causation, statistical significance, confidence intervals, and regression analysis enables sophisticated investigation of relationships

---

[105] *Network for Greening the Financial System (NGFS), NGFS Climate Scenarios for Central Banks and Supervisors, NGFS, 2023, https://www.ngfs.net/ngfs-scenarios-portal/ , accessed 23 December 2024.*

between sustainability performance and financial outcomes. These capabilities allow professionals to move beyond anecdotal evidence toward systematic analysis that withstands critical scrutiny.

The table below outlines data competencies across different applications:

Data Skill	Application in Green Finance	Tools/Frameworks	Development Pathway
Data Quality Assessment	Validating sustainability disclosures and ESG ratings	Materiality frameworks, audit standards	Training in data verification, working with auditors
Scenario Analysis	Evaluating climate risks across pathways	NGFS scenarios, TCFD framework	Workshops on scenario planning, practical application
Impact Measurement	Quantifying environmental and social outcomes	IRIS+ metrics, GRI standards	Impact assessment courses, project experience
Data Visualization	Communicating findings to stakeholders	Tableau, Power BI, Python	Data visualization training, practice with real datasets
Statistical Analysis	Identifying performance correlations	R, Python, SPSS	Statistics coursework, applied

			research projects

This structured view helps professionals identify which data capabilities most directly support their target roles and development priorities.

Interdisciplinary Collaboration Skills: Bridging Knowledge Domains

Sustainability challenges transcend traditional disciplinary boundaries, requiring seamless collaboration between professionals with diverse expertise. Developing strong interdisciplinary skills multiplies individual effectiveness and expands career opportunities as organizations increasingly value professionals who bridge technical specializations.

Effective collaboration begins with recognizing that different disciplines offer unique, complementary perspectives on shared challenges. Engineers understand technical feasibility and operational constraints. Environmental scientists grasp ecological systems and planetary boundaries.

Finance professionals assess economic viability and investment requirements. Social scientists consider community impacts and equity dimensions. Policy specialists navigate regulatory frameworks and governmental processes. Success emerges when teams harness these diverse viewpoints rather than privileging single perspectives or allowing disciplinary silos to fragment understanding.

Active listening forms the foundation of productive interdisciplinary work. This involves seeking to understand colleagues' perspectives fully before evaluating how they relate to one's own expertise, asking clarifying questions that surface underlying assumptions, probing analytical frameworks informing different viewpoints, and recognizing valid insights even when framed in unfamiliar language. Active listening requires intellectual humility, acknowledging that no single discipline possesses complete understanding of complex sustainability challenges.

Professional language varies significantly across disciplines, creating potential communication barriers.

Skilled collaborators learn to translate between disciplinary vocabularies, explaining technical concepts in accessible terms while maintaining precision, identifying when seemingly different terminology refers to similar concepts, and bridging analytical frameworks that structure thinking differently across fields. This translation capability proves especially valuable when facilitating cross-functional teams or presenting technical work to diverse audiences.

Structured collaboration approaches enhance effectiveness. Regular cross-functional meetings with clear agendas maintain alignment. Shared documentation platforms ensure information accessibility. Defined roles clarify responsibilities while allowing flexibility.

Explicit decision-making processes prevent confusion about authority and accountability. Post-project reviews capture lessons improving future collaboration. These structures support productive teamwork without stifling creativity or imposing unnecessary bureaucracy.

Large-scale sustainability initiatives demonstrate interdisciplinary collaboration principles. Urban sustainability projects require coordination between urban planners, architects, engineers, economists, social scientists, and policy specialists. Renewable energy transitions engage electrical engineers, financial analysts, environmental scientists, community organizers, and regulatory experts.

Nature-based solution projects integrate ecologists, hydrologists, agricultural specialists, carbon accountants, and indigenous knowledge holders. These examples illustrate how ambitious goals necessitate diverse expertise working in concert rather than parallel.

Professional development in collaboration skills combines deliberate practice with reflection. Volunteering for cross-functional projects builds experience.

Attending interdisciplinary conferences exposes professionals to different analytical approaches. Reading outside one's discipline develops broader perspective. Seeking feedback on communication effectiveness from colleagues in other fields identifies improvement opportunities.

Reflecting on collaborative experiences, what worked well, what created friction, how processes might improve, transforms experience into learning.

Project-Based Learning Approaches: Accelerating Development Through Application

Project-based learning accelerates professional development by engaging individuals in authentic challenges requiring applied knowledge and producing tangible outcomes.

Rather than passively consuming information through lectures or reading, learners actively construct understanding through hands-on experience addressing realistic problems with uncertain solutions and multiple constraints.

Sustainable finance provides rich opportunities for project-based learning across different scales and contexts.

Projects might involve analyzing corporate sustainability performance using established frameworks, designing green financial products for specific market segments, creating impact measurement systems for investment portfolios, evaluating climate risks in existing asset holdings, developing sustainable supply chain finance programs, or preparing green bond frameworks for potential issuers. Each project type develops distinct yet transferable capabilities.

Effective project design incorporates several elements. Clear objectives specify what participants should accomplish and learn. Realistic constraints mirror actual professional challenges including time limitations, data availability, stakeholder requirements, and resource constraints.

Collaborative requirements encourage teamwork and diverse perspective integration. Feedback mechanisms enable course correction and continuous improvement. Presentation components develop communication skills alongside technical capabilities. Reflection activities help participants extract generalizable lessons from specific experiences.

Organizations implement project-based learning through various structures. Rotation programs move early-career professionals through different functions via substantial project assignments. Innovation challenges invite employees to propose and develop sustainability initiatives.

Consulting projects connect professionals with external organizations seeking solutions. Hackathons compress intensive problem-solving into short timeframes encouraging creativity. Strategic task forces address specific organizational challenges through cross-functional collaboration. Each format offers distinct learning opportunities suited to different objectives and organizational contexts.

Academic institutions increasingly embrace project-based pedagogies in sustainability programs. Capstone projects require students to apply integrated knowledge toward solving actual problems presented by partner organizations.

Studio courses structure semester-long engagement with community or corporate partners. Consulting practicums place student teams with clients requiring sustainability analysis or strategy development. These approaches develop professional capabilities alongside academic knowledge, preparing graduates for immediate contribution rather than requiring extended onboarding.

Self-directed project-based learning proves accessible for motivated professionals at any career stage. Identifying a sustainability challenge within one's organization or community creates the project foundation.

Assembling a small team representing different perspectives brings diverse capabilities. Conducting thorough research into best practices, local context, and stakeholder needs builds understanding. Developing detailed implementation proposals with financial analysis, impact projections, and execution plans demonstrates professional quality work. Presenting recommendations to decision-makers provides authentic communication practice.

Documenting lessons learned regardless of adoption creates knowledge artifacts for future reference.

The value of project-based learning extends beyond immediate skill development. Projects create portfolio artifacts demonstrating capabilities to potential employers or clients.

They build professional networks through collaboration and stakeholder engagement. They generate confidence from successfully navigating ambiguous challenges. They reveal personal interests and strengths informing career direction. They produce tangible impacts when projects achieve implementation.

These multifaceted benefits explain why experiential learning accelerates professional development more effectively than purely didactic approaches.

Key Takeaways

- Financial literacy enables non-finance professionals to using business language that resonates with decision-makers and influences capital allocation.
- Sustainability frameworks provide finance professionals with structured approaches for integrating environmental and social factors systematically into investment analysis and risk management.
- Data capabilities, quality assessment, scenario analysis, impact measurement, visualization, statistical analysis, transform sustainability claims from aspirational statements into credible, measurable performance tracking.
- Interdisciplinary collaboration skills prove essential as sustainability challenges transcend traditional disciplinary boundaries, requiring professionals who bridge technical specializations effectively.
- Project-based learning accelerates professional development through authentic challenges that develop applied capabilities, build confidence, and create tangible portfolio artifacts.
- Professional readiness requires integrated skill sets where financial analysis, sustainability frameworks, data literacy, collaboration capabilities, and practical application reinforce each other rather than existing in isolation.
- Global labor markets increasingly reward sustainability competencies, with green skills appearing in growing percentages of job postings across financial services, professional services, and corporate functions.
- Different learning pathways, formal education, certifications, online courses, mentorship, conferences, self-directed projects,

serve varied professional contexts and development stages with distinct benefits.

- Active listening, professional language translation, and structured collaboration approaches enhance interdisciplinary team effectiveness across complex sustainability initiatives.
- Continuous capability building positions communicate sustainability value
- professionals for emerging opportunities as green finance evolves, creates new roles, and expands across geographies and sectors globally.

20

Careers and Capacity Building in Green Finance

The green finance profession has evolved into a dynamic career landscape offering diverse opportunities across financial institutions, corporations, public agencies, advisory firms, and research organizations. Professionals entering this field contribute to one of the most consequential economic transformations in human history, redirecting capital flows toward sustainable development while building resilient financial systems aligned with planetary boundaries.

Career pathways in sustainable finance blend traditional financial expertise with specialized knowledge in climate science, environmental policy, impact measurement, and sectoral transitions. This interdisciplinary nature creates opportunities for professionals from varied backgrounds, finance graduates seeking purpose-driven careers, engineers translating technical knowledge into investment frameworks, policy experts shaping regulatory landscapes, and data scientists building analytical tools that measure sustainability performance.

The field's rapid growth creates substantial demand for skilled professionals. LinkedIn's 2023 Global Green Skills Report indicates that **green finance roles grew by 40% annually between 2020 and 2023, significantly outpacing overall financial sector job growth**[106]. This expansion reflects how sustainability considerations have moved from specialized functions to core business operations across the financial ecosystem.

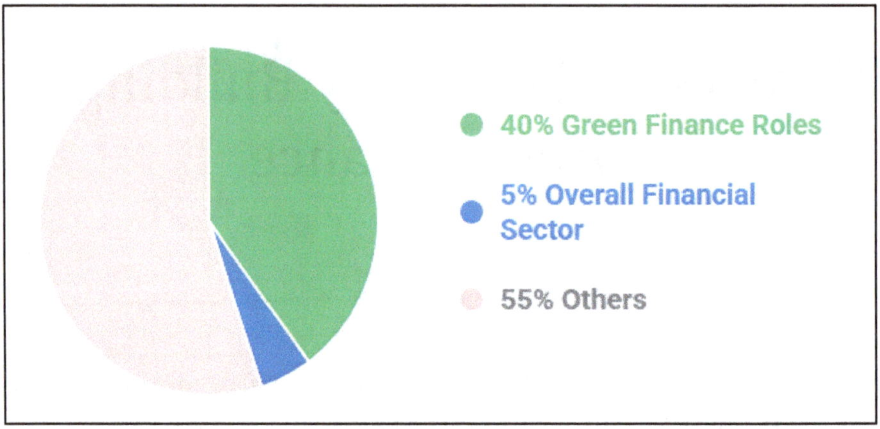

Source: Global Green Skills Report 2023

Successful careers in green finance require continuous learning because the field evolves rapidly through regulatory changes, technological innovations, methodological refinements, and shifting market expectations. Professionals who cultivate adaptability, interdisciplinary thinking, and commitment to lifelong learning position themselves for sustained success and meaningful impact.

This chapter explores career opportunities across institutional settings, examines capacity-building pathways through training and certification, and provides frameworks for designing personal learning strategies that support long-term professional development in sustainable finance.

---

[106] *LinkedIn Economic Graph, Global Green Skills Report 2023, LinkedIn Corporation, 2023, https://economicgraph.linkedin.com/research/global-green-skills-report, accessed 24 December 2024.*

OBJECTIVES OF THE CHAPTER

This chapter will help individuals:

- Explore emerging roles in banks, asset management firms, and corporate sustainability departments.
- Understand career opportunities within public institutions and development finance organizations.
- Examine advisory, consulting, and research pathways in sustainable finance.
- Learn about training programs, professional certifications, and continuous learning resources.
- Develop frameworks for designing personalized learning roadmaps aligned with career objectives.
- Recognize how diverse professional backgrounds contribute value to green finance teams.
- Build confidence in navigating career transitions into sustainable finance roles.
- Understand skills combinations that create competitive advantages in the job market.
- Appreciate how green finance careers balance financial performance with environmental impact.
- See capacity building as an ongoing process rather than a destination.

1. Emerging Roles in Banks, Asset Management and Corporate Settings

Financial institutions have created specialized roles that integrate sustainability into core business functions. Sustainable finance relationship managers work with corporate clients to structure green loans, sustainability-linked facilities, and transition finance arrangements. These professionals combine credit analysis skills with understanding of environmental frameworks, sectoral transition pathways, and sustainability performance metrics. They serve as trusted advisors helping clients access sustainable finance while strengthening their own environmental strategies.

ESG analysts within banks evaluate climate risks, assess sustainability performance of borrowers, and contribute to portfolio alignment strategies. They build models that quantify emissions exposure, conduct scenario analysis, and support credit decision-making through sustainability lenses. Strong ESG analysts blend financial modeling capabilities with environmental knowledge and data analytics skills.

Green bond specialists manage labelled bond issuances from framework development through post-issuance reporting. They coordinate with external reviewers, ensure regulatory compliance, track use of proceeds, and measure impact. This role requires understanding of bond markets, familiarity with sustainable finance principles, and project management capabilities.

Asset management firms employ portfolio managers focused on sustainable investment strategies, thematic funds targeting renewable energy or circular economy opportunities, impact investment vehicles delivering measurable environmental outcomes, and ESG-integrated strategies applying sustainability analysis across traditional asset classes. These roles demand investment acumen combined with deep sustainability expertise.

Climate risk officers within asset managers assess physical and transition risks across portfolios, implement scenario analysis frameworks, and engage companies on climate strategy. They work at the intersection of risk management, climate science, and investment analysis.

Corporate sustainability teams have expanded beyond compliance functions to strategic roles influencing capital allocation. Sustainability directors develop transition plans, set science-based targets, coordinate cross-functional implementation, and communicate progress to stakeholders. Corporate green finance managers structure sustainability-linked financing, prepare green bond frameworks, and manage investor relationships around ESG topics.

Supply chain sustainability managers work with suppliers to reduce emissions, improve environmental performance, and build resilience. This role combines procurement expertise with sustainability knowledge and relationship management skills.

Role Category	Key Functions	Essential Skills	Career Entry Points
Relationship Management	Client advisory, product structuring	Credit analysis, sustainability frameworks	Banking, corporate finance
ESG Analysis	Risk assessment, performance evaluation	Financial modeling, environmental metrics	Equity research, credit analysis
Portfolio Management	Investment selection, strategy execution	Investment analysis, sustainability expertise	Asset management, financial analysis
Corporate Sustainability	Strategy development, implementation coordination	Project management, stakeholder engagement	Operations, strategy consulting
Risk Management	Climate scenario analysis, exposure assessment	Risk modeling, climate science	Risk functions, quantitative analysis

This table illustrates how green finance roles combine traditional financial capabilities with specialized sustainability knowledge, creating career opportunities for professionals with diverse skill combinations.

2. Opportunities in Public Institutions and Development Finance

Public sector institutions offer meaningful career pathways for professionals seeking to shape policy frameworks, deploy catalytic capital, and support sustainable development at systemic levels. Central banks hire specialists in climate risk supervision who develop regulatory guidance, conduct stress testing exercises, and assess system-wide exposures. These roles suit professionals with backgrounds in banking supervision, risk management, or macroeconomic analysis who want to influence financial stability frameworks.

Securities regulators employ sustainable finance experts who design disclosure requirements, review green bond frameworks, and monitor market integrity. This work shapes information architecture that guides trillions in capital allocation decisions. Regulatory roles often attract lawyers, accountants, and financial analysts seeking to build market infrastructure.

Development finance institutions maintain large teams focused on sustainable finance across project evaluation, transaction structuring, risk management, and impact measurement. Project officers assess renewable energy proposals, sustainable infrastructure projects, and conservation initiatives. They conduct technical due diligence, structure financing arrangements, and monitor implementation. These roles combine financial analysis with sectoral expertise in energy, infrastructure, agriculture, or natural resource management.

Policy analysts within development banks research best practices, evaluate program effectiveness, and design new financial instruments. They contribute to knowledge products that advance the field while supporting operational teams with strategic insights. Strong analytical and writing skills prove essential.

Multilateral institutions recruit economists who study climate finance flows, assess policy effectiveness, and contribute to international coordination. These positions suit professionals with advanced degrees in economics or public policy seeking to influence global frameworks.

National green investment banks and climate funds employ investment professionals who deploy public capital strategically to catalyze private investment. Fund managers structure blended finance vehicles, negotiate co-investment arrangements, and monitor portfolio performance. These roles blend public purpose with private sector investment disciplines.

Technical assistance programs within development organizations hire advisors who build capacity in partner countries, supporting taxonomy development, training financial supervisors, or strengthening corporate sustainability reporting. These roles suit experienced professionals ready to share expertise internationally.

3. Advisory, Consulting and Research Pathways

Sustainability advisory firms guide clients through strategy development, framework design, and implementation planning. Consultants help corporates set science-based targets, develop transition plans, and prepare for evolving stakeholder expectations. They support financial institutions building sustainable finance capabilities through governance design, product development, and risk integration. Advisory work demands strong analytical abilities, excellent communication skills, and practical understanding of implementation challenges across diverse organizational contexts.

Independent verification providers employ reviewers who assess green bond frameworks, evaluate sustainability-linked loan structures, and provide assurance on sustainability reports. Second-party opinion work requires rigorous analytical thinking, attention to detail, and ability to apply complex standards consistently. Many reviewers have backgrounds in environmental science, engineering, or financial analysis.

Impact measurement specialists develop methodologies, conduct evaluations, and quantify environmental outcomes. They work with project developers, investors, and financial institutions to demonstrate credibility through robust impact assessment. This field attracts professionals with skills in statistics, environmental science, and program evaluation.

Climate risk consulting addresses growing demand from financial institutions implementing scenario analysis, measuring portfolio emissions, or integrating climate considerations into risk frameworks. Consultants bring expertise in climate science, financial modeling, and data analytics. Many firms seek professionals who can translate complex climate information into actionable financial insights.

Research institutions and think tanks employ researchers studying green finance evolution, policy effectiveness, and market development. Academic researchers contribute through peer-reviewed publications that advance theoretical understanding. Policy researchers produce reports influencing regulatory design and institutional practice. Research careers suit individuals passionate about generating knowledge that shapes the field's development.

Data providers building ESG databases and analytical platforms hire specialists in data science, software development, and sustainability expertise. These roles support the infrastructure enabling systematic sustainability analysis across global markets.

Universities increasingly offer faculty positions in sustainable finance, creating opportunities for scholars combining research excellence with teaching commitment. Academic careers allow deep investigation of specific questions while mentoring next-generation professionals.

4. Training Programs, Certifications and Continuous Learning Resources

Professional development in green finance occurs through multiple channels that serve different learning objectives and career stages. University degree programs offer comprehensive foundation, specialized master's degrees in sustainable finance, climate finance, or ESG investing provide structured curricula, research opportunities, and peer networks. These programs suit early-career professionals or those making significant career transitions.

Executive education programs deliver intensive learning experiences for mid-career professionals. Leading business schools offer short courses on sustainable finance topics, climate risk management, impact investing, or ESG integration. These programs balance theoretical frameworks with practical applications, often featuring case studies and practitioner perspectives.

Professional certifications signal specialized expertise to employers and clients. The CFA Institute offers the Certificate in ESG Investing covering analysis frameworks, portfolio construction, and stewardship. The Global Association of Risk Professionals (GARP) provides the Sustainability and Climate Risk Certificate focusing on risk management applications. These certifications require structured study and examinations demonstrating competency.

Industry associations deliver training aligned with professional standards. The Loan Market Association and International Capital Market Association offer programs on sustainable finance principles, transaction structuring, and reporting requirements. These practical courses help professionals implement green finance products within their institutions.

Online learning platforms democratize access to green finance education. Coursera, edX, and specialized providers offer courses ranging from introductory overviews to advanced technical topics. Self-paced learning suits professionals balancing education with work responsibilities.

Webinars and conferences provide continuing education on emerging topics. Organizations like the Climate Bonds Initiative, Principles for Responsible Investment, and regional sustainable finance networks host regular events featuring latest research, policy developments, and market innovations.

Internal training programs within financial institutions build organizational capability systematically. Leading banks and asset managers invest substantially in employee development through customized curricula, expert speakers, and experiential learning opportunities.

Mentorship relationships accelerate learning by connecting less experienced professionals with seasoned practitioners who share insights, provide guidance, and open networks. Formal mentorship programs and informal relationships both contribute to professional growth. Reading remains fundamental to staying current. Academic journals, industry publications, regulatory guidance, and thought leadership from consulting firms all contribute to professional knowledge. Allocating time for regular reading demonstrates commitment to continuous learning.

5. Designing a Personal Learning Roadmap: Strategic Approaches to Skill Development

Effective capacity building begins with honest self-assessment of current capabilities, clear articulation of career objectives, and realistic planning for skill development. A structured learning roadmap provides direction while remaining flexible enough to adapt as interests evolve and opportunities emerge.

Step 1: Assess Current Position

Begin by evaluating existing skills across relevant dimensions, financial analysis capabilities, sustainability knowledge, sectoral expertise, data analytics skills, regulatory understanding, and stakeholder engagement abilities. Identify strengths to leverage and gaps to address. Consider both technical competencies and soft skills like communication, collaboration, and leadership that enable effectiveness.

Reflect on professional experience and how it translates to green finance. Traditional banking skills apply directly to sustainable finance roles. Engineering backgrounds support technical project evaluation. Policy experience informs regulatory strategy work. Most professional backgrounds offer transferable value when combined with targeted sustainability learning.

Step 2: Define Career Objectives

Articulate where you want to contribute within the green finance ecosystem. Interest in direct investment roles suggests pursuing asset management or corporate development pathways. Passion for systemic change points toward policy, research, or development finance. Preference for advisory work indicates consulting or verification careers. Clear objectives guide learning priorities and networking strategies.

Consider time horizons, immediate next steps, medium-term positioning, and long-term aspirations. This temporal perspective helps sequence learning investments appropriately.

Step 3: Identify Priority Skill Gaps

Compare current capabilities against requirements for target roles. This gap analysis reveals where focused development delivers highest return. Prioritize gaps that represent prerequisites for advancement versus those representing competitive advantages once in position.

Distinguish between foundational knowledge requiring systematic study and emerging topics where staying current through regular reading suffices. Balance depth in core areas with breadth across adjacent topics.

Step 4: Select Learning Modalities

Choose development approaches matching your learning style, budget constraints, and time availability. Formal degree programs provide comprehensive foundation and credentials but require significant time and financial investment. Professional certifications offer focused learning and market-recognized validation at moderate cost. Online courses allow flexible, self-paced learning. Conferences and networking build relationships alongside knowledge.

Most effective learning strategies combine multiple modalities, perhaps a certification program for structured foundation, regular webinar attendance for current developments, and active reading to deepen specific areas of interest.

Step 5: Build Practical Experience

Seek opportunities to apply developing skills through project involvement, volunteer roles, or pilot initiatives within current organizations. Practical application accelerates learning and demonstrates capability to future employers. Offer to support green finance initiatives, join sustainability committees, or contribute to climate-related projects.

Step 6: Develop Network Connections

Relationships with professionals working in green finance provide insights, mentorship, and career opportunities. Attend industry events, participate in professional associations, engage through social media platforms, and request informational interviews with people in roles you find interesting.

Step 7: Create Implementation Timeline

Establish realistic timeline for learning activities with specific milestones. Perhaps: complete certification within six months, attend two major conferences annually, read one green finance book monthly, and complete online course quarterly. Concrete goals create accountability and momentum.

Schedule regular reviews, quarterly or semi-annually, to assess progress, celebrate achievements, and adjust plans based on experience and evolving interests.

Step 8: Document and Share Learning

Maintain records of completed training, certifications earned, and skills developed. Update professional profiles to reflect growing expertise. Consider writing about learning experiences through articles, blog posts, or social media to solidify understanding while building professional visibility.

Step 9: Seek Feedback and Mentorship

Engage mentors or trusted colleagues to provide perspective on development and identify blind spots. External feedback helps calibrate self-assessment and reveals opportunities you might overlook.

Step 10: Remain Adaptable

Green finance evolves rapidly, creating new opportunities while shifting priorities. Maintain flexibility to adjust plans as the field develops and your interests crystallize through experience. View the roadmap as a living document rather than fixed prescription.

This systematic approach to capacity building transforms vague aspirations into actionable strategies while maintaining adaptability essential in dynamic fields. The investment in continuous learning compounds over career spans, enabling sustained contribution to green finance transformation.

Key Takeaways

- Green finance careers span diverse institutional settings, banks, asset managers, corporations, public institutions, advisory firms, and research organizations.
- Emerging roles combine traditional financial expertise with specialized sustainability knowledge across relationship management, analysis, risk assessment, and strategic planning.
- Public sector and development finance opportunities allow professionals to shape policy frameworks and deploy catalytic capital supporting systemic change.
- Advisory, consulting, and research pathways serve clients and advance knowledge through specialized expertise and rigorous analysis.
- Professional development occurs through university programs, certifications, executive education, online learning, and practical experience.
- Continuous learning remains essential because green finance evolves rapidly through regulatory changes, technological innovations, and market developments.
- Effective capacity building begins with self-assessment, clear objectives, gap analysis, and strategic learning plans combining multiple modalities.
- Practical experience and network development complement formal education in building competitive professional capabilities.
- Diverse professional backgrounds contribute value to green finance when combined with targeted sustainability learning and genuine commitment.

- Personal learning roadmaps provide structure while maintaining flexibility to adapt as careers evolve and interests deepen.

21

Future Directions in Green Finance

Green finance stands at a transformative moment where established practices meet emerging innovations that will shape the next decade of sustainable development.

This chapter explores frontiers expanding across capital markets, new instruments reshaping investment flows, equity considerations ensuring inclusive transitions, technological advances enabling unprecedented transparency, and fundamental questions guiding continued evolution. Together, these elements reveal pathways through which finance can accelerate global sustainability while creating shared prosperity.

The pace of innovation accelerates as practitioners gain experience, technologies mature, and stakeholder expectations evolve. What seemed experimental five years ago now operates at scale. What appears ambitious today will likely become standard practice tomorrow. This momentum creates opportunities for professionals entering the field to shape emerging conventions rather than simply adopting established ones.

Understanding future directions requires examining multiple dimensions simultaneously, financial innovation, social equity, technological capability, and strategic uncertainty. Each dimension influences the others, creating dynamic interactions that define how sustainable finance evolves. The World Economic Forum estimates that **achieving global climate and nature goals will require mobilizing USD 125-140 trillion in capital by 2050, representing the largest economic transformation in human history**[107]. This scale underscores both the opportunity and responsibility facing financial professionals.

This chapter invites reflection on where green finance travels next and how current decisions shape that trajectory. It balances optimism about progress with realistic assessment of remaining challenges, maintaining focus on actionable pathways that accelerate positive change.

OBJECTIVES OF THE CHAPTER

This chapter will help individuals:

- Explore innovative financial instruments and structures expanding sustainable finance capabilities.
- Understand just transition principles and equity considerations that ensure inclusive transformation.
- Examine how emerging technologies reshape measurement, verification, and market access in green finance.
- Engage with open questions that will define the field's evolution over the next decade.

---

[107] *World Economic Forum, The Global Risks Report 2023, World Economic Forum, 2023, https://www.weforum.org/publications/global-risks-report-2023/, accessed 24 December 2024.*

- Develop strategic thinking skills for navigating uncertainty and complexity in sustainable finance.
- Build confidence in contributing to green finance innovation through practical exercises and frameworks.
- Recognize how professional choices connect to broader transformation toward sustainable economies.
- Appreciate the integration of environmental, social, and technological dimensions in future finance systems.
- Understand personal roles in advancing sustainable finance through commitments and collaborative action.
- See green finance as an evolving discipline where continued learning and adaptation remain essential.

1. Innovation in Instruments and Structures: Expanding the Financial Toolkit

Financial innovation continuously expands mechanisms for channeling capital toward sustainable outcomes. Sustainability-linked bonds represent significant evolution where coupon rates tie directly to issuers achieving predetermined sustainability targets.

This structure creates financial incentives for performance improvement while maintaining flexibility in fund utilization. Companies across manufacturing, energy, and infrastructure sectors increasingly adopt these instruments, demonstrating market appetite for performance-based sustainable finance.

Transition bonds finance activities enabling high-emitting sectors to reduce environmental impact progressively over time. These instruments recognize that decarbonization requires supporting companies on transformation journeys rather than excluding them from capital markets.

Steel manufacturers, cement producers, and chemical companies utilize transition bonds to fund efficiency improvements, fuel switching, and technology adoption, creating measurable progress toward net-zero goals while maintaining operational continuity.

Blue bonds finance marine and ocean-related projects that protect coastal ecosystems, support sustainable fisheries, and preserve marine biodiversity. The Seychelles pioneered sovereign blue bonds for conservation, creating templates that other island nations and coastal countries now adapt. These instruments address growing recognition that ocean health connects directly to climate stability, food security, and economic opportunity for billions of people globally.

Gender bonds link financial markets with social equity objectives by raising capital specifically for women's economic empowerment. These instruments support women-led enterprises, expand financial inclusion, and address systemic barriers that limit women's access to capital. They demonstrate how financial innovation addresses multiple sustainable development dimensions simultaneously, recognizing interconnections between environmental sustainability and social equity.

Debt-for-nature swaps restructure sovereign debt in exchange for conservation commitments, creating fiscal space for environmental protection while reducing debt burdens. Belize, Ecuador, and Gabon completed significant swaps that protect marine ecosystems, rainforests, and critical habitats. These mechanisms show how creative financial engineering can address both economic and environmental priorities, particularly benefiting countries with substantial debt loads and globally significant ecosystems.

Blended finance combines concessional capital from development institutions with commercial capital to improve project economics in challenging markets or emerging technologies. This approach proved particularly effective in renewable energy deployment across developing countries, enabling projects that become commercially viable once risks reduce through initial implementation. The Innovation Exercise below invites readers to design new sustainable finance instruments for their own sectors.

Innovation Exercise: Identify an industry or sector you work with that faces significant sustainability challenges, construction, transportation, manufacturing, or agriculture. Design a hypothetical sustainable finance instrument that could accelerate transition toward more sustainable practices.

Consider what specific metrics would define success, how performance would be measured reliably and transparently, what financial incentives would effectively drive meaningful change, and who the likely investors might be given risk-return profiles.

Share your concept with colleagues, professional associations, or industry forums to refine it through constructive feedback and diverse perspectives. This exercise develops financial innovation skills essential for advancing sustainable finance.

Instrument Type	Primary Purpose	Key Feature	Target Sectors	Innovation Potential
Sustainability-Linked Bonds	Performance incentives	Coupon tied to KPIs	Cross-sector	High, flexible structure
Transition Bonds	Support transformation	Gradual improvement	Heavy industry	High, enables hard-to-abate sectors

Blue Bonds	Ocean conservation	Marine ecosystem focus	Coastal, maritime	Medium, emerging market
Gender Bonds	Social equity	Women's empowerment	Cross-sector	High, addresses systemic gaps
Debt-for-Nature Swaps	Fiscal-environmental link	Debt restructuring	Sovereign, conservation	Medium, complex structuring

This table clarifies how different innovative instruments serve distinct purposes while collectively expanding the sustainable finance toolkit beyond traditional green bonds and loans.

2. Just Transition, Equity and Inclusion: Ensuring Shared Benefits

Transformation toward sustainable economies must ensure benefits distribute broadly and affected workers receive meaningful support through economic change. Just transition principles recognize that environmental progress creates both opportunities and disruptions across communities, sectors, and regions. Successful transitions require proactive strategies that support workers, diversify local economies, and maintain social cohesion during periods of significant change.

Just transition frameworks emphasize several interconnected elements, worker retraining programs that build skills for emerging sectors, community economic diversification that reduces dependence on single industries, social safety nets that provide security during transitions, and inclusive planning processes that give affected stakeholders voice in shaping pathways forward. Countries implementing coal phase-downs, for example, invest heavily in alternative employment creation, education systems, and infrastructure that positions communities for future prosperity.

Access to green finance remains unevenly distributed across geographies, enterprise sizes, and demographic groups. Small and medium enterprises often lack resources to navigate complex sustainable finance application processes, limiting their participation despite strong potential for impact. Microfinance institutions increasingly integrate environmental considerations, enabling smallholder farmers to adopt solar irrigation, supporting small businesses to improve energy efficiency, and financing community-level renewable energy systems.

Gender equity in green finance encompasses multiple dimensions, expanding women's access to capital through dedicated programs and supportive policies, ensuring women participate in green economy employment opportunities, and recognizing that women entrepreneurs demonstrate particularly strong commitment to sustainable practices. Research consistently shows women invest business profits in community wellbeing at higher rates than men, making investments in women-led green businesses impactful across environmental and social dimensions.

Indigenous knowledge and community participation prove essential for effective environmental finance, particularly in projects involving land use, forestry, and conservation. Indigenous communities steward much of the world's remaining intact ecosystems, bringing generations of ecological knowledge to sustainable resource management. Projects that engage these communities as genuine partners, respecting traditional knowledge, ensuring benefit sharing, and supporting self-determination, achieve superior outcomes through contextual understanding and stakeholder commitment.

Youth engagement grows increasingly important as young people inherit both environmental challenges and opportunities created by sustainable transitions. Educational programs build next-generation capacity in green finance. Youth-focused investment products enable young people to align savings with values. Leadership opportunities in sustainability initiatives prepare emerging professionals to drive continued innovation.

The Equity Reflection Exercise invites deeper thinking about inclusive transitions:

Equity Reflection Exercise: Consider a sustainability transition occurring in your sector or community, the shift to renewable energy, adoption of circular economy practices, or implementation of sustainable agriculture.

List all stakeholder groups affected by this transition, not just owners and investors, but workers at different skill levels, local communities, supply chain participants, and consumers. For each group, identify potential benefits and challenges from the transition, considering both immediate and long-term impacts. Develop three specific, actionable strategies for ensuring equitable outcomes across these diverse stakeholders. This exercise builds essential capacity for inclusive sustainability planning that considers social dimensions alongside environmental objectives.

Inclusive growth ensures green finance contributes to poverty alleviation and shared prosperity rather than concentrating benefits among already-advantaged groups.

When renewable energy projects create local employment, green buildings include affordable housing components, and sustainable agriculture raises smallholder incomes, green finance becomes comprehensive sustainable development that strengthens both environmental and social outcomes simultaneously.

3. The Role of Technology in Next-Generation Solutions: Digital Transformation

Technological innovation fundamentally transforms green finance practices, enabling new approaches to measurement, verification, transparency, and market access. The next generation of sustainable finance will be increasingly digital, data-driven, and accessible through platforms that democratize participation.

Blockchain technology offers compelling applications for tracking and verifying environmental claims with unprecedented transparency. When renewable energy certificates are issued on blockchain, their authenticity becomes transparent and immutable, eliminating double-counting risks and streamlining trading. Carbon credit registries exploring blockchain implementation aim to increase market integrity and reduce transaction costs. Supply chain traceability applications demonstrate product sustainability credentials from origin to consumer, building trust in environmental claims.

Artificial intelligence enhances ESG analysis by processing vast quantities of unstructured data, news articles, satellite imagery, social media, regulatory filings, to assess sustainability performance and identify risks more comprehensively than traditional methods allow. Machine learning algorithms detect patterns in emissions data, predict climate impacts on asset values, and identify investment opportunities aligned with sustainability themes. Natural language processing extracts sustainability information from corporate disclosures, creating structured datasets for systematic analysis.

Satellite technology revolutionizes environmental monitoring by providing independent verification of sustainability claims. Satellites track deforestation in near real-time, measure agricultural productivity, monitor industrial emissions, assess climate vulnerability, and verify conservation efforts. This remote sensing capability reduces monitoring costs while increasing coverage, making verification economically viable for projects and geographies previously difficult to assess systematically.

Digital platforms democratize sustainable investment access by reducing minimum investment thresholds and simplifying participation processes. Where green bonds traditionally required million-dollar minimums accessible only to institutional investors, digital platforms enable retail participation with modest amounts. This democratization expands market depth while allowing individuals to align investments with personal values. Fractional ownership models further lower barriers, enabling participation in large-scale sustainable infrastructure projects.

Internet of Things devices generate continuous environmental performance data through sensors, smart meters, and connected equipment. Buildings equipped with IoT sensors provide real-time energy consumption data that supports performance verification for green building certifications. Industrial facilities monitor emissions continuously rather than through periodic sampling. Smart agriculture systems track water usage, soil conditions, and crop health, creating data streams that support sustainable farming verification and optimization.

The Technology Foresight Exercise encourages forward-thinking exploration:

Technology Foresight Exercise: Select one emerging technology, blockchain, artificial intelligence, Internet of Things, quantum computing, or another frontier technology. Research its current development stage and potential applications. Then imagine how this technology might transform green finance practices in five to ten years. What new possibilities would it create? What current limitations would it overcome? What new considerations might it introduce? Document your insights in brief memo format suitable for sharing with professional networks.

Fintech innovations reduce transaction costs and expand access to financial services in ways that particularly benefit sustainable finance. Digital verification systems automate compliance checking, making smaller transactions economically viable. Automated reporting reduces administrative burden for issuers. Mobile payment systems reach populations without traditional banking access, enabling participation in community renewable energy or sustainable agriculture finance.

Climate fintech, the convergence of climate action and financial technology, attracts significant venture capital investment as entrepreneurs develop solutions for carbon accounting, climate risk analytics, green investment platforms, and impact measurement. This innovation ecosystem accelerates sustainable finance capabilities through competitive experimentation and rapid iteration that brings new tools to market continuously.

4. Open Questions for the Coming Decade: Navigating Uncertainty

Despite remarkable progress, significant questions remain about green finance's future trajectory and optimal pathways forward. Honest engagement with these uncertainties directs research and innovation toward critical gaps while maintaining appropriate humility about what we know and don't know.

How do we ensure green finance remains truly additional, funding projects that wouldn't proceed otherwise rather than simply relabeling conventional activities? This fundamental question challenges the field to demonstrate genuine impact beyond sophisticated marketing. Answering requires combining regulatory requirements that set clear standards, investor scrutiny that demands credible evidence, and institutional integrity that prioritizes substance over appearance. Market discipline strengthens as participants gain experience distinguishing meaningful impact from greenwashing.

Can market-based approaches alone drive the required speed and scale of change, or do they need complementary policy frameworks? Historical evidence suggests successful transitions combine market innovation with supportive policy structures, carbon pricing that internalizes environmental costs, subsidies that support emerging technologies, regulations that phase out harmful activities, and public investment that demonstrates viability. The optimal policy mix likely varies by sector, geography, and development stage, requiring experimentation and adaptation.

How do we measure and compare impact across vastly different activities and contexts? Comparing emissions reductions from renewable energy against biodiversity protection from forest conservation or social benefits from affordable housing requires common metrics that may not exist or involve difficult value judgments. Impact measurement methodologies represent an active innovation area where standardization efforts balance comprehensiveness with practical feasibility.

The Strategic Thinking Exercise develops analytical capabilities:

Strategic Thinking Exercise: Choose one open question that particularly interests you from those discussed or identify another critical uncertainty facing green finance. Research diverse perspectives on this question from academics, practitioners, policymakers, and civil society representatives. Synthesize these viewpoints into balanced analysis presenting various arguments fairly. Then articulate your own position with clear reasoning and supporting evidence. This exercise develops critical thinking skills essential for leadership in complex, evolving fields like sustainable finance.

What role should sustainable finance play in addressing historical inequities between developed and developing nations regarding climate responsibility and capacity? Climate change results largely from historical emissions by industrialized countries, yet impacts fall disproportionately on developing nations with limited adaptive capacity. International climate finance negotiations attempt to address these justice dimensions, but adequate mechanisms remain under development. Green finance evolution must grapple with equity questions that extend beyond individual transactions to systemic fairness.

How do we accelerate innovation while ensuring sufficient governance and risk management? Moving too slowly means missing opportunities and delaying necessary transformation. Moving too quickly without adequate safeguards risks repeating financial crises or creating unintended consequences. Finding appropriate pace requires balancing innovation's potential with governance's protective functions, enabling experimentation within guardrails that evolve based on experience.

Will green finance remain a specialized practice or become fully integrated into mainstream finance where all decisions automatically incorporate environmental and social considerations? Current trends suggest progressive integration, but timeline and completeness remain uncertain. Full integration would fundamentally transform financial practice, making sustainability lens as natural as risk-return analysis. This evolution depends on data availability, methodological maturity, regulatory requirements, and cultural shifts within financial institutions.

How can green finance better support adaptation alongside mitigation, recognizing that climate impacts require both reducing future warming and managing inevitable changes? Adaptation finance historically received less attention than mitigation, yet vulnerable communities need resources for resilience building. Innovative instruments that finance adaptation infrastructure, support community resilience, and protect natural systems against climate impacts represent important growth areas.

5. Closing Reflections on Capital, Responsibility and the World We Build

As this exploration of green finance concludes, fundamental questions about capital's purpose and our responsibility in directing financial flows deserve reflection. How we deploy capital shapes the physical, economic, and social reality we inhabit. Green finance ultimately reflects choices about what world we want to build and what legacy we want to create.

Every investment decision contributes to particular outcomes whether intentionally or inadvertently. When capital flows toward renewable energy, it accelerates clean energy transitions that reduce emissions and create employment. When it finances green buildings, it creates healthier indoor environments and reduces operating costs. When it supports sustainable agriculture, it protects soil health and supports farming livelihoods. These aggregated choices determine whether humanity successfully navigates environmental challenges while creating broadly shared prosperity.

Nations, institutions, and individuals worldwide demonstrate that economic prosperity and environmental stewardship can advance together rather than requiring trade-offs. Ambitious sustainability goals increasingly drive innovation, create competitive advantages, and attract investment. This alignment offers hope that transformation remains achievable through coordinated effort across public, private, and civil society sectors.

Responsibility in green finance operates at multiple levels that reinforce each other. Financial professionals maintain integrity, develop expertise, and apply it with care. Institutions establish governance structures and allocate capital consistent with stated values. Governments create enabling policy frameworks and ensure accountability.

Civil society organizations monitor progress and advocate for stronger action. These overlapping responsibilities create mutual accountability that strengthens the entire system.

The urgency of environmental challenges demands action while complexity requires humility about what we know and continued openness to learning. We understand enough to begin meaningful transformation yet recognize significant uncertainties.

Success requires combining confidence to act with willingness to adapt based on evidence, maintaining high standards while remaining pragmatic about implementation realities.

Hope remains essential yet insufficient by itself. Optimism without action leads to complacency. Action without hope leads to burnout and cynicism. The sustainable finance professional must cultivate realistic hope, grounded in evidence of progress, aware of remaining challenges, and motivated by the conviction that individual and collective efforts make meaningful differences. Green finance's growth over the past decade demonstrates that transformative change is possible when vision combines with sustained effort.

You now possess comprehensive understanding of green finance principles, practices, and possibilities. You have frameworks for continuing your learning journey, tools for navigating complexity, and inspiration for the vital work ahead. The knowledge gained through these chapters provides foundation, but lasting impact comes through application and continued development.

The world needs the skills, dedication, and creativity you bring to sustainable finance. Every project you evaluate, investment you recommend, policy you shape, and innovation you support contributes to transformation toward a sustainable global economy. Your work matters because collective impact emerges from countless individual decisions and actions.

Green finance's future will be written by professionals who combine technical expertise with genuine commitment to positive change, maintain ethical standards while achieving financial results, collaborate generously across disciplines and sectors, and persist through inevitable setbacks.

The next chapter of this field's evolution begins with actions taken tomorrow and decisions made next week by you and thousands of colleagues worldwide.

The opportunity to participate in this transformation represents both privilege and responsibility. Previous generations lacked our knowledge, tools, and understanding of environmental imperatives. Future generations will inherit the consequences of choices we make today.

We stand in a unique moment where our actions can decisively shape humanity's trajectory toward sustainable prosperity or continuing environmental degradation.

The Personal Commitment Exercise translates knowledge into action:

Personal Commitment Exercise: Having completed this exploration of green finance, articulate your personal commitment to advancing sustainable finance.

Write three specific, measurable commitments you will fulfill over the next twelve months, relating to skills development, professional activities, or direct project involvement.

Share these with someone who will hold you accountable, a colleague, mentor, or friend. Schedule quarterly check-ins to assess progress and adjust approaches as needed. Transform knowledge into action through deliberate commitment.

As you move forward in your green finance journey, carry confidence in your capabilities, commitment to continuous improvement, willingness to collaborate with diverse partners, and courage to challenge conventional approaches when necessary. You join a global community united by shared purpose, professionals across continents, sectors, and disciplines working toward sustainable development that respects planetary boundaries while creating opportunity for all.

The world we build through capital allocation becomes the world our children inherit. This profound responsibility should inspire our highest efforts and deepest creativity. Green finance provides powerful tools for building a world characterized by clean energy and healthy ecosystems, prosperous communities and equitable opportunities, innovation and resilience.

Your journey continues beyond these pages. Armed with knowledge, inspired by possibility, and called to meaningful work, you are ready to make your unique contribution to transformation toward a sustainable global economy. The field needs diverse voices, fresh perspectives, and dedicated professionals bringing their full capabilities to shared challenges.

Go forward with confidence in your preparation, competence in your skills, and commitment to values that transcend immediate self-interest. The future awaits your contribution. The work is urgent yet rewarding. The destination, truly sustainable global economy-remains achievable through collective effort. And the journey begins now, with you.

Appendix

Glossary of Key Terms in Green Finance

Additionality: The extent to which an investment or intervention creates environmental or social benefits beyond what would have occurred without it.

Adaptation Finance: Capital allocated to reduce vulnerability and increase resilience to climate impacts such as floods, heat stress, or water scarcity.

Asset-Level Risk: Climate or sustainability risk assessed at the level of individual facilities, projects, or physical assets.

Blended Finance: The strategic use of public, concessional, or philanthropic capital to mobilise private investment into sustainable projects.

Carbon Budget: The maximum amount of cumulative greenhouse-gas emissions permitted to meet specific climate targets.

Carbon Capture and Storage (CCS): Technologies that capture carbon dioxide emissions and store them underground to prevent atmospheric release.

Carbon Credit: A tradable unit representing one tonne of carbon dioxide equivalent reduced or removed through verified activities.

Carbon Intensity: A measure of emissions relative to output, revenue, or production volume.

Carbon Markets: Trading systems where carbon credits or emission allowances are bought and sold.

Carbon Pricing: Assigning a monetary value to greenhouse-gas emissions through taxes, emissions trading systems, or internal pricing.

Circular Economy: An economic system focused on reuse, recycling, material efficiency, and waste reduction.

Climate Adaptation: Actions that reduce exposure and sensitivity to climate impacts.

Climate Finance: Financial flows that support mitigation, adaptation, and resilience aligned with climate goals.

Climate Mitigation: Efforts aimed at reducing or preventing greenhouse-gas emissions.

Climate Risk: Financial risk arising from climate-related physical and transition factors.

Concessional Capital: Capital provided at below-market terms to support high-impact or early-stage sustainable investments.

Credit Enhancement: Financial mechanisms such as guarantees or insurance that improve project creditworthiness.

Disclosure Frameworks: Structured systems guiding how organisations report sustainability-related risks, governance, and performance.

Do No Significant Harm (DNSH): A principle ensuring that sustainable activities do not undermine other environmental or social objectives.

Double Materiality: A concept recognising both financial impact on the company and the company's impact on society and the environment.

Environmental, Social, and Governance (ESG): A framework used to evaluate non-financial factors influencing long-term value, risk, and resilience.

ESG Integration: The systematic inclusion of ESG factors into financial analysis and investment decisions.

ESG Rating: A score or assessment evaluating a company's ESG performance based on defined methodologies.

External Review: Independent assessment of sustainability frameworks, instruments, or disclosures.

Forward-Looking Analysis: Evaluation based on future scenarios rather than historical data alone.

Green Bonds: Bonds where proceeds are allocated to environmentally beneficial projects.

Green Buildings: Buildings designed or retrofitted to reduce energy use, emissions, and resource consumption.

Green Loans: Loan facilities financing eligible green activities aligned with recognised principles.

Green Taxonomy: A classification system defining environmentally sustainable economic activities.

Impact Investing: Investments made with the intention to generate measurable social or environmental impact alongside financial returns.

Internal Carbon Pricing: A self-imposed carbon cost used by organisations for planning and investment decisions.

Just Transition: A framework ensuring fairness, inclusion, and economic opportunity during the shift to a low-carbon economy.

s Performance Indicators (KPIs): Quantifiable metrics used to track sustainability performance.

Labelled Bonds: Bonds identified as green, social, sustainability, or transition based on defined criteria.

Long-Term Value Creation: Value generated through sustainable business models, resilience, and strategic alignment.

Macroprudential Risk: System-wide financial risk affecting overall economic stability.

Materiality Assessment: The process of identifying sustainability issues most relevant to decision-making.

Mitigation Finance: Capital directed toward emissions reduction activities.

Municipal Finance: Financing mechanisms used by cities and local governments.

Nature-Based Solutions: Actions that protect, restore, or manage ecosystems to address climate and environmental challenges.

Net-Zero: Achieving a balance between emissions produced and emissions removed from the atmosphere.

Physical Risk: Risk arising from climate hazards such as floods, storms, heatwaves, or sea-level rise.

Portfolio Alignment: The degree to which investments align with climate or sustainability targets.

Project Finance: A financing structure reliant primarily on project cash flows rather than sponsor balance sheets.

Public-Private Partnership (PPP): Long-term collaboration between public and private entities to deliver infrastructure or services.

Scenario Analysis: A tool assessing performance under different climate or policy pathways.

Science-Based Targets: Emissions reduction goals aligned with climate science.

Social Bonds: Bonds financing projects with positive social outcomes.

Stakeholder Engagement: Interaction with affected parties to inform strategy and decision-making.

Stranded Assets: Assets that lose value due to regulatory, technological, or market shifts.

Sustainability Bonds: Bonds financing both environmental and social projects.

Sustainability-Linked Bonds (SLBs): Bonds where financial terms depend on sustainability performance.

Sustainability-Linked Loans (SLLs): Loans with pricing linked to sustainability KPIs.

Systemic Risk: Risk that threatens the stability of the entire financial system.

Taxonomy Alignment: The degree to which activities meet taxonomy-defined sustainability criteria.

Transition Finance: Capital supporting emissions reduction in carbon-intensive sectors through measurable pathways.

Transition Risk: Risk arising from policy, technology, and market changes during decarbonisation.

Use of Proceeds: Specification of how raised capital must be allocated.

Verification: Independent confirmation of sustainability claims, data, or performance.